arihant
SUCCESS AND NOTHING LESS

AF819981

Niharika yadav

Be a TOP SCORER
in ICSE Exams 2025

i Succeed

15 Sample Question Papers

with Quick Study Notes

History & Civics 10th

AUTHORS
Charu Tripathi,
Nazma Ansari

List of *i Succeed* Sample Papers for ICSE 10

- Physics
- Chemistry
- Maths
- Biology
- History & Civics
- Geography
- English Language
- Literature in English
- हिंदी
- Computer Applications

Arihant Prakashan
(School Division Series)

Administrative & Production Offices

Regd. Office
'Ramchhaya' 4577/15, Agarwal Road, Darya Ganj, New Delhi -110002
Tele: 011- 47630600, 43518550

Head Office
Kalindi, TP Nagar, Meerut (UP) - 250002
Tel: 0121-7156203, 7156204

Sales & Support Offices
Agra, Ahmedabad, Bengaluru, Bareilly, Chennai, Delhi, Guwahati, Hyderabad, Jaipur, Jhansi, Kolkata, Lucknow, Nagpur & Pune.

PRICE ₹185.00

PO No : TXT-XX-XXXXXXX-X-XX

Published by Arihant Publications (India) Ltd.

For further information about the books published by Arihant, log on to www.arihantbooks.com or e-mail at info@arihantbooks.com

Follow us on

i Succeed

SAMPLE QUESTION PAPERS

THE **BEST CHOICE** OF TEACHERS & STUDENTS, Why?

01 Exact Exam Pattern

All Sample Papers have been designed on the actual exam format of ICSE.

02 Complete Syllabus

Complete coverage of syllabus through different types of questions across all the sample papers.

03 Latest Specimen Question Paper

Latest Specimen Question Paper with detailed answers.

04 Detailed Answers

Step-by-step answer to help you understand concepts and improve problem-solving skills.

05 Quick Study Notes

Focused revision of the whole syllabus through Quick Study Notes.

06 All Types of Questions

Coverage of all types of exam pattern questions based on, recall, analysis, understanding, application & evaluation.

i Succeed

History & Civics Class 10

Course Structure
2024-25

*There will be one paper of **two hours** duration of 80 marks and Internal Assessment of practical work carrying 20 marks.*

SECTION A : CIVICS

1. The Union Legislature

Meaning of the federal setup in India.

(i) Lok Sabha - Term, composition, qualifications for membership. Parliamentary procedures: a brief idea of sessions, quorum, question hour, adjournment and no-confidence motion. Speaker – election and functions.

(ii) Rajya Sabha – Composition, qualifications for membership, election, term, Presiding Officer.

Powers and functions of Union Parliament – (legislative, financial, judicial, electoral, amendment of the Constitution, control over executive). Exclusive powers of the two Houses.

2. The Union Executive

(i) The President: Qualifications for election, composition of Electoral College, reason for indirect election, term of office, procedure for impeachment.

Powers (executive, legislative, financial, judicial, discretionary and emergency)

(ii) The Vice-President: Qualifications for election, term of office and powers.

(iii) Prime Minister and Council of Ministers: Appointment, formation of Council of Ministers, tenure, functions - policy making, administrative, legislative, financial, emergency. Position and powers of the Prime Minister. Collective and individual responsibility of the members of the Cabinet. Distinction between the Council of Ministers and the Cabinet.

3. The Judiciary

(i) The Supreme Court: Composition, qualifications of judges, appointment, independence of judiciary from the control of executive and legislature; Jurisdiction and functions: Original, Appellate, Advisory, Revisory, Judicial Review and Court of Record. Enforcement of Fundamental Rights and Writs.

(ii) The High Courts: Composition, qualifications of judges, appointment; Jurisdiction and functions: Original, Appellate, Revisory, Judicial Review and Court of Record. Enforcement of Fundamental Rights and Writs.

(iii) Subordinate Courts: Distinction between Court of the District Judge and Sessions Court.

Lok Adalats: Meaning and advantages.

SECTION B : HISTORY

1. The Indian National Movement (1857 – 1917)

(i) The First War of Independence, 1857
Only the causes (political, socio-religious, economic and military) and consequences will be tested. [The events, however, need to be mentioned in order to maintain continuity and for a more comprehensive understanding.]

(ii) Factors leading to the growth of Nationalism – economic exploitation, repressive colonial policies, socio-religious reform movements (brief mention of contribution of Raja Ram Mohan Roy and Jyotiba Phule) and role of the Press.

Foundation of the Indian National Congress - the Indian National Association (Surendranath Banerjee) and the East India Association (Dadabhai Naoroji) as precursors. Immediate objectives of the Indian National Congress - the first two sessions and their Presidents should be mentioned.

(iii) First Phase of the Indian National Movement (1885-1907) - Objectives and methods of struggle of the Early Nationalists. Any two contributions of Dadabhai Naoroji, Surendranath Banerjee and Gopal Krishna Gokhale.

Second Phase of the Indian National Movement (1905-1916) - Brief mention of the causes of the Partition of Bengal and its perspective by the Nationalists. Brief mention of Surat Split of 1907; objectives and methods of struggle of the Radicals. Any two contributions of Bal Gangadhar Tilak, Bipin Chandra Pal and Lala Lajpat Rai. The Muslim League; Factors leading to the formation of the Muslim League and its objectives. Brief mention of the significance of the Lucknow Pact - 1916.

2. Mass Phase of the National Movement (1915-1947)

(i) Mahatma Gandhi:- Non-Cooperation Movement : causes (Khilafat Movement, Rowlatt Act, Jallianwala Bagh Tragedy), programme and suspension – Chauri Chaura incident and impact of the Movement; the Civil Disobedience Movement: causes (reaction to the Simon Commission, Declaration of Poorna Swaraj at the Lahore Session of 1929), Dandi March, programme and impact of the Movement, Gandhi-Irwin Pact and the Second Round Table Conference; the Quit India Movement: causes (failure of the Cripps Mission, Japanese threat), Quit India Resolution and the significance of the Movement.

(ii) Forward Bloc (objectives) and INA (objectives and contribution of Subhas Chandra Bose).

(iii) Independence and Partition of India – Cabinet Mission Plan (clauses only); Mountbatten Plan (clauses and its acceptance); and the Indian Independence Act of 1947 (clauses only).

3. The Contemporary World

(i) The First World War :
Causes (Nationalism and Imperialism, Armament Race, division of Europe and Sarajevo crisis) and Results (Treaty of Versailles, territorial rearrangements, formation of League of Nations).

(ii) Rise of Dictatorships :

Causes for the rise of Fascism in Italy and the rise of Nazism in Germany. A comparative study of Mussolini's Fascist and Hitler's Nazi ideologies.

(iii) The Second World War :

Causes (Dissatisfaction with the Treaty of Versailles, Rise of Fascism and Nazism, Policy of Appeasement, Japanese invasion of China, Failure of League of Nations and Hitler's invasion of Poland). Brief mention of the attack on Pearl Harbour and bombing of Hiroshima and Nagasaki. Consequences (Defeat of Axis Powers, Formation of the United Nations and Cold War).

(iv) United Nations

(a) The objectives of the U.N. :

The composition and functions of the General Assembly, the Security Council and the International Court of Justice.

(b) Major agencies of the United Nations:

NICEF, WHO and UNESCO - functions only.

(v) Non-Aligned Movement : Brief meaning; objectives; Panchsheel; role of Jawaharlal Nehru; Names of the architects of NAM.

Preparation Assessment Zone

Welcome to the Preparation Assessment Zone !

In this section, you'll find **ICSE Specimen Paper** and **ICSE Solved Paper 2024** to help you assess your readiness.
Attempt these papers to familiarise yourself with the exam format and identify areas that need improvement.

Progress Tracker Tick the papers as you complete them.

- ☐ ICSE Specimen Paper 2025
- ☐ Board Examination Paper 2024

ICSE Specimen Paper 2025

History & Civics (Code 50)

Class 10

General Instructions

1. Part I is compulsory. All questions from Part I are to be attempted.
2. A total of 5 questions are to be attempted from Part II, 2 out of 3 questions from Section A and out of 5 questions from Section B.
3. The intended marks for questions or part of questions are given in brackets [ ].

- No. of Questions : 10
- No. of Parts : 2
- Time Alloted : 2 Hrs.
- Max. Marks : 80

Part-I Attempt all questions from this part

Que 1.

Choose the correct answers to the questions from the given options. (16)

(Do not copy the question, write the correct answers only.)

(i) On 19th May, 2023, the President of India exercised legislative power under Article 123 of the Constitution, during the period Parliament was in recess, to promulgate The Government of National Capital Territory of Delhi Ordinance, 2023. *–The Hindu, 26th May, 2023*

What information about an ordinance can be obtain from the above passage? (1)

(a) The ordinance must be approved within six weeks.
(b) Only the Cabinet can prepare an ordinance.
(c) It is issued when the Parliament is not functioning.
(d) If the Parliament does not approve it within six weeks it becomes inoperative.

[Application]

(ii) Given below are details of few Indian citizens.

Person	Age [In years]	Description
W	34	Is a Professor in the Government College
X	35	Has taken up the citizenship of the United States of America
Y	27	Is a reputed sportsperson
Z	36	Is a scientist

Select the person who fulfils the eligibility criteria to become the President of India. [Understanding] (1)

(a) W (b) X
(c) Y (d) Z

(iii) Who made the amendment which resulted in the below headline? [Application] (1)

THE TIMES OF INDIA

In Historic Move Within 100 Days Of Modi-2, Govt Bifurcates State Into 2 UTs, Defangs Article 370 & Scraps 35A

KASHMIR IS NOW UNION'S TERRITORY

J&K To Lose Special Status, Centre To Directly Rule Ladakh

INDIA'S NORTH POLE SHIFTS TO CENTRE

Why now? PM, Shah felt political tide and timing favoured action

(a) The Supreme Court
(b) The President
(c) The Parliament
(d) The Prime Minister

(iv) Residents of Jodhpur, X and Y got married in the year 2014 and after 4 months of wedlock, petty family issues and arguments resulted in their separation for 6 years. The matter was placed before the Bench of Lok Adalat Family Court, Jodhpur wherein all efforts were made to reunite the family again. With constant efforts of counselling parties agreed to live together and withdraw their Divorce Petition

Case Study, Lok Adalat, District - Jodhpur.

Which advantage of the Lok Adalat is highlighted in the above case? [Application] (1)

(a) Saves money

(b) Speedy justice

(c) Works on the spirit of compromise

(d) Reduces the burden on High Courts

(v) District Judge : Cases :: Sessions Judge : Criminal Cases [Recall] (1)

(a) Advisory (b) Civil

(c) Constitutional (d) Appellate

(vi) Identify the exclusive powers of the Rajya Sabha.

P : Can introduce a new All India Service

Q : Can impeach the President

R : Can never be dissolved as a whole

S : Can introduce a Money Bill [Recall] (1)

(a) P and Q (b) R and S

(c) P and R (d) Q and S

(vii) Read the two statements given below about the Civil Disobedience Movement and select the option that shows the correct relationship between (A) and (R).

Assertion (A) The Civil Disobedience Movement was renewed by Mahatma Gandhi.

Reason (R) The Second Round Table Conference was a failure. [Analysis] (1)

(a) R contradicts A

(b) R is the reason for A

(c) A is true but R is false

(d) A and R are independent of each other

(viii) The government of Country X has introduced a law similar to Ilbert Bill introduced in 1883. Who will be impacted by this Bill? [Understanding] (1)

(a) The Farmers

(b) The Artisans

(c) The Soldiers

(d) The Judges

(ix) The area in which Anand stays has had no water supply for three days in spite of repeated complaints. The residents have a meeting and discuss a few methods to resolve this problem. Being a follower of the beliefs and methods of the Early Nationalists, which of the following methods is Anand not likely to approve? [Application] (1)

(a) Peaceful procession by the residents

(b) Follow the method of boycott

(c) Write a petition to the government

(d) Write an article in the newspaper highlighting the problem.

(x) Which of the given policies is not aligned with the ideologies of the leader seen in the picture? [Understanding] (1)

(a) Prioritising military expansion

(b) Promoting racist policies

(c) Hosting an anti-communist seminar

(d) Holding pro-democracy rallies

(xi) Identify the odd one out of the following objectives of the Muslim League. [Analysis] (1)

(a) To promote among Muslims of India, support for the British.

(b) To promote cultural and socio-economic cooperation among Muslims.

(c) To protect and advance political rights and interests of the Muslims.

(d) To present the needs and demands of the Muslims to the government.

(xii) Your school has organised a poster making competition on the topic - Education empowerment for girls in India. Which of the following leaders would most likely be part of the poster? [Understanding] (1)

(a) Surendranath Banerjee

(b) Pherozeshah Mehta

(c) Dadabhai Naoroji

(d) Jyotiba Phule

(xiii) Read the description and identify the person–

He established the Forward Bloc and coined the slogan, 'Delhi Chalo'. [Recall] (1)

(a) Mahatma Gandhi (b) Subhash Chandra Bose

(c) Bal Gangadhar Tilak (d) Dadabhai Naoroji

(xiv) Which of the following countries will not be part of this cartoon? [Application] (1)

(a) China (b) Japan (c) Russia (d) Britain

(xv) Identify the cities most affected by American action in World War II. [Recall] (1)

(a) Rome, Berlin (b) Tokyo, Berlin
(c) Hiroshima, Nagasaki (d) Tokyo, Rome

(xvi) Which of the following scenarios describes the Non-Alignment Policy (NAM)? [Understanding] (1)

(a) A country forms a military alliance only with the United States.
(b) A country maintains relations with both factions during the Cold War and does not take sides.
(c) A country is part of a religious movement advocating non-violence.
(d) A country aligns with Soviet Union and receives military aid.

Que 2.

Read the extract given below and answer the question which follows.

Congress member's adjournment motion disallowed. The notice, along with another moved demanding a discussion on China, was disallowed in the Lok Sabha. *The Times of India, 10th Feb, 2023*

(i) Who can allow or disallow the above motion? What does this motion mean? [Understanding] (2)

(ii) Which category of power is being exercised by the President in the following. [Recall] (2)
(a) Approval of Bills
(b) Appointment of the Supreme Court judges

(iii) Imagine you were an artisan, in the year 1856. Mention any two ways in which the economic policies of the British would have affected you. [Understanding] (2)

(iv) Give two reasons for the acceptance of the Mountbatten Plan by the Congress. [Recall] (2)

(v) Mention any two leaders of the Assertive Nationalists. [Recall] (2)

(vi) Mention any two objectives of the League of Nations. [Recall] (2)

(vii) Name the two alliances formed in Europe before the beginning of the First World War. [Recall] (2)

Part-II Section A (Civics) Attempt any two questions from this section

Que 3.

The Union Legislature of India is not only the law-making body, but the center of all democratic political process. With reference to the Parliament, answer the following questions.

(i) The Lok Sabha is more powerful than the Rajya Sabha. Justify this by mentioning any three points. [Analysis] (3)

(ii) Rajya Sabha adjourned sine die, overall productivity at 79 percent.

–Deccan Herald, 21st December, 2023

Who can adjourn the above session? Explain the composition of this house. [Recall] (3)

(iii) Mention any four legislative powers of the Parliament. [Recall] (4)

Que 4.

The President is the nominal head of the executive, the first citizen of the country, as well as the commander-in-chief of the Indian Armed Forces. With reference to this, answer the following questions.

(i) The President is the nominal head of the country and cannot act independently.
Mention any three legislative powers of the President which justifies the nominal position. [Understanding] (3)

(ii) Mention any three financial powers of the President. [Recall] (3)

(iii) Describe the procedure of impeachment of the President. [Recall] (4)

Que 5.

The Supreme Court of India is the supreme judicial authority and the highest court of the Republic of India. It is the final court of appeal for all civil and criminal cases. With reference to the Supreme Court, answer the following questions.

(i) Who appoints the judges of the Supreme Court?

Mention any two qualifications required for a person to be appointed as a judge of the Supreme Court. [Recall] (3)

(ii) Under Article 129, the Supreme Court of India is called a Court of Record.

Justify this statement with any three points. [Analysis] (3)

(iii) Explain the following terms.

(a) Revisory Jurisdiction

(b) Advisory Jurisdiction [Recall] (4)

Section B (History) Attempt any three questions from this section

Que 6.

The Indian Rebellion of 1857 was a major uprising against the rule of the British East India Company, which functioned as a sovereign power on behalf of the British Crown. With reference to this, answer the following questions.

(i) The British used many policies of expansion. Mention any three such policies. [Recall] (3)

(ii) How did the failure of this Revolt impact the Mughals and the Peshwas? [Recall] (3)

(iii) The India army was reorganised after 1858, to prevent the reoccurrence of another uprising. Analyse this statement by stating any four changes made in the army after the Revolt. [Analysis] (4)

Que 7.

Nationalism refers to the feeling of oneness that emerges when people consider themselves as one nation. With reference to the growth of nationalism, answer the following.

(i) Name the first President of Congress. Mention any two of its objectives. [Recall] (3)

(ii) The press played an important role in the growth of Indian Nationalism. Thus, the British saw the need for curbs on the press. Mention any three points to analyse the role of the press in the growth of nationalism. [Analysis] (3)

(iii) Lord Lytton's repressive policies led to the growth of Nationalism. Mention any four policies enforced by him. [Recall] (4)

Que 8.

Read the excerpt given below and answer the questions that follow

The March, which took place in India, was led by Mohandas Gandhi to protest British rule in India. During the march, thousands of Indians followed Gandhi from his religious retreat near Ahmedabad to the Arabian Sea coast, a distance of some 240 miles. The march resulted in the arrest of nearly 60,000 people, including Gandhi himself.

–The Marion (Ohio) Star [Edited]

(i) Name the march being discussed above. Which movement did this march lead to? In which year was that movement launched? [Recall] (3)

(ii) The movement which began with this march made a considerable impact on the social and political surroundings of the country. Analyse this statement by mentioning any three impacts. [Analysis] (3)

(iii) Mention any four clauses of the Gandhi Irwin Pact. [Recall] (4)

Que 9.

Look at the picture given and answer the following questions. [Recall] (3)

(i) Describe the incident depicted in the cartoon.

(ii) Mention any three points to analyse how Europe was rearranged as a consequence of the war caused by this incident. Consequence of the war caused by this incident. [Recall] (3)

(iii) The Germans described the Treaty of Versailles as harsh and humiliating.

Give any four reasons that justify this statement. [Analysis] (4)

Que 10.

The United Nations Organisation aims to maintain international peace. With reference to its organs and agencies, answer the following.

(i) What is the composition of the International Court of Justice? [Recall] (3)

(ii) Mention any three functions of the General Assembly. [Recall] (3)

(iii) Gujarat's famed garba dance received the intangible heritage tag. Which agency of the United Nations is authorized to give this tag? Mention any three other contributions of that agency in the preservation of culture. [Application & Recall] (4)

Answers in Topper's Style

1. (i) (c) It is issued when the Parliament is not functioning.
   (ii) (d) Z
   (iii) (c) The Parliament
   (iv) (c) Works on the spirit of compromise
   (v) (b) Civil
   (vi) (c) P and R
   (vii) (b) R is the reason for A
   (viii) (d) The Judges
   (ix) (b) Follow the method of boycott
   (x) (d) Holding pro-democracy rallies
   (xi) (a) To promote among Muslims of India, support for the British.
   (xii) (d) Jyotiba Phule
   (xiii) (b) Subhash Chandra Bose
   (xiv) (b) Japan
   (xv) (c) Hiroshima, Nagasaki
   (xvi) (b) A country maintains relations with both factions during the Cold War and does not take sides.

2. (i) The Speaker of the Lok Sabha has the authority to allow or disallow an adjournment motion. This power is crucial for maintaining order and focusing the discussion in the house.

   An adjournment motion is used to temporarily stop proceedings to discuss a matter of urgent public importance. The discussion must be specific and is intended to draw the government's attention to a particular issue that needs immediate attention.

   (ii) (a) The President of India exercises legislative powers under Article 111 of the Constitution to approve bills passed by both houses of Parliament.

   (b) The President exercises executive power to appoints judges to the Supreme Court of India under Article 124 of the Constitution.

   (iii) An artisan in the year 1856 would have been affected by the British policies in the following ways
   - **Reduced demand for local goods** As an artisan in 1856, British economic policies such as the promotion of British-made goods would have severely affected his/her livelihood by reducing the demand for locally made products.
   - **Taxation and raw material supply** One would likely face heavy taxes imposed by the British, which would diminish their earnings. Additionally, the colonial focus on raw material exportation would limit his/her access to necessary resources, further impacting his/her ability to produce and sell.

   (iv) Two reasons for the acceptance of the Mountbatten Plan by the Congress were

   (a) **Immediate Transfer of Power** One of the primary reasons Congress accepted the Mountbatten Plan was the provision for immediate transfer of power from British to Indian hands, which promised a quicker end to British rule.

   (b) **Avoidance of Civil War** The plan proposed the partition of India into two dominions, which, despite being a painful decision, was seen by Congress leaders as a necessary compromise to prevent a civil war between different communal groups.

   (v) Two leaders of the Assertive Nationalists were

   (a) **Bal Gangadhar Tilak** Often referred to as 'Lokmanya, Tilak' was a prominent leader of the Assertive Nationalists, advocating for Swaraj as a birthright of Indians. He initiated the Shivaji festival in 1896 to inspire nationalism in addition to the Ganesh festival.

(b) **Lala Lajpat Rai** He was also called 'Punjab Kesari' and 'Lion of Punjab' and was instrumental in the freedom struggle and was known for his advocacy of aggressive policies against British rule. Along with Bipin Chandra Pal and Bal Gangadhar Tilak, he formed the Lal-Bal-Pal trio of extremist leaders.

(vi) Following are the two main objectives of League of Nations.

(a) **Prevention of wars** The League of Nations aimed to maintain peace and prevent wars through collective security and disarmament and settling international disputes through negotiation and arbitration.

(b) **Promotion of international cooperation** The league of Nations aimed to foster cooperation among nations in solving international problems of an economic, social, or humanitarian nature and to achieve international peace and security.

(vii) Before the beginning of the First World War, two major alliances were formed in Europe. These were

(a) **The Triple Entente** This alliance, established in the early 20th century, included France, Russia and the United Kingdom. It was formed through a series of agreements that aimed to counterbalance the growing strength of the Triple Alliance and provide mutual support and cooperation among the member nations.

(b) **The Triple Alliance** This alliance was formed in 1882 and comprised and Germany, Austria-Hungary and Italy. It was intended primarily as a defensive pact, where each member promised to support the others in case of an attack by two or more powers, or in case of aggression by France against Germany or Italy.

3. (i) The Lok Sabha is more powerful than the Rajya Sabha because it has

- **Legislative Power over Money Bills** The Lok Sabha holds exclusive powers to introduce and make decisions on money bills.
  While the Rajya Sabha can suggest amendments, it cannot reject or indefinitely withhold its approval of money bills, which must be returned within 14 days.
- **Major Role in Government Formation** The Lok Sabha is directly involved in the formation of the government, as the Prime Minister and the majority of the cabinet ministers are typically from the Lok Sabha. This house reflects the direct choice of the electorate.
- **Motion of No-Confidence** Only the Lok Sabha has the power to move and pass a motion of no confidence against the sitting government.
  If such a motion passes, it necessitates the resignation of the entire cabinet, underscoring the greater political power of the Lok Sabha.

(ii) The session of the Rajya Sabha can be adjourned sine die by the Chairman of the Rajya Sabha, who is the Vice-President of India. This type of adjournment marks the end of a session without any definite date for resumption.

The Rajya Sabha, or the Upper House of Parliament, is composed of representatives from the states and union territories. 238 members are elected by the state legislative assemblies, and 12 members are nominated by the President of India.

The total membership is limited by the Constitution, which allocates seats based on the population of each state and territory.

(iii) The four legislative powers of the Parliament are as follows

(a) **Amendment of the Constitution** Parliament can amend the Constitution, subject to the provisions of Article 368.

(b) **Passing Laws** Parliament can legislate on subjects listed in the Union List and, under certain circumstances, on the Concurrent List shared with states.

(c) **National Emergency** During a national emergency, Parliament assumes the power to make laws on any subject, including those normally reserved for states.

(d) **Creation or Abolition of States** Parliament can pass laws changing the boundaries of states or creating new ones.

4. (i) The three legislative powers of the President that justify the nominal position are as follows

- **Bill Assent** The President has the power to give assent to bills passed by Parliament, which is required for a bill to become law. This role is largely ceremonial as refusal to assent is rare and usually done on the advice of the cabinet.
- **Ordinance Issuance** The President can issue ordinances under article 123, when Parliament or any of the two houses are not in session, which have the same force as laws passed by Parliament.
- **Summoning and Proroguing Parliament** The President summons and prorogues the sessions of Parliament, but these actions are typically performed on the advice of the Prime Minister and the cabinet.

(ii) The three financial powers of the President are as follows

(a) **Budget Presentation** The budget is presented in the Parliament with the President's prior recommendation, necessary for any proposals involving expenditure from the Consolidated Fund of India.

(b) **Financial Bills** No financial bills involving expenditure can be introduced in Parliament without the President's recommendation.

(c) **Contingency Fund** The President is the custodian of the Contingency Fund of India (Article 267(1) of the Indian Constitution), allowing him to make advances to meet unforeseen expenses.

(iii) Impeachment procedure of the President is discussed below

- **Initiation** The process can be initiated by either house of Parliament i.e Rajya Sabha or Lok Sabha. The motion to impeach must be supported by at least one-fourth of the total number of members of that house.
- **Investigation** The charges are investigated, and the President has the right to appear and to be represented at the investigation.
- **Decision** For the impeachment to succeed, it must be passed by a two-thirds majority of the total membership of each house of the Parliament.

This rigorous procedure emphasises the stability of the executive head and ensures that impeachment is a measure of last resort based on substantial misdeeds or incapacity.

5. (i) Appointment and Qualifications of Supreme Court Judges.

The Judges of the Supreme Court are appointed by the President of India after consulting the Chief Justice of the Supreme Court.

The qualifications required for being a Supreme Court Judge are

(a) **Experience in the Judiciary** A person must have been a judge of one or more high courts for at least five years, or an advocate there for at least ten years.

(b) **Distinguished Jurist** Alternatively, a person must be a distinguished jurist in the opinion of the President, recognised for their expertise and contributions to the legal field.

(ii) Under Article 129, the Supreme Court of India is called a Court of Record. This statement can be justified the rough the following points

(a) **Permanent Record Keeping** As a Court of Record, all judgments, proceedings, and acts of the Supreme Court are recorded for perpetual memory and testimony.

These records are recognised as legal precedents and authoritative references.

(b) **Power to Punish for Contempt** The Court of Record status grants the Supreme Court the authority to punish for contempt of itself. This power helps maintain the respect and authority of the court.

(c) **Precedential Value** Decisions made by the Supreme Court as a Court of Record are binding on all lower courts within the territory of India. This ensures consistency and predictability in the application of the law across the country.

(iii) (a) Revisory jurisdiction refers to the power of the Supreme Court to review, revisit and possibly overturn its own decisions or those of lower courts. This jurisdiction is exercised to correct errors or injustices in judgments and to ensure that justice is served in accordance with law and evolving legal standards.

(b) Under Article 143 of the Constitution, the President of India can seek the advice of the Supreme Court on any question of law or fact that is of public importance or that which involves interpretation of the Constitution. This is known as the Advisory Jurisdiction. While the advice provided by the Supreme Court is generally respected, it is not binding on the President. This jurisdiction helps in clarifying legal issues and aiding executive decisions with judicial insight.

6. (i) The three British Policies of expansion were as follows

(a) **Doctrine of Lapse** Introduced by Lord Dalhousie, this policy allowed the British to annex any princely state where the ruler died without a direct heir.

(b) **Subsidiary Alliance** This strategy, pioneered by Lord Wellesley, involved placing British forces in a princely state and making it a protectorate of the British Empire, effectively controlling its external affairs.

(c) **Direct Conquest** Several regions of India were directly conquered through military force, expanding British territorial holdings and control over resources.

(ii) The impacts of the failure of Revolt of 1857 on the Mughals and Peshwas were

- **End of the Mughal Empire** The failure of the Revolt marked the end of the Mughal Empire, with Emperor Bahadur Shah II being deposed and exiled. This effectively eliminated the Mughal Empire as a political entity and symbol of authority in India.
- **Decline of the Peshwas** The Peshwas, who were leaders of the Maratha Empire, also faced decline as their power had been waning through earlier defeats. After the Revolt, any remaining influence or claims to authority by the Peshwas were further diminished, consolidating British dominance.

(iii) The Indian army was reorganised after the Revolt of 1857 in the following ways

- **Reduction of Indian Troops** The proportion of Indian soldiers in the army was reduced, and the number of European troops was increased to prevent future revolts.

- **Strategic Placement of Troops** The artillery units, which were crucial in any military engagement, were placed under direct British control and Indians were largely removed from these key positions.
- **Enhanced Segregation** The troops were reorganised based on ethnicity and religion to divide and rule by fostering distrust among different groups.
- **Improved Communication** The British improved infrastructure, like roads and telegraphs, to facilitate faster movement and communication of their forces across the country.

7. (i) The first President of the Indian National Congress was Womesh Chunder Bonnerjee.
The Objectives of Congress were
(a) **Promote Political Education and Unity** One of the main objectives was to promote political education among Indians and to foster a sense of unity against colonial rule.
(b) **Formulate and Present Demands** The Congress aimed to provide a platform for all Indians to discuss public matters and to formulate demands for greater civil and political rights from the British administration.

(ii) The role of the Press in the Growth of Nationalism was
(a) **Educating the Masses** Newspapers and periodicals played a critical role in educating the masses about political ideas and the impacts of colonial policies.
(b) **Fostering Unity** The press helped in creating a shared sense of identity and purpose among diverse linguistic and cultural groups across India.
(c) **Exposing Injustices** The press was instrumental in exposing the injustices and exploitation under British rule, which galvanised support for nationalist movements.

(iii) The four policies enforced by Lord Lytton's were
(a) **Vernacular Press Act (1878)** This act aimed to curb the freedom of the Indian press, particularly vernacular newspapers, to prevent the spread of nationalist ideas.
(b) **Arms Act (1878)** This law prohibited Indians from possessing arms without a licence.
(c) **Reduction of Maximum Age for Civil Service Examinations** Lord Lytton reduced the maximum age for appearing in civil service exams, making it difficult for Indians to enter the service.
(d) **Imperial Assemblies** Lord Lytton hosted luxurious assemblies and durbar to reinforce the might of the British Empire, even during famines and hardships faced by Indians, showing a stark disconnect and fueling resentment.

8. (i) The Salt March, also known as the Dandi March, is one of the most iconic events in the history of India's struggle for independence.
This march was a key part of the Civil Disobedience Movement, where Indians were encouraged to disobey British laws non-violently to press for independence.
The Civil Disobedience Movement was officially launched in 1930 following the culmination of the Salt March. The march itself began on 12th March, 1930.

(ii) The impacts of the Civil Disobedience Movement were as follows
- **Increased National Unity** The Civil Disobedience Movement, sparked by the Salt March, played a crucial role in bringing together Indians from different backgrounds. It transcended regional, caste and religious boundaries, creating a widespread collective consciousness against British rule.
This unity was pivotal in strengthening the national movement and making it a mass movement rather than being limited to the intellectuals and the elite.
- **Economic Impact** By boycotting British goods, refusing to pay taxes, and halting other economic activities that benefited the British economically, the movement delivered a blow to the British economy in India.
These boycotts were effective in reducing the revenue the British could extract from India.
- **International Attention** The non-violent nature of the protest drew widespread international attention, particularly from the Western world. Reports of British repression during the movement helped gain sympathy for the Indian cause, boosting support for Indian independence on an international level.

(iii) The four clauses of the Gandhi-Irwin Pact were
(a) **Release of Political Prisoners** A significant achievement of the pact was the release of thousands of political prisoners who were imprisoned for participating in the Civil Disobedience Movement. However, those convicted of violence were not included in this amnesty, which was a point of contention among some nationalists.
(b) **Salt Manufacture** The agreement allowed the collection and manufacture of salt by the coastal communities, which was crucial since the Salt March was specifically initiated against the salt tax imposed by the British.

(c) **Return of Confiscated Properties** Under the pact, the British agreed to return the confiscated lands and properties of the satyagrahis, although properties seized directly by the government were not returned. This clause aimed at alleviating some of the financial strains on the protesters who had sacrificed much in their fight against British laws.

(d) **Right to Peaceful Protests** The pact acknowledged the right of Indians to conduct peaceful protests. It also allowed Gandhi to represent the Indian National Congress at the Round Table Conference in London, marking a significant step toward negotiations for Indian self-rule.

9. (i) The cartoon likely illustrates the assassination of Archduke Franz Ferdinand of Austria in Sarajevo. This event occurred on 28th June, 1914, when the heir to the Austro-Hungarian throne was assassinated by Gavrilo Princip, a Bosnian Serb nationalist.

This assassination is widely acknowledged as the spark that ignited the First World War I, leading to the mobilisation of allied and central powers into one of the deadliest conflicts in human history.

(ii) Europe was rearranged as a consequence of the first world war in the following ways

(a) **New Nations Formed** The map of Europe was dramatically redrawn with several new nations emerging, such as Czechoslovakia, Poland and Yugoslavia, as multi-ethnic empires like Austro-Hungarian and Ottoman were dismantled.

(b) **Territorial Losses for Central Powers** Countries like Germany and Austria-Hungary lost significant territories to neighbouring states and new nations, altering the political landscape of Europe.

(c) **New Blocks Formed** There were formation of new blocks in Europe along with other non-European countries for example; UK sided with USA etc.

(iii) The Treaty of Versailles was viewed as Harsh and humiliating by Germans due to the following reasons

(a) **Territorial Losses** Germany lost significant territories, such as Alsace-Lorraine to France and parts of Prussia to the new Polish state, reducing its size and economic power.

(b) **War Guilt Clause** Article 231, known as the War Guilt Clause, forced Germany to accept sole responsibility for starting the war, a point of national humiliation.

(c) **Reparations** Germany was required to pay huge reparations, which strained its economy and contributed to severe economic hardships during the interwar period.

(d) **Military Restrictions** The treaty drastically limited the size and capability of the German military, undermining national defence and pride.

10. (i) The International Court of Justice (ICJ) is composed of 15 judges elected to nine-year terms by the United Nations General Assembly and the Security Council. These judges represent the principal legal systems of the world and no two judges may be from the same country, ensuring a diversity of legal traditions.

(ii) The three functions of the General Assembly are

(a) **Legislative Functions** The General Assembly passes resolutions that influence international law and practices.

(b) **Budgetary Functions** It approves the budget of the United Nations and determines the financial contributions of member states.

(c) **Electoral Functions** The General Assembly elects non-permanent members of the Security Council, judges of the International Court of Justice and other key officials within the UN system.

(iii) UNESCO (United Nations Educational, Scientific and Cultural Organisation) is authorised to give the intangible heritage tag.

The contributions of UNESCO in the preservation of culture are as follows

(a) **World Heritage Sites** It identifies and preserves cultural sites and natural wonders around the world that are of outstanding value to humanity.

(b) **Preserves Heritage** It aims at preserving the rich cultural heritage of the countries and focuses on preserving its significance.

(c) **Intangible Heritage** It also maintains a list of Intangible heritage for example, Garba, Vedic Chanting etc from India to preserve their cultural significance.

Write your Roll No.

Board Examination Paper 2024

History & Civics 10th (Code 50)

No. of Ques : 10 | No. of Parts : 2 | Time : 2 Hrs. | Max. Marks : 80

General Instructions

1. Attempt all questions from Part I (Compulsory).
2. A total of 5 questions are to be attempted from Part II, 2 out of 3 questions from Section A and 3 out of 5 questions from Section B.
3. The intended marks for questions or parts of questions are given in brackets [].

Part-I Attempt all questions from this part

(30 Marks)

Que 1.

Select the correct answers to the questions from the given options. [16 ×1]

(i) The salaries and allowances of the ministers are decided by the

(a) Parliament (b) Finance Minister
(c) President (d) Prime Minister

(ii) Civil Cases: Court of District Judge: : Criminal Cases:

(a) Revenue Court (b) Family Court
(c) Sessions Court (d) Commissioner's Court

(iii)

The Lok Adalat has many advantages. Which of the following statements about the advantages of the Lok Adalat is best described in the picture given above?

(a) It is inexpensive
(b) It is organised in various parts of the country
(c) It works on the spirit of compromise
(d) It reduces the burden of the higher courts

(iv) Given below are details of Indian citizens. Select the ones who are eligible for appointment as a High Court Judge.

Candidate	Age	Details
P	65	Is a distinguished jurist
Q	61	Has been a High Court Advocate for 10 years
R	67	Has been a High Court Advocate for 5 years
S	56	Has held a judicial office for at least 10 years

(a) P and R (b) Q and S
(c) R and P (d) Q and R

(v) The strength of the house is 550. On a particular day 50 members are present. The speaker decides to adjourn the house. Identify the most likely reason for the adjournment.

(a) Disorder in the house
(b) Lack of quorum
(c) Breach of privilege
(d) Contempt of the House

(vi) During a hung assembly when no party gets the majority, the President appoints the Prime Minister. What power is the President exercising?

(a) Legislative (b) Executive
(c) Discretionary (d) Judicial

(vii) Read the two statements given below and select the option that shows the correct relationship between (A) and (R).

Assertion (A) Forward Bloc had the objective of abolishing Zamindari System.

Reason (R) Subhash Chandra Bose wanted to establish a socialist state.

Codes

(a) A is true but R is false
(b) R is the reason for A
(c) Both A and R are false
(d) Only R is true, A is false

(viii) The ...... aimed to introduce equality between British and Indian Judges.

(a) Vernacular Press Act
(b) Gagging Act
(c) Indian Universities Act
(d) Ilbert Bill

(ix) The Rowlatt Act was called the Black Act because the Indians

(a) could not possess any arms.
(b) could not export any goods.
(c) could be arrested without a warrant.
(d) could be sent overseas on duty.

(x) Who organised the Grand Delhi Durbar?

(a) Lord Curzon (b) Lord Canning
(c) Lord Lytton (d) Lord Dalhousie

(xi) Tina is inspired by the methods of the Early Nationalists and wants to follow them. She notices that the road leading to her school is damaged and has many potholes. Which of the following methods is she most likely to follow, to solve this problem?

(a) Boycott the civic authorities
(b) Gather a group of students and protest
(c) Write a petition to the authorities highlighting the problem
(d) Block the entrance to the road

(xii) Given below are the objectives of the Indian National Army. Identify the odd one out of the following.

(a) To organise a provisional government of Free India.
(b) Total mobilisation of Indian manpower and money.
(c) Unity, faith and sacrifice.
(d) To train and organise public opinion in the country.

(xiii) Tahir is preparing to give a speech about the Sati system in India. Which of the following Indian leader's contribution must he mentions in his speech?

(a) Raja Rammohan Roy
(b) WC Bonerjee
(c) Bipin Chandra Pal
(d) Jyotiba Phule

(xiv) Which of the following is not a consequence of the Second World War?

(a) Austria and Hungary became separate states
(b) Defeat of the Axis powers
(c) Beginning of the Cold War
(d) Formation of the United Nations

(xv) Identify the principle of Panchsheel.

(a) Mutual non-aggression
(b) Regulate armaments
(c) Take action against aggressor
(d) Recommend admission of members

(xvi)

Which incident depicted in the above cartoon led to the beginning of the Second World War?

(a) Hitler's policy of Imperialism
(b) Hitler's attack on Poland
(c) Hitler's annexation of Austria
(d) Hitler's attack on Czechoslovakia

Que 2.

(i) Mention any two writs issued by the High Court. [2]

(ii) Imagine you are an Indian ruler who has signed the Subsidiary Alliance. Mention any two conditions of this agreement which will affect you. [2]

(iii) Mention any two causes of the Quit India Movement. [2]

(iv) In which year did the *Surat Split* happen? What was the result of this split? [2]

(v) Mention any two common ideologies of Fascism and Nazism. [2]

(vi) Name the two cities of Japan which were bombed by America in the year 1945. [2]

(vii) Read the given news carefully and answer the question that follows.

Government's power to promulgate, repromulgate Ordinances _ why and how

An Ordinance "shall have the same force and effect as an Act of Parliament". But the government is required to bring an Ordinance before Parliament for ratification - and failure to do so will lead to its lapsing "at the expiration of six weeks from the reassembly of Parliament". *The Indian Express - 25th May, 2023*

Mention any two points regarding an ordinance that can be deduced from the above news. [2]

Part-II Section A (Civics) Attempt any two questions from this section

(20 Marks)

Que 3.

The Union Parliament is the supreme legislative body in the country. With reference to the Indian Parliament answer the following questions.

(i) The Rajya Sabha is called a Permanent House. Explain this statement. [3]

(ii) Explain the composition of the Rajya Sabha. [3]

(iii) Mention any two exclusive powers of the Lok Sabha and two powers exclusive to the Rajya Sabha. [4]

Que 4.

The Council of Ministers headed by the Prime Minister aids and advises the President. In this context, answer the following questions.

(i) Mention any three points to distinguish between the Council of Ministers and the Cabinet [3]

(ii) Who appoints the Cabinet Ministers? Mention any two administrative powers of the Cabinet. [3]

(iii) The President is the nominal head of the Indian Union. Mention any four functions of the Prime Minister with reference to the President. [4]

Que 5.

The judiciary is the system of courts that interprets and guards the Indian Constitution. With reference to the Supreme Court of India, answer the following.

(i) What is the composition of the Supreme Court? Why is it called the Court of Record? [3]

(ii) Explain the power of Judicial Review. [3]

(iii) What is meant by the term Original Jurisdiction? Mention any three cases which come under this jurisdiction. [4]

Section B (History) Attempt any three questions from this section

(30 Marks)

Que 6.

The Revolt of 1857 was the beginning of the independence struggle against the colonial rule of the British. With reference to the consequences of the Revolt, answer the following.

(i) Mention any three changes made in the administration with the end of the Company's Rule. [3]

(ii) State any three policies promised to Indians in Queen Victoria's Proclamation. [3]

(iii) Mention any four changes made in the army after the Revolt. [4]

Que 7.

The Indian National Movement is divided into three phases. With reference to the Second Phase of the Indian National Movement, answer the following questions.

(i) Who partitioned Bengal? Mention any two points to explain the perspective of the Nationalists regarding the actual motive behind the decision of Partition. [3]

(ii) What was the objective of the Assertive Nationalists? Mention any two contributions of Bal Gangadhar Tilak. [3]

(iii) In which year was the Muslim League formed? Mention any three objectives of the Muslim League. [4]

Que 8.

Look at the picture given and answer the following questions.

The Times of India

WAY OUT OF INDIAN DEADLOCK

BRITAIN'S PLAN FOR SMOOTH TRANSFER OF POWER

Immediate Dominion Status Granted

PEOPLE ASKED TO DECIDE PARTITION QUESTION

Present Constituent Assembly Not Disturbed

Only Practical Method

PREMIER'S VIEW

Plan Commended To Commons

MR. NEHRU COMMENDS PLAN TO NATION

Mr. Jinnah Hopeful Of League's Acceptance

SARDAR BALDEV SINGH CALLS IT "SETTLEMENT"

"UNIFIED INDIA BEST SOLUTION"

Viceroy's Appeal

"THERE IS INDIAN CONSCIOUSNESS"

(i) Name the Viceroy who announced the plan for smooth transfer of power. Mention any two clauses of his plan with reference to the Princely States. [3]

(ii) Mention any three reasons for the acceptance of his plan by the Congress. [3]

(iii) Mention any four provisions of the Indian Independence Act of 1947. [4]

Que 9.

The final act of the long-drawn-out negotiations took place at Versailles on Saturday afternoon, and to-day Germany and the Allies - always with the exception of America - are at peace. Peace is a blessed word, and both the word and the fact are welcome to-day. So far as Germany is concerned there is for the present an end of strife, and at least a formal return to the decent relations of civilised states.

Editorial : Peace in force (12th January, 1920)

The Guardian

(i) Mention any three causes of the World War which ended with the signing of the treaty being discussed in the passage above. [3]

(ii) Name the organisation which was established in 1920 to maintain peace after this war. Mention any two of its objectives. [3]

(iii) Mention any four clauses of the Treaty which affected Germany. [4]

Que 10.

Both the United Nations Organisation and the Non-Aligned Movement aim to achieve international peace and security. In this context, answer the following.

(i) Mention any three functions of the Security Council. [3]

(ii) Mention any three functions of the World Health Organisation. [3]

(iii) Name any two founders of the Non-Aligned Movement. Mention any two of its objectives. [4]

Answers in Topper's Style

1. (i) (a) Parliament

(ii) (c) Sessions Court

(iii) (c) It works on the spirit of compromise

(iv) (b) Q and S

(v) (b) Lack of quorum

(vi) (c) Discretionary

(vii) (b) R is the reason for A

(viii) (d) Ilbert Bill

(ix) (c) could be arrested without a warrant.

(x) (a) Lord Curzon

(xi) (c) Write a petition to the authorities highlighting the problem

(xii) (b) Total mobilisation of Indian manpower and money.

(xiii) (a) Raja Rammohan Roy

(xiv) (a) Austria and Hungary became separate states

(xv) (a) Mutual non-aggression

(xvi) (b) Hitler's attack on Poland

2. (i) Two writs of High Court are as follows

(a) **Writ of Prohibition** This writ is designed to prevent a subordinate court or tribunal from exceeding its authority or its scope of jurisdiction.

(b) **Writ of Quo Warranto** It is used to judicially control executive activities in the matter of making nominations for public posts, in accordance with the applicable statutory provisions.

(ii) As an Indian ruler who has signed the Subsidiary Alliance, two conditions of this agreement that would significantly affect me are

(a) Military control and presence

(b) Financial burden

(iii) The two causes of the Quit India Movement were

(a) Failure of Cripps Mission

(b) Hardships caused during World War II

(iv) The Surat split happened on 26th December, 1907. The result of this split was the division of the Indian National Congress into Moderates and Radicals (extremists).

(v) The two common ideologies of Fascism and Nazism are as follows

(a) Both Mussolini and Hitler aimed at restoring the status and dignity of their nations by making them strong powers.

(b) Both aimed at providing strong, stable and efficient Governments.

(vi) Hiroshima and Nagasaki were the cities of Japan which were bombed by America in 1945.

(vii) The two points regarding an ordinance that can be deduced from the given news are

- Ordinance are temporary in nature.
- Parliamentary Approval is necessary for an ordinance to remain in effect.

3. (i) The Rajya Sabha is called a Permanent House as it is the upper house of the Indian Parliament. Since, it is a permanent assembly, it cannot be dissolved. The Lok Sabha is the only body that can be dissolved. One-third members of Rajya Sabha retire every two years.

(ii) The composition of Rajya Sabha at present includes 245 members. Out of which 233 members are elected from States and Union Territories of Delhi and Puducherry and 12 are nominated by the President. These 12 nominated members are distinguished people in the field of Literature, Science, Art and Social Sciences.

(iii) The two exclusive powers of the Lok Sabha are

(a) Only the Lok Sabha can vote on the demands for grants in the budget.

(b) The Council of Ministers is collectively responsible only to the Lok Sabha. Thus, the Lok Sabha alone can vote a minister out of office.

The two exclusive powers of Rajya Sabha are

(a) The Parliament can assume temporary power to legislate on State List subjects (Article 249) only if Rajya Sabha passes a resolution, which is supported by two-third (2/3rd) majority of its members present and voting.

(b) The All-India Services can be established only if the Rajya Sabha passes a resolution for it, which is supported by two-third (2/3rd) majority of its members present and voting.

4. (i) The three points to distinguish between the Councils of Ministers and the Cabinet are

Council of Ministers	Cabinet Ministers
(a) It is a wider body.	It is a smaller body.
(b) It includes all three categories of ministers, Cabinet members, ministers of state and deputy ministers.	It includes the ministers holding important ministries.
(c) It does not meet, as a body,to transact government business.It has no collective functions.	It meets as a body usually once a week to take decisions regarding the transactions of government business.

(ii) The Cabinet Ministers are appointed by the President on the advice of the Prime Minister.

The two administrative powers of the cabinet are

(a) **Policy Making** The Council of Ministers is mainly a policy formulating body. It formulates both external and domestic policies of the government on important matters.

(b) **Implementation of Policies** When the policy decision on any subject is taken by the Cabinet, then, the Minister of State and the Deputy Minister of the concerned ministry examine the policies.

(iii) The President is the nominal head of the Indian Union. The four functions of the Prime Ministers with reference to the President are as follows

(a) The Prime Minister is the principal advisor to the President.

(b) The Prime Minister chooses the ministers and on his advice the President appoints them.

(c) The Prime Minister acts as a link between the President and the Council of Ministers as it communicates all the decisions of the Council of Ministers to the President on administration of the Union.

(d) The Prime Minister advises the President with regard to the appointment of important officials, such as CAG, members of UPSC, Election Commission, etc.

5. (i) The Composition of the Supreme Court consists of 34 judges including 1 Chief Justice and 33 other Judges. Originally the strength was fixed at 8 (1 Chief Justice and 7 other Judges).

The Supreme Court is called the Court of Record because the judgments, proceedings and acts of the Supreme Court are recorded for perpetual memory and testimony. These records cannot be questioned when produced before any court.

(ii) Judicial Review is a power given to the courts of India to examine the actions of the legislatures, executive and administrative arms of the centre and state government. It is to ensure that such actions comply with the provisions of the Constitution.

If the enactments and orders are found to be violative of the Constitution, they can be declared as illegal, unconstitutional and invalid (null and void) by the judiciary.

(iii) The term Original Jurisdiction refers to the power to hear and determine a dispute in the first instance. It happens in those cases, which cannot be transferred in any court other than the Supreme Court.

Three cases which come under this jurisdiction include

(a) Centre-State or Inter-State Disputes

(b) Transfer of cases

(c) Protection of Fundamental Rights

6. (i) Three changes made in the administration with the end of the Company's Rule

(a) **Establishment of the British Raj** The British government took direct control over India, replacing the rule of the East India Company.

(b) **Centralisation of Power** Authority was concentrated in the hands of British administrators appointed by the Crown.

(c) **Implementation of British Policies** New policies were introduced to impose British dominance.

(ii) The three policies promised to Indians in Queen Victoria's Proclamation are as follows

(a) Treat all subjects i.e. Indians and Europeans as equal (education and ability would be the basis of all appointments).

(b) Follow a policy of non-intervention in social and religious matters of Indians.

(c) A general pardon was granted to all those who laid down arms by 2nd January, 1859, except those who were found guilty of murder of British subjects.

(iii) The four changes made in the army after the Revolt were

(a) The proportion of the Europeans to Indians in the army was raised.

(b) Artillery and other effective weapons of war were placed exclusively under the charge of the Europeans.

(c) To curb nationalism, Indian soldiers of different communities, castes and religions were all mixed up and they were kept away in remote places.

(d) Indian soldiers were not provided newspapers, journals and nationalist publications to keep them separated from the life of the rest of the population.

7. (i) Bengal was partitioned by the Viceroy Lord Curzon. The two major points to explain the perspective of the Nationalists regarding the actual motive behind the decision of partition were as follows

(a) At that period, Bengal had become the main centre of the Indian politics and Indian nationalism. So, the British expected to regulate the rising tide of nationalism by the division of Bengal.

(b) Another reason of the Partition of Bengal was to destroy the political influence of the educated middle class, among whom the Bengali intellectuals was the most prominent.

(ii) The objectives of Assertive Nationalists were to achieve 'Swaraj' by self-reliant methods and sacrifices.

The major contributions of Bal Gangadhar Tilak were

(a) In 1880, he started the Poona New English School with a view to educate Indians by charging small fees.

(b) He started two newspapers i.e. Maratha (English) and Kesari (Marathi) in order to spread the idea of nationalism.

(iii) The Muslim League was formed on 1st October, 1906.

The three objectives of the Muslim League were

(a) To promote the feelings of loyalty towards the British Government amongst the Indian Muslims.

(b) To remove any misconception regarding the intentions of the government in relation to the Indian Muslim.

(c) To protect and advance the political rights and other interests of the Muslims of India.

8. (i) Lord Mountbatten was the Viceroy who announced the plan for smooth transfer of power. The two clauses of his plan with reference to the Princely states were as follows

(a) India would be divided into two dominions, i.e. India and Pakistan.

(b) It was up to the two Dominions, i.e. India and Pakistan, to decide what relations they would have with the British Commonwealth and with each other.

(ii) The three reasons for the acceptance of his plan by the Congress were

(a) The Congress leaders realised that the large-scale communal riots and mass killing could be prevented only by accepting the Muslim League's demand for Pakistan.

(b) The Congress believed that it could not have the joint administration with the Muslim League as it had bitter experience in interim government of 1946.

(c) The Congress leaders realised that the extension of the British rule would be harmful to India. By applying the 'Divide and Rule Policy' the Britishers divided Hindu and Muslim community in India.

(iii) The four major provisions of Indian Independence Act of 1947 were

(a) India would be partitioned and two independent dominions i.e. India and Pakistan would be created from 15th August, 1947. The act provided the legislative supremacy of both the dominions.

(b) The territories of the two dominions were divided in such terms that Pakistan would comprise of Sindh, British Baluchistan, North-West Frontier Province, the West Punjab and East Bengal. The exact boundaries of the dominions would be determined by a Boundary Commission.

(c) For each of the two dominions, there would be a Governor-General who would be appointed by the British King and who would represent the king for the purposes of the government of the dominions.

(d) Each of the Dominions and all Provinces were to be governed in accordance with the Act of 1935 till the new Constitution was formed.

9. (i) The three main causes of the World War which ended with the signing of the treaty being discussed in the passage are

(a) **Military** The First World War was fought not only by the soldiers but also by the civilians. The use of arms and the spreading of new types of weapons by every nation made the situation unfavourable for peace. To protect their colonies the European powers developed their defence system in the colonies. This created an atmosphere of fear, insecurity and mutual hatred.

(b) **Alliance System** The war was fought between allied powers (Britain, France, Russia and their allies) and central powers (Germany, Austria and their allies). These alliances have their benefits for which they allied together and fought on different fronts.

(c) **Imperialism** Germany, Italy, Russia and Japan worked to increase their influence over the colonies in the least developed continents like Asia and Africa. Competition between European powers for colonies and resources around the world exacerbated tensions.

(ii) In 1920, the League of Nations was established. The main objectives of this organisation were

(a) To ensure disarmament, war prevention through collective security.

(b) It also focuses on international conflict resolution through conversation and diplomacy and global well-being.

(iii) The four clauses of the Treaty which affected Germany were

(a) **War Guilt Clause** This clause assigned full responsibility for the war and its damages to Germany and its allies.

(b) **Territorial Losses** The mineral-rich land of Ruhr was given to France, which further deteriorated the conditions for Germany.

(c) **Reparations** A huge sum of money was signed to give as the war guilt by the winning parties. It put an additional pressure on the economy of Germany.

(d) **Demilitarisation and Military Restrictions** Germany was demilitarised and only a small number of the police force was allowed to be formed. This condition was given to reduce the chance of war initiation by Germany.

10. (i) The three main functions of the Security Council are

(a) It maintains international peace and security in accordance with the principles and purposes of the United Nations.

(b) It investigates any dispute or situation which might lead to international friction.

(c) It recommends methods of adjusting such disputes or the terms of settlement.

(ii) The three main functions of World Health Organisation are as follows

(a) It helps countries to improve their health system by building up infrastructure.

(b) It gives important drugs needed for medical care.

(c) It launches programmes to immunise children against 6 major diseases such as measles, diphtheria, tetanus, tuberculosis, polio and whooping cough.

(iii) The two founders of the Non-Aligned Movement were Jawaharlal Nehru of India and Kwame Nkrumah of Ghana.

The two main objectives of Non-Aligned Movement are

(a) To remove all those factors and tendencies that could lead to war.

(b) To project the growing freedom of the newly independent Asian and African countries and help them to keep away from colonial domination.

Proficiency Building Zone

Welcome to the Proficiency Building Zone !

This section contains **15 Sample Question Papers** designed to enhance your problem-solving skills and proficiency. Use these papers to practice regularly and track your progress. Remember, consistent practice is key to mastering ICSE History & Civics.

Progress Tracker Tick the papers as you complete them.

- ☐ Sample Paper 1 _____ (Fill your score)
- ☐ Sample Paper 2 _____ (Fill your score)
- ☐ Sample Paper 3 _____ (Fill your score)
- ☐ Sample Paper 4 _____ (Fill your score)
- ☐ Sample Paper 5 _____ (Fill your score)
- ☐ Sample Paper 6 _____ (Fill your score)
- ☐ Sample Paper 7 _____ (Fill your score)
- ☐ Sample Paper 8 _____ (Fill your score)
- ☐ Sample Paper 9 _____ (Fill your score)
- ☐ Sample Paper 10 _____ (Fill your score)
- ☐ Sample Paper 11 _____ (Fill your score)
- ☐ Sample Paper 12 _____ (Fill your score)
- ☐ Sample Paper 13 _____ (Fill your score)
- ☐ Sample Paper 14 _____ (Fill your score)
- ☐ Sample Paper 15 _____ (Fill your score)

SQP Code : **PB-1/15** Series ***i*-Succeed 1-25/15** Roll No. | | | | | | | | |

Sample Question Paper 01

History & Civics 10th (Code 50)

General Instructions

1. Attempt all questions from Part I (Compulsory).
2. A total of 5 questions are to be attempted from Part II, 2 out of 3 questions from Section A and 3 out of 5 questions from Section B.
3. The intended marks for questions or parts of questions are given in brackets ( ).

Time : 2 Hrs.

Max. Marks : 80

Part-I Attempt all questions from this part

Que 1.

Choose the correct option. (16)

(i) India is federal in form and unitary in spirit. Which among the following best describes the same? [Application]

(a) India has certain unitary features which limit the powers of the State Governments.

(b) Constitution of India is both rigid and flexible.

(c) India has a federal form of Government.

(d) Both Union and State Governments draw their power and the authority from the Constitution.

(ii) Given below are the details of few citizens (1)

Candidate	Age	Details
A	31	Bankrupt
B	35	Belongs to rural areas
C	30	Actor
D	32	Member of Lok Sabha

Select the candidate who fulfills the criteria of becoming the Vice-President of India. [Understanding]

(a) A (b) B

(c) C (d) D

(iii) If any question arises whether a bill is a money bill or not, the decision of the X thereon will be final and with the prior recommendation of the Y for introduction in Lok sabha. [Analyse]

Identify the X and Y in the above given information. (1)

(a) Prime Minister and the Home Minister

(b) Speaker and Finance Minister

(c) Cabinet Secretary and Speaker

(d) Speaker and the President

(iv) The given below image depicts the oath taking ceremony. Who among the following administers the oath to the office of the President of India? [Understanding] (1)

(a) Prime Minister

(b) Vice- President

(c) Chief Justice of India

(d) Speaker of Lok Sabha

(v) A person is under a trial for theft. He will be tried in which court? [Recall] (1)

P. District Court
Q. Sessions Court
R. Court of Chief Judicial Magistrate
S. Court of First Class Magistrate

(a) P and Q (b) R and S
(c) P and S (d) Q and R

(vi) Parliamentary Government: India : : Presidential : ? [Recall] (1)

(a) Canada (b) USA
(c) Britain (d) Israel

(vii) Read the two statements below about Non-Cooperation Movement and select the option that shows the correct relationship between A and R. [Analyse] (1)

Assertion (A) The Non-Cooperation Movement emphasised on the use of Swadeshi and boycott programmes.

Reason (R) The concept of Swadeshi and the boycott of foreign goods gave impetus to the handicraft and local industries.

(a) R contradicts A
(b) R is the reason for A
(c) A is true, but R is false
(d) A and R are independent of each other

(viii) Country A wants to gain independence and wants to use the methods similar to the ones used by Indian Assertive Nationalists. [Analyse] (1)

Based on the information which methods would not fit the ones used by Country A?

(a) National Education
(b) Swadeshi
(c) Prayers and Petition
(d) Boycott

(ix) There was a continuous shortage of water supply in the area where Mayank resided. Soon, there was a rally organised by a Minister of that area, Mayank sat with a placard in his hand with "To make the deaf hear" written on it. He was following the ideology of [Application] (1)

(a) Bhagat Singh
(b) Lala Lajpat Rai
(c) Subhash Chandra Bose
(d) Mahatma Gandhi

(x) What was the immediate cause of the given below incidence? [Application](1)

EXTRA
Baltimore American
FINAL EDITION
ENGLAND, FRANCE DECLARE WAR

(a) Invasion of Poland by Hitler
(b) Bombing of Hiroshima and Nagasaki
(c) Murder of Archeduke of Austria
(d) None of the above

(xi) The Non-Permanent members of the Security Council are elected for a period of [Recall] (1)

(a) two years
(b) one year
(c) three years
(d) four years

(xii) Siya, a school girl is doing a research on an Assertive Nationalist who said "Swaraj is my birthright and I shall have it". Who is Siya researching about? [Understanding] (1)

(a) Bipin Chandra Pal
(b) Lala Lajpat Rai
(c) Bal Gangadhar Tilak
(d) Dadabhai Naoroji

(xiii) Which of the following is not correct about Treaty of Versailles? [Understanding] (1)

(a) Germany was held responsible for the war.
(b) Rhine Valley was given to the Allied Powers.
(c) League of Nations was created.
(d) It was signed on 28th July, 1919.

(xiv) Which of the following factors led to the formation of NAM? [Understanding] (1)

(a) Formation of collective forces
(b) Poverty of newly independent nations
(c) Struggle against Imperialism
(d) All of the above

(xv) Fascism : Nationalism and Individual Institutions :: Nazism :: .... [Recall] (1)

(a) Extreme Nationalism and Dictatorship
(b) Equality and Political freedom
(c) Democracy and Sovereignty
(d) Both (b) and (c)

(xvi) Identify the odd one out. Which among the following is not the part of NAM? (1) [Analyse]

(a) India
(b) Indonesia
(c) Sri Lanka
(d) USA

Que 2.

(i) Read the extract given below and answer the question which follows.

Headline : Did the Supreme Court Truly Give the Delhi Government a 'Big Win'?

The order leaves the most pertinent question hanging in the balance: Is the Union government constitutionally barred from Legislative and Executive power over 'Services' under Article 239AA(3)?

Source: The Wire

On the basis of above information, enumerate any two legislative powers of Union Legislature. [Recall] (2)

(ii) Explain the following terms in short. [Recall] (2)

(a) Zero Hour
(b) Adjournment Motion

(iii) Mention two reasons for the faith of the Moderates in the British sense of justice. [Recall] (2)

(iv) State the reason due to which the British revoke the partition of Bengal. [Recall] (2)

(v) Why was the Simon Commission boycotted by the Indians? [Recall] (2)

(vi) Mention any two functions of World Health Organisation (WHO). [Recall] (2)

(vii) Mention any two ways through which the Treaty of Versailles benefitted France. [Recall] (2)

Part-II Section A (Civics) Attempt any two questions from this section

Que 3.

The Parliament of India (Union Parliament) is supreme power holding body of the country. In this context, answer the following questions.

(i) The Union Legislature do not just possess law making authority but also has a lot of financial power as well. Enumerate some of the financial powers of the Union Parliament. [Analyse] (3)

(ii) Mention three instances when the Parliament can make laws on the subjects entered in the State List. [Recall] (3)

(iii) What do you mean by Council of States? What are the qualifications necessary to become a member of the Upper house of the Parliament in the Rajya Sabha? [Analyse] (1+3)

Que 4.

Article 63 stipulates that there shall be a Vice-President of India. Vice-President act as President in the absence of the President.
In this context, answer the following questions.

(i) Other than citizenship of India, mention the qualifications of the Vice-President. [Recall](3)

(ii) Mention any three points regarding the term of office of the Vice-President. [Recall] (3)

(iii) In which cases, the Vice-President acts as the President or discharges the functions of the President? How does his emoluments are justified? [Analyse] (2+2)

Que 5.

An independent judiciary is a feature of federal governance. With reference to the Supreme Court, answer the following questions

(i) What do you mean by appellate jurisdiction? State any two types of cases over which the Supreme Court has appellate jurisdiction. [Analyse] (1+2)

(ii) Mention the qualifications required to become a Supreme Court Judge. [Recall] (3)

(iii) (a) The Judiciary is kept independent from the control of the Executive and Legislature. Give reasons. [Recall] (2)

(b) Explain the procedure for the removal of the Supreme Court Judge? [Recall] (2)

Section B (History) Attempt any three questions from this section

Que 6.

Nationalism is an idea and movement that holds that the nation should be congruent with the state. In the context of nationalism, explain each of the following.

(i) Discuss the impacts of socio-religious reform movement on nationalism. [Recall] (3)

(ii) Explain the role of press during this period. [Recall] (3)

(iii) Discuss the reaction of Britishers with the formation of Indian National Congress. State the appropriate reason for their change of attitude later. [Recall] (2+2)

Que 7.

European countries suffered from unemployment, social unrest and different nationalist aspirations which led to the rise of dictatorship. With reference to this, answer the following questions.

(i) Explain briefly the rise of Fascism in Italy. State any two impacts on Italy. [Analyse] (1+2)

(ii) What do you mean by Fascism? How the ideologies of Fascism were similar to Nazism? [Analyse] (1+3)

(iii) Why did Italy and Germany lose faith in post World War I democratic governments? [Recall] (3)

SP-01 **Que 8.**

Read the excerpt given below and answer the questions that follow.

The movement democratised India's freedom struggle and saw the participation of women, peasants, workers, students, and people from all castes and religions. It energised the Congress leadership and base. The British were stunned. And then a violent incident in Chauri Chaura saw Gandhi withdraw the movement on principle, much to the disappointment of even his colleagues.

Source : Hindustan Times

(i) Which movement was combined with this movement? When was this movement started? Explain about it. (1+2)

(ii) Mention any three impacts of this movement. [Recall] (3)

(iii) Describe any three programs undertaken in this movement. [Recall] (4)

Que 9.

Look at the picture carefully, the picture is one of the most prominent moderate leaders. In context to this picture, explain the following.

(i) (a) Identify the person given in the picture. [Recall] (1+2)

(b) Throw light on his early life.

(ii) Why was he known as the forerunner of Mahatma Gandhi? [Recall] (3)

(iii) Write about his contribution to the National Movement. [Application & Recall] (4)

Que 10.

With reference to United Nations as an organisation, answer the following questions.

(i) How international organisations like United Nations are helpful to Nations? [Analyse] (3)

(ii) What is the major difference in the privileges given to its permanent and non-permanent members by UN Charter? [Analyse] (3)

(iii) When was UNESCO formed and for what purpose? Write down any four functions of UNICEF as an agency of UN. [Recall] (1+3)

Answers in Topper's Style

My Commitment *I affirm that I am reviewing these answers only after I have solved the Sample Question Paper 1 on my own. My purpose of looking the answers is solely to verify whether my answers were correct or not and to identify my mistakes in case my answers were wrong or I could not answer that.*

1. (i) (a) India has certain unitary features which limit the powers of the State Governments.
   (ii) (b) B
   (iii) (d) Speaker and the President
   (iv) (c) Chief Justice of India
   (v) (b) R and S
   (vi) (b) USA
   (vii) (d) A and R are independent of each other
   (viii) (c) Prayers and Petition
   (ix) (a) Bhagat Singh
   (x) (a) Invasion of Poland by Hitler
   (xi) (a) two years
   (xii) (c) Bal Gangadhar Tilak
   (xiii) (d) It was signed on 28th July, 1919.
   (xiv) (d) All of the above
   (xv) (a) Extreme Nationalism and Dictatorship
   (xvi) (d) USA

2. (i) Two legislative powers of Union Legislature are
   (a) The Lok Sabha and the Rajya Sabha make laws on the Union List on important subjects such as foreign policy and defence.
   (b) The Houses can make laws on the matters which are not included in any of the three lists. This power is known as residuary powers.

   (ii) (a) Zero Hour is the time when Members of Parliament (MPs) can raise issues of urgent public importance. For raising matters during the Zero Hour, MPs must give the notice before 10 am to the Speaker/Chairman on the day of the sitting.
   (b) The adjournment motion is introduced in the Parliament to draw the attention of the House to a definite matter of urgent public importance. It requires the support of 50 members to be admitted.

   (iii) Two reasons for the faith of the Moderates in the British sense of Justice were as follows
   (a) The Moderates thought that the Englishmen will work towards the progress of India by putting it on the path of democracy and self- governance.
   (b) The Moderates thought that English rule had conferred benefits upon them, especially the English language and the modern means of communication and transport.

   (iv) The British revoke the partition of Bengal, due to the widespread agitation in the form of Swadeshi and Boycott movements. These movements were supported by all sections of the society. The movements rapidly gained momentum and rose to their peak within a short span of time.

   (v) The Simon Commission (1927) was boycotted by the Indians because
   - This commission consisted of all the Englishmen; no Indian was associated with it. It deeply hurt the self-respect of the Indians.
   - The government showed no inclination towards accepting the demand for Swaraj.

   (vi) Two functions of the World Health Organisation are
   (a) It helps countries to improve their health system by building up infrastructure.
   (b) It organises conferences, seminars and training activities for healthcare personnel to raise awareness.

   (vii) Two ways through which the Treaty of Versailles benefitted France were
   (a) Through the Treaty of Versailles France got more colonies as all the German colonies were taken and given to Britain and France.
   (b) As per the demand made by France, the Rhineland, the area between France and Germany was demilitarised. The German army could no longer get into this territory.

3. (i) Financial powers of the Union Parliament are as follows
   - **Annual Budget** The Parliament passes the Union Budget which contains the estimates of receipts and expenditure of the government for a financial year. The Union Finance Minister with the prior approval of the President presents the budget in the Parliament.
   - **Supplementary Demands** If the amount authorised for the current financial year is not sufficient, the Finance Minister (who is part of Union Parliament) may put up some supplementary demands during the course of the financial year.
   - **Money Bill** It can only be introduced in the Lok Sabha. Rajya Sabha cannot reject or amend it by the virtue of its own powers.

   (ii) The three instances when the Parliament can make laws on the subjects entered in the State List are as follows
   (a) If the Rajya Sabha passes a resolution by a two-third majority to the effect that a particular subject on the State List has assumed national importance.

(b) Two or more states request the centre to pass a law mutually agreed upon, regarding a particular subject in the State List. Such a law will be applicable to the requesting states.

(c) If a state of National Emergency is proclaimed by the President.

(iii) The Rajya Sabha is also called the Council of States. It is the Upper house of the Indian Parliament.

The qualifications necessary to become a member of the Rajya Sabha are as follows

- He/she should be an Indian citizen.
- He/she must be not less than 30 years of age.
- Should have his/her name in the electoral roll in any part of the country.
- He/she should not hold any office of profit under the Central or the State Government.
- He/she should not be a proclaimed criminal.
- He/she should be of sound mind.

4. (i) A person shall be eligible for election as Vice-President, if he/she

- has completed the age of 35 years.
- is qualified for election as a member of the Rajya Sabha.
- does not hold any office of profit under the Government of India or Government of any state or local authority.

(ii) Three important points regarding the term of office of the Vice-President are

(a) The Vice-President shall hold office for a term of five years from date on which he enters upon his office.

(b) The Vice-President may resign from his office by writing his resignation addressed to the President.

(c) The Vice-President shall continue to hold office, not withstanding the expiry of his term, until his successor enters upon his office.

(iii) The Vice-President acts as President or discharge his functions when

- the office of the President is vacant by reason of death, resignation, removal or otherwise.
- the President is unable to discharge his functions owing to absence, illness or any other cause.

The Vice-President, while acting as or performing the duties of the office, shall have all the powers and immunities of the President. He is entitled to such emoluments, allowances and privileges as may be determined by Parliament for the President, until provision is not made on this behalf.

5. (i) Appellate jurisdiction means the power of granting special leave to appeal against the judgement delivered by a High Court.

The Supreme Court enjoys a wide appellate jurisdiction which can be understood through the following two cases over which the Supreme Court has appellate jurisdiction.

(a) **Constitutional Matters** In these cases, an appeal can be made to the Supreme Court against the judgement of a High Court. If the High Court certifies that the case involves a substantial question of law regarding interpretation of the Constitution.

(b) **Civil Matters** In this case, an appeal lies to the Supreme Court from any judgement of the High Court, if the High Court certifies that the case involves a substantial question of law of general importance.

(ii) The qualifications required to become a Supreme Court Judge are as follows

- He/she must be a citizen of India.
- He/she has been for atleast 5 years as a Judge of a High Court or two or more such courts in succession.

Or He/she has been for atleast 10 years as an advocate of a High Court or two or more such courts in succession.

Or He/she is in the opinion of the President, a distinguished jurist.

(iii) (a) Judiciary is kept independent from the control of the Executive and the Legislature because of the following reasons

- India opted for a Federal System of administration. To protect the constitutional division of powers, an independent judiciary is an essential requirement.
- It is an essential requisite for ensuring human rights and protecting democracy.
- In a representative democracy, administration of justice assumes special significance in view of the rights of individuals, which needs protection against executive or legislative interference.

(b) A Supreme Court judge may be removed from office in the following manner which is commonly known as impeachment

- A motion addressed to the President signed by atleast 100 members of the Lok Sabha or 50 members of the Rajya Sabha is delivered to the Speaker or the Chairman.
- The motion is to be investigated by a Committee of three i.e. two judges of the Supreme Court and a distinguished jurist.
- If the Committee finds the judge guilty of misbehaviour or that he suffers incapacity, the motion together with the report of the committee is taken up for consideration in the House where the motion is pending.
- The judge will be removed after the President gives his order of removal on the said address.

6. (i) The socio-religious reform movement influenced the growth of nationalism in the following ways
- It showed the ways of reform to Indian masses.
- People started to believe in Indian leadership.
- It infused the sense of belongingness among Indian masses.

(ii) The press played an enormous role in fostering national unity and creating consciousness among the Indians. A large number of newspapers were started in the later half of the 18th century.

Some of the prominent newspapers were The Amrit Bazar Patrika, The Bengali, The Tribune, The Pioneer, The Times of India, The Hindu and The Statesman in English.

(iii) When the Indian National Congress (INC) was formed (1885), the British Government displayed a friendly and sympathetic attitude towards it. Lord Dufferin, the Viceroy of India at the time, supported the formation of the Congress, perceiving it as a means to act as a 'safety valve' for releasing popular discontent and thus safeguarding British interests in India. This supportive stance was based on the belief that the Congress would provide a platform for Indians to express their grievances and aspirations in a controlled and moderate manner, thereby preventing more radical and potentially destabilising actions.

The sympathetic attitude of the British Government changed later when the Congress began to demand more rights for the people and also when they saw the growth of Nationalism. The Britishers began to criticise the Congress leaders and branded them as 'Disloyal Babus, Seditious Brahmins and Violent Villians'.

7. (i) Fascism was a political ideology and a mass movement that dominated many parts of Central, Southern and Eastern Europe. Italy got nothing out of Treaty of Versailles. Thus, dictatorship got established in Italy under the powerful leadership of Benito Mussolini. People in Italy wanted bold and efficient governments which further led to the rise of Fascism.
Two impacts of Fascism on Italy are as follows
(a) It improved the economy, reduced unemployment and illiteracy.
(b) It curbed political freedom, censored press, prohibited freedom of speech.

(ii) Fascism is a form of dictatorship in which all the power is in one hand and it is compulsory for all the others to respect its orders.

The ideologies of Fascism were similar to Nazism in the following ways
- Both ideologies had faith in totalitarian rule.
- Both were against the democratic political systems.
- Both ideologies held the view that the state is supreme and it could suppress the fundamental rights and freedoms of the individual.
- Both believed in aggressive nationalism and imperialism.
- Both regarded war as an instrument for furthering national interests.
- Both preferred ultra nationalistic, anti-communist and anti-democratic rule.

(iii) Italy and Germany lose faith in the post World War-I democratic governments because they were weak and thus, could not respond properly to the needs and aspirations of the people. In the case of Italy, between 1919 and 1922, more than six coalition governments were formed. The government was divided into different policies and could not find any riots. Economic conditions became worse as trade and business got ruined leading to large-scale unemployment. There was shortage of food grains that had led to price rise. War debts and budget deficits caused a lot of difficulty. On the other hand, Germany had to pay a huge sum as war-indemnity, which led to a financial crisis. Therefore, the people were looking for a strong government with a firmer economic programme.

8. (i) Khilafat Movement was combined with Non-Cooperation Movement.
The Khilafat and Non-Cooperation Movement thus started on 31st August, 1921.
In the First World War, the Ottoman Turkey was defeated. There were rumours that a harsh peace treaty was going to be imposed on the Ottoman emperor, who was the spiritual head (Khalifa) of the Islamic world.
Thus, the Muslims of India decided to force Britain to change its Turkish policy and a Khilafat Committee was formed under the leadership of Maulana Azad, Hakim Ajmal Khan and Hasrat Mohani. Some young Muslim leaders like the brothers Muhammad Ali and Shaukat Ali also started discussing with Mahatma Gandhi about the possibility of a united mass action on the Khilafat issue. Gandhiji saw this as an opportunity of uniting Hindus and Muslims together and this led to beginning of the Khilafat Movement.

(ii) Three impacts of this movement were
(a) It fostered Hindu-Muslim unity.
(b) People started to resign from government services. The necessities like buying and selling of goods, schools were put on hold.
(c) The Khilafat Movement and the Congress Non-Cooperation Movement merged into one nationwide movement by the year-end of 1920.

In 1921, the Khilafat Committee noted that all Muslims are asking not to join the police and armed forces and not pay taxes. This outraged the government and the popular Ali brothers were arrested on charges of sedition.

(iii) Three programs undertaken in this movement were

(a) To boycott government-run schools, colleges and courts.

(b) To boycott foreign goods and resign from nominated seats in local bodies.

(c) To surrender titles and honorary offices and popularise the use of swadeshi and khadi clothes Charkha became a household article.

9. (i) (a) The person in the picture is Bal Gangadhar Tilak.

(b) Bal Gangadhar Tilak was born in Ratnagiri on 23rd July, 1856. He obtained his Graduation degree in Mathematics from Deccan College of Pune. After graduation, Tilak began teaching mathematics in a private school in Pune and later became a journalist. He became a strong critic for the Western education system and felt that it deteriorated the Indian students and disrespected India's heritage. He organised the Deccan Education Society to improve the quality of education for India's youth. He taught mathematics at the Fergusson College.

(ii) Bal Gangadhar Tilak is known as the forerunner of Mahatma Gandhi in a number of ways as follows

- Tilak's idea of Swaraj was akin to Mahatma Gandhi's idea of complete independence.
- Tilak sought close contact with the masses as Mahatma Gandhi did.
- Tilak preached the idea of Swadeshi, Boycott and Prohibition. These ideas were preached and followed by Mahatma Gandhi later on.
- Tilak had to suffer several terms of imprisonment for the sake of the country, an example followed by Mahatma Gandhi and other nationalist leaders.

(iii) Tilak's contribution was immense towards the Indian Society and National Movement. The Britishers called him "The Leader of the Indian unrest." He was one of the most important leaders of the second phase of Indian National Congress. Tilak was the leader of the radical section in the Congress who popularised the concept of patriotism by saying, "Swaraj is my birthright and I Shall have it." He started two newspapers Kesari written in Marathi and The Mahratta written in English which spread the idea of nationalism, courage and self-defence.

In 1893, he started the traditional religious Ganpati festival and in 1895 started Shivaji festival to encourage patriotism and the spirit of glory. His no-rent campaign in 1896 exposed the misrule of the British in India.

When famine and plague broke out in various parts of the country in 1896-97, Tilak criticised the British Government for not helping the people. It was because of him that the Congress adopted a resolution making Swaraj the aim of Congress in its Annual Session in 1906.

10. (i) International organisations like United Nations can be helpful to nations in the following ways

- They help to develop friendly relations among nations based on respect for the principle of equal rights and self-determination of people.
- They provide mechanisms, rules and human resources to the member states to deal with issues and problems of global concern.

(ii) The UN Charter gave the permanent members a privileged position to bring about stability in the world. After the Second World War, the main privileges enjoyed by the permanent members include permanency and veto power.

By application of Veto power, a permanent member may reject any decision in the Security Council. Any decision of Security Council is held once a month, but in case of Emergency, it can be held whenever required.

On the other hand, the non-permanent members are elected only for two years at a time and cannot be re-elected immediately after completing two years. They are elected in a manner so that they represent all continents of the world. The non-permanent members do not have the veto power.

(iii) UNESCO was established on 16th November, 1946 with the main objective to contribute the peace and security in the world, by promoting collaboration among nations through education, science, culture and communication.

The four functions of UNICEF are

(a) It works for the protection of children in respect of their survival, health and well-being. It also supports child-immunisation programmes.

(b) It provides technical supplies, equipments and other aids to villages.

(c) It provides basic social services for children in developing countries including campaigns against endemic and preventable diseases, as well as efforts to combat malnutrition. Emergency assistance is provided to victims of floods, earthquakes, droughts and other disasters.

(d) It provides support to the interests of women and facilities for pregnant women. Conventions aimed at suppressing trafficking in women and children, as well as crime prevention, are also supported.

SQP Code : **PB-2/15** Series ***i*-Succeed 2-25/15** Roll No.

Sample Question Paper 02

History & Civics 10th (Code 50)

General Instructions

1. Attempt all questions from Part I (Compulsory).
2. A total of 5 questions are to be attempted from Part II, 2 out of 3 questions from Section A and 3 out of 5 questions from Section B.
3. The intended marks for questions or parts of questions are given in brackets ( ).

Time : 2 Hrs.

Max. Marks : 80

Part-I Attempt all questions from this part

Que 1.

Choose the correct option. (16)

(i) If a significant policy fails to pass in the legislature, what is likely to be the immediate consequence for a Prime Minister in a parliamentary system? [Application] (1)

(a) The Prime Minister must resign immediately.
(b) The Prime Minister may face a vote of no confidence.
(c) The Prime Minister can dissolve the opposition.
(d) The Prime Minister will automatically get an extended term.

(ii) Consider the following details. [Understanding] (1)

Candidate	Age	Details
P	25	Postgraduate
Q	37	Qualified as member of Lok Sabha
R	44	Businessman
S	31	Charges of corruption

Select the person who fulfills the eligibility criteria to become President of India.

(a) P (b) Q (c) R (d) S

(iii) What was the main purpose of the Cripps Mission to India in 1942? [Understanding] (1)

(a) To offer India independence after World War II.
(b) To divide India into separate countries.
(c) To stop Indian support for the war.
(d) To change the education system in India.

(iv) **Assertion** (A) The Supreme Court's judgements and orders can be produced in any court as precedents. [Analyse] (1)

Reason (R) A Court of Record implies that its judgements and orders are preserved as a record and it has the authority to punish for contempt of court.

(a) R contradicts A
(b) R is the reason for A
(c) A is true, but R is false
(d) A and R are independent of each other

(v) Identify the individual in this image who is known as the "Father of the Indian Constitution." [Understanding] (1)

(a) BN Rau (b) TT Krishnamachari
(c) N. Madhava Rao (d) BR Ambedkar

(vi) Residents of Pune, A and B, entered into a business partnership in 2016. Disputes over financial management and profit sharing arose within two years, leading to severe disagreements and the threat of legal action. Before the case escalated to the regular courts, it was brought to the Pune District Lok Adalat. The Lok Adalat facilitated a mediation session where both parties were encouraged to discuss their issues openly. With guided mediation, A and B reached an amicable settlement that allowed them to adjust their financial contributions and profit shares, thereby preserving their business partnership. Both parties agreed to drop their legal claims against each other.

Which advantage of the Lok Adalat is highlighted in the above case? [Application] (1)

(a) It saves money
(b) It delivers speedy justice
(c) It works on the spirit of compromise
(d) It reduces the burden on High Courts

(vii) Read the two statements given below about the Second World War and select the option that shows the correct relationship between A and R.

Assertion (A) America remained neutral during the beginning of the Second World War.

Reason (R) USA dropped atomic bomb on Nagasaki on 9th August, 1945. The Japanese government surrendered without any conditions. This brought an end to the Second World War. [Analyse] (1)

(a) R contradicts A
(b) R is the reason for A
(c) A is true, but R is false
(d) A and R are independent of each other

(viii) The rulers of Country X introduced a policy similar to Doctrine of Lapse in India. Which states were annexed under Doctrine of Lapse in India? [Analyse] (1)

(a) Satara (b) Jhansi
(c) Nagpur (d) All of these

(ix) In a small village facing regular power outages, Priya, an advocate of Gandhian principles, attends a community meeting to discuss potential solutions. Which of the following solutions is Priya not likely to support? [Application] (1)

(a) Organising a peaceful sit-in protest at the local government office.
(b) Calling for a Non-Cooperation Movement against paying electricity bills.
(c) Sending a collective letter of appeal to the electricity board.
(d) Engaging in dialogue with the electricity board officials to find a solution.

(x) It was a bundle of sticks bound to an axe. It was referred to as the ancient Roman symbol of power. Which political ideology closely describes this symbol? [Understanding] (1)

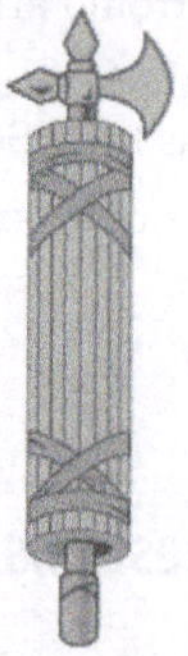

(a) Nazism (b) Fascism
(c) Marxism (d) Leninism

(xi) Identify the odd one out of the following objectives of the Indian National Congress. [Analyse] (1)

(a) To obtain a greater share in government for educated Indians.
(b) To promote the interests of the British in India.
(c) To foster a sense of national unity among all sections of Indian society.
(d) To formulate policies and programs that benefit the Indian population.

(xii) Mangesh is doing a research on Quit India Movement. It was launched at the Bombay session of All India Congress Committee in 1942. Who among the following were the prominent leaders of the Movement? [Analyse] (1)

(a) Aruna Asaf Ali
(b) Jayaprakash Narayan
(c) Ram Manohar Lohia
(d) All of the above

SP-02

(xiii) Which of the following was not an objective of the League of Nations?

P. States were prohibited from entering into secret treaties and alliances.

Q. Member states were restricted in maintaining armies, warships and destructive armaments.

R. All the states were to respect each other's independence.

S. It provides directions to disturb world peace and order. [Recall] (1)

Codes

(a) P and Q (b) R and S

(c) P and R (d) Only S

(xiv) The given below image depicts "Lal Bal Pal" of extremist group, who among the following was not the part of it.

(a) Lal Bahadur Shastri [Analyse] (1)

(b) Vipin Chandra Pal

(c) Balgangadhar Tilak

(d) Lala Lajpat Rai

(xv) The Nazi Party had become the largest party by the end of .... [Recall] (1)

(a) 1921 (b) 1932

(c) 1930 (d) 1925

(xvi) Identify the main policy-making organ of the United Nations from the given options. [Analyse] (1)

(a) The Security Council

(b) The General Assembly

(c) International Court of Justice

(d) The Secretariat

Que 2.

(i) Read the extract given below and answer the question which follows.

Headline : Extraordinary Writ Jurisdiction under Article 226 can't be invoked if Appellate Jurisdiction u/s 107 is available: Madras HC

The single bench of Madras High Court presided by Mr. Justice R Suresh Kumar has held that extraordinary Writ Jurisdiction under Article 226 can't be invoked if Appellate Jurisdiction under Section 107 is available.

Source : *Taxscan, 15th July, 2022*

On the basis of above news discuss in brief about Appellate Jurisdiction of High Court. [Understanding] (2)

(ii) Explain the following in short [Recall] (2)

(a) No-confidence motion

(b) Quorum

(iii) What was Nana Sahib's grievance against the British? [Analyse] (2)

(iv) State any two repressive policies of Lord Curzon. [Recall] (2)

(v) Name any two leaders of the moderates. Mention any two demands of them. [Recall] (2)

(vi) Give two similarities in the Foreign Policies of Mussolini and Hitler. [Recall] (2)

(vii) Name the principal organs of the UN. [Recall] (2)

Part-II Section A (Civics) Attempt any two questions from this section

Que 3.

Parliament is the Supreme Legislative body of India. Indian Parliament comprises of the President and two Houses – Rajya Sabha and Lok Sabha. With reference to the Indian Parliament, explain the following.

(i) The tenure of the members of the Lok Sabha and the Rajya Sabha. [Recall] (3)

(ii) The composition of the Lok Sabha and the Rajya Sabha. [Recall] (3)

(iii) Powers to make laws on subjects mentioned in the [Recall] (2+2)

(a) Union List

(b) Concurrent List

Que 4.

The President of India is the head of the Indian Republic. In this context, answer the following questions.

(i) Write three points to explain the position of the President in the Indian Constitution. [Recall] (3)

(ii) What is the procedure of election of the President in India? [Analyse] (3)

(iii) Under what circumstances can the President of India declare an emergency in the country? [Recall] (4)

Que 5.

The Supreme Court is the apex court of our country. It is the final court of appeal for all civil and criminal cases in India. In this context, explain the following questions.

(i) The composition of the Supreme Court of India. [Recall] (3)

(ii) The meaning of independence of the Judiciary and the need to do so. [Recall] (3)

(iii) In which manner, the Supreme Court maintains its independence from the hand of the Executive and the Legislative? Discuss. [Analyse] (4)

Section B (History) Attempt any three questions from this section

Que 6.

The establishment of the Indian National Congress led to the development of the National Movement in India. In this context, answer the following questions.

(i) When was the Indian National Congress established? Discuss the First and Second Congress Session. [Recall] (3)

(ii) What were the main aims of the Congress? Discuss any three. [Recall] (3)

(iii) Mention four basic beliefs of the Early Nationalists. [Recall] (4)

Que 7.

Treaty of Versailles was signed after the end of World War I with reference to the explain each of the following questions.

(i) Discuss the economic impacts of the Treaty of Versailles on Germany after World War I. [Analyse] (3)

(ii) Explain how the League of Nations aimed to prevent future conflicts but ultimately failed to stop the aggression of Axis powers. [Understanding] (3)

(iii) Analyse the rise of totalitarian regimes in Europe during the interwar period, focusing on the factors that contributed to their emergence. [Analyse & Recall] (4)

Que 8.

Read the excerpt given below and answer the questions that follow.

On 23rd March, 1946, the Cabinet Mission arrived in Karachi, which consisted of the Secretary of State Pethick-Lawrence, President of the Board of Trade Sir Stafford Cripps and the First Lord of the Admiralty Mr. AV Alexander. "As the Viceroy's Executive Council told the Mission, the main obstacle to a compromise was an issue which for long had been swept under the carpet: the need to redraw provincial boundaries if the Muslim provinces were to be given more autonomy than they had previously possessed. The Mission could not be allowed to fail; the Executive Council insisted, it 'must refuse to permit a breakdown.'" (The Sole Spokesman : Jinnah, the Muslim League and the Demand for Pakistan, by Dr Ayesha Jalal, Sang-e-Meel Publication, pp. 176-178)

***Source**: Al Hakam, July 2022*

(i) Name any two events that led to arrival of Cabinet Mission in India. Who sent Cabinet Mission to India and why? [Recall] (2+1)

(ii) Mention the reaction of Indian leaders to Cabinet Mission. [Recall] (3)

(iii) Mention any four clauses of Cabinet Mission Plan. [Recall] (4)

Que 9.

Look at the picture given below and answer the following questions.

(i) Identify the famous personalities in the above picture. Mention ideological views of the Indian leader. [Recall] (1+2)

(ii) Explain the reason behind the launching of the Khilafat Movement in India. How did the Khilafat and Non-Cooperation Movement merge in 1920? [Application & Recall] (1+2)

(iii) Why did Mahatma Gandhi withdraw the Non-Cooperation Movement? How did this decision influence the formation of the Swaraj Party? [Analyse] (2+2)

Que 10.

The United Nations Organisation was established to maintain peace and promote social progress and better standards of life in larger freedom. With reference to this, explain the following.

(i) The composition of the Security Council. [Recall] (3)

(ii) The functions of Security Council related to maintaining world peace. [Recall] (3)

(iii) The role of UNESCO in the development of science and technology. [Recall] (4)

Answers *in Topper's Style*

My Commitment *I affirm that I am reviewing these answers only after I have solved the Sample Question Paper 2 on my own. My purpose of looking the answers is solely to verify whether my answers were correct or not and to identify my mistakes in case my answers were wrong or I could not answer that.*

1. (i) (b) The Prime Minister may face a vote of no confidence.

(ii) (b) Q

(iii) (a) To offer India independence after World War II.

(iv) (b) R is the reason for A

(v) (d) BR Ambedkar

(vi) (c) It works on the spirit of compromise

(vii) (d) A and R are independent of each other

(viii) (d) All of these

(ix) (b) Calling for a Non-Cooperation Movement against paying electricity bills.

(x) (b) Fascism

(xi) (b) To promote the interests of the British in India.

(xii) (d) All of the above

(xiii) (d) Only S

(xiv) (a) Lal Bahadur Shastri

(xv) (b) 1932

(xvi) (b) The General Assembly

2. (i) The High Court can hear appeals against the decisions of the District Courts in civil and criminal matters. Only those civil cases which are decided by the District Courts under the Jurisdiction of the District Court can be brought before the High Court by an appeal. In civil cases, only those which are concerned with land revenues and where injustice has been made by the tribunal court can be brought before the High Court.

(ii) (a) A motion or vote of No-confidence is a formal expression by a deliberative body (often a legislature) as to whether an officeholder (typically an executive) is deemed fit to continue to occupy their office. A no-confidence motion can be moved only in the Lok Sabha. It cannot be moved in the Rajya Sabha.

(b) Quorum is the minimum number of members required to be present in the House before it can transact any business. It is 1/10th of the total number of members of the House (including the presiding officer).

(iii) Nana Sahib was the adopted son of Peshwa Baji Rao II. Lord Dalhousie's Doctrine of Lapse refused to accept Nana Sahib as the next Peshwa and stopped his pension because according to Doctrine of Lapse when an Indian ruler dies without having a natural son, then the state under the policy of annexation will merge with the British rule. This was the main grievance of Nana Sahib against the British.

(iv) Two repressive policies of Lord Curzon were as follows

(a) The Indian Universities Act, (1904) imposed strict control over the Indian Universities and reduced their autonomy.

(b) The Seditious Meeting Act, (1907) was enacted to prevent political meetings against the Government.

(v) Two leaders of the moderates were Dadabhai Naoroji and Surendranath Banerjee.

Two demands of the moderates were

(a) The Moderates wanted a reduction in land revenue and protection of peasants against the unjust demands of the Zamindars.

(b) Moderates demanded for the Indianisation of services through simultaneous Indian Civil Services Examination in England and India.

(vi) Two similarities in the Foreign Policies of Mussolini and Hitler are as follows

(a) Both aimed at resorting the status and dignity of their nations amongst the community of nations by making them strong powers.

(b) Both aimed at providing strong, stable and efficient Government.

(vii) The principal organs of the UN are the Secretariat, the General Assembly, the Security Council, the International Court of Justice, the Trusteeship Council and the Economic and Social Council.

3. (i) The tenure of the members of the Lok Sabha is 5 years. However, it can be dissolved earlier by the President or can be extended for 1 year at the time of proclamation of an emergency by the Parliament. Rajya Sabha, the Upper House of the Parliament is a permanent house and thus not subjected to dissolution. Members sit for 6 years term, with one-third of the members retiring every 2 years.

(ii) **Composition of Lok Sabha** The maximum strength of Lok Sabha, (the Lower House of Parliament), envisaged by the Constitution of India is 552, where 530 members are Representative of States, 20 of Union Territories. In January 2020, the Anglo-Indian reserved seats in the Parliament and State Legislatures of India were abolished by the 104th Constitutional Amendment Act, 2019.

Composition of Rajya Sabha The Rajya Sabha has 250 members, 12 of whom are nominated by the President of India for their contributions to Art, Literature, Science and Social Science. The remaining 238 of the body are elected by the States and Territorial Legislatures. At present, the strength of Rajya Sabha is 245, where 233 are elected and 12 are nominated.

(iii) (a) **Union List** The Parliament has exclusive powers to make laws with respect to matters mentioned in the Union List of 100 items. Union List includes defence, armed forces, arms and ammunition, atomic energy, finance, communication, foreign policy, etc.

(b) **Concurrent List** It is a list of 52 items concerned with relations between the Union and the States. This list includes criminal law, criminal procedure, marriage and divorce, population control and family planning, price control, electricity, etc. In the case of conflict between a Centre and State Law, the laws made by the Parliament shall prevail and the laws made by the Legislature of a state shall be void.

4. (i) The following three points throw light on the position of the President in the Indian Constitution are

(a) The President is required to exercise his/her powers on the aid and advice of the Council of Ministers. The 42nd Amendment Act makes it binding on the President to accept such advice.

(b) The 44th Constitutional Amendment Act of 1978 authorised the President to ask the Council of Ministers to reconsider such advice, if necessary.

(c) Though the President is only a Constitutional Head of States and has little effective power at his/her disposal, the office of the President is one of great honour, prestige and dignity.

(ii) The system of election to the office of the President of India is Proportional Representation by Means of Single Transferable Vote.

President is elected by the electoral college of

- elected members of both house of the parliament.
- elected members of state legislatures.
- elected members of the legislative assemblies of the Delhi and Puducherry (added by 70th amendment Act, 1992).

Value of the vote of an MLA

$$= \frac{\text{Total Population of State}}{\text{Total Number of Elected Members in State Legislative Assembly}} \times \frac{1}{1000}$$

Value of Vote of an MP

$$= \frac{\text{Total Number of Votes of all the MLAs of all States}}{\text{Total Number of Elected MPs}}$$

(iii) President can proclaim an emergency in the following cases

- **National Emergency (Article 352)** The President, if satisfied that the security of the nation is threatened by war or external aggression or an armed rebellion, he/she can issue the proclamation of National Emergency. Every such proclamation must be approved by Parliament within 1 month by a special majority.

- **President Rule (Article 356)** On a receipt of a report from the Governor, if the President is satisfied that there is a breakdown of constitutional machinery in the state, he may declare an emergency in state assuming all functions of state to himself.
- **Financial Emergency (Article 360)** If a situation has arisen whereby the financial stability or credit of the nation is threatened, the President can declare Financial Emergency.

5. (i) According to Article 124 of the Indian Constitution, there were 8 judges including the Chief Justice in the Supreme Court at the time of its formation. The article also provide power to the Parliament to increase or decrease the number of judges as and when required. At present, there are 30 other judges and 1 Chief Justice in the Supreme Court.

Besides, the Chief Justice of India has the power, with the previous consent of the President to request a retired Supreme Court judge to act as a judge of the Supreme Court for a temporary period. Similarly, a High Court judge may be appointed as an adhoc judge of the Supreme Court for a temporary period whenever required.

(ii) Independence of Judiciary means the system which is not influenced either by the Legislative or Executive. It is free to make decisions based upon law and not upon any individual or any other groups. An independent Judiciary is created to guarantee equal justice to all. Judges and juries are free from any influence and can make fair and honest decisions about cases.

The basic needs for the independence of the Judiciary rests upon the following points

- Judiciary acts as a watch dog by ensuring that all the organs of the state function within their respective areas and according to the Constitution.
- Judiciary is given the job to interpret the Constitution according to the constitutional philosophy and the constitutional norms.

(iii) To ensure the independence of the courts, the following measures were taken

- Appointment of the judges is not left in the hands of the Executive. The President appoints the judges after consulting people from the Judiciary itself.
- A judge to the Supreme Court once appointed, cannot be removed from office normally until he completes the age of 65 years.
- The judges of the Supreme Court cannot practice in any court of India after their retirement.
- The Supreme Court has total control over its establishment.
- The Constitution empowers the Supreme Court to punish any person for its contempt irrespective of his post or power.

6. (i) The Indian National Congress was established in 1885 by AO Hume. WC Bonnerjee was the President of its First Session.

The first session of the Congress took place in Bombay (Mumbai). 72 delegates attended the conference from all over the nation. This meeting was held in December 1885, meanwhile the All-India National Conference was also held in Calcutta.

The Second Congress Session was held at Kolkata in 1886 under the Presidentship of Dadabhai Naoroji. Some of the delegates were also received by Lord Dufferin as distinguished visitors to the capital.

(ii) The three main aims of the Congress were

(a) Promotion of close relations between nationalistic workers from different parts of the country.

(b) Formulation of popular demands and their presentation before the government.

(c) Development and consolidation of a feeling of national unity irrespective of caste, religion or province.

(iii) Early years of the Congress were dominated by the early nationalist leaders like, Dadabhai Naoroji, Surendranath Banerjee, WC Bonnerjee, Pherozeshah Mehta, Madan Mohan Malaviya, etc.

Four basic beliefs of the Early Nationalists were as follows

(a) They had faith in constitutional remedies by building public opinion in favour of their demands.

(b) They believed that the British Government could be persuaded by arguments and that it would respond to Indian public opinion.

(c) They did not want to overthrow British rule by violence. Their chief demand was self-government within the British regime.

(d) They believed that the British rule was boon for Indians. According to them, Britishers familiarised us with the English language, means of communication and transport.

7. (i) The Treaty of Versailles had a profoundly negative economic impact on Germany after World War I. It demanded huge reparations (payments for war damages) that Germany couldn't afford, leading to economic chaos like hyperinflation in 1923.

This hyperinflation destroyed people's savings and made life very hard for the middle class.

Additionally, Germany lost important industrial areas, which made unemployment worse and weakened its economy.

These economic problems created anger and desperation among people, helping extremist groups like the Nazis gain support by promising to fix the economy and restore Germany's pride.

(ii) The League of Nations aimed to prevent wars by promoting peaceful resolutions to disputes among countries. However, it failed to stop the aggression of Axis powers. Axis powers like the United States never joined the League of Nations, which limited its global influence. The League's decision-making required unanimous agreement, making it slow to respond in crises. It also lacked its own military force and struggled to enforce its decisions. These weaknesses were evident when it failed to stop Japan's invasion of Manchuria and Italy's attack on Ethiopia, allowing aggressive actions that led to World War II.

(iii) During the interwar period in Europe, the rise of totalitarian regimes was driven by several critical factors, such as

- Economic devastation after World War I and the Great Depression left many disillusioned with democratic solutions, paving the way for leaders like Hitler and Mussolini who promised strong leadership and national revival.
- In Germany, the Treaty of Versailles fueled resentment and a desire to reclaim lost pride and territory. Mussolini capitalised on economic hardships and fears of socialism in Italy to establish fascism as a solution for stability.
- The fear of communism also pushed conservative forces to support authoritarian regimes.
- Through effective propaganda, charismatic leadership and nationalist appeals, these regimes gained power, controlling all aspects of society and laying the groundwork for the conflicts that erupted in World War II.

8. (i) Two events that led to arrival of Cabinet Mission in India were

(a) Protests by Indian Civil Servants against discriminatory policies and look of representation in government decision.

(b) Workers in India protested with strike and demonstrations for better wages improved working conditions and political rights.

Clement Attlee, the new Prime Minister of Britain, sent the Cabinet Mission Plan to India from the transfer of powers from the British Indian Government to Indian leaders.

(ii) The reaction of Indian leaders to Cabinet Mission was

- The Congress accepted the proposals with certain reservations. While it accepted the scheme which dealt with the Constituent Assembly, it rejected the proposals of the Viceroy to form an interim government as it would have limited powers.
- The Muslim League accepted the proposals completely. It felt that the grouping together of Muslim majority provinces would anyway lead to the formation of Pakistan.

(iii) Four clauses of Cabinet Mission Plan were

(a) The Cabinet mission proposed the formation of the federal union of the British Provinces and Princely States in India. The Central Government was to have control of the defence, foreign affairs and communications in the country.

(b) It was laid down that the Indian Union was to have its own executive and legislature and provinces had the power to enjoy complete autonomy for all subjects other than union subjects.

(c) The British Provinces were to be divided into groups. There were three major groups and a province could opt out of any group and join another by a majority of votes.

(d) It proposed the setting up of a Constituent Assembly to frame the Constitution of India.

9. (i) The famous personalities in the above picture are Lord Mountbatten, his wife Edwina Mountbatten and Mahatma Gandhi.

Ideological views of Mahatma Gandhi were

- **Satyagraha** It was a novel method of mass agitation, which stressed the principle of truth, tolerance, non-violence and peaceful protests.
- **Swadeshi** It meant the use of things that were produced in one's own country to encourage Atmanirbharta.
- **Swaraj** The word 'swaraj' implies self-rule. Gandhiji provided it with the substance of vital unrest that includes all circles of life. It also includes self-control and could be likened to moksha or salvation.
- **Concern for the Poor and Oppressed** Gandhiji worked for the abolition of untouchability which would improve the life of poor and oppressed.

(ii) The reason behind the launching of the Khilafat Movement was the abolish of Khalifa.

Turkey was defeated in the First World War. Consequently, Britain and its allies divided the territories of the Turkish Empire and abolished the office of the Khalifa who was regarded as the spiritual head of the Muslims all over the world. It was not acceptable by the Muslims. To defend the Khalifa's temporal powers, a Khilafat Committee was formed in Bombay in 1919.

A young generation of Muslim leaders like the brothers Muhammad Ali and Shaukat Ali began discussing with Mahatma Gandhi about the possibility of a united mass action on the issue. Gandhiji saw this as an opportunity to bring Muslims under the umbrella of a Unified National Movement.

In 1920, at the Calcutta Session of Congress, Gandhiji convinced the Congress members to start a Non-Cooperation Movement in support of Khilafat as well as for Swaraj. Both movements sought to challenge British rule.

Gandhiji saw an opportunity to unite Hindus and Muslims in a common cause against colonialism. In 1920, the Congress officially adopted the Non-Cooperation Movement, integrating the demand of Khilafat Movement.

(iii) Gandhiji decided to withdraw the Non-Cooperation Movement due to various incidents of violence by the masses, particularly the Chauri Chaura incident in 1922, where people clashed with the police and set a police station on fire. Gandhiji believed that the people were not yet prepared for a mass struggle and that satyagrahis needed proper training for non-violent demonstrations.

Disappointed with the withdrawal of movement, a section of the Congress led by CR Das and Motilal Nehru organised a separate party called the Swaraj Party within the Congress. They wanted to participate in elections to the provincial councils that had been set up by the Government of India Act of 1919. They felt that it was important to oppose British policies within the councils, to argue for reforms and also to demonstrate that these councils were not truly democratic.

10. (i) The United Nations Security Council (UNSC) is one of the six principal organs of the United Nations and is responsible for maintaining peace and security. The Security Council consists of fifteen members, among them five are permanent. The five permanent members are Russia, the United Kingdom, the United States, France and China.

These permanent members can veto any substantive Security Council resolution, including those on the admission of new member states or candidates for Secretary-General. The Security Council also has ten non-permanent members, elected on a regional basis to serve two-year term. The body's presidency rotates monthly between its members.

(ii) The functions of Security Council related to maintaining world peace as follows

- To maintain international peace and security in accordance with the principles and purposes of the United Nations.
- To investigate the cause of disputes which might lead to international tension.
- To recommend ways of settling such disputes.
- To take military action against an aggressor.
- To suggest remedial action in order to prevent aggression.

(iii) The role of UNESCO in the sphere of science and technology is stated in the points below

- To promote cooperation of scientific pursuits by bringing scientists of various countries together and by circulating information through journals, press and exhibitions.
- To encourage basic research by providing research fellowships in Mathematics, Physics, Geology, Oceanography, etc.
- To organise seminars and conferences among world scientists and encourage them to cooperate in various spheres.
- To help developing countries to set up infrastructural facilities in the field of communications.

SQP Code : **PB-3/15**　　Series *i*-**Succeed 3-25/15**　　Roll No. | | | | | | | |

Sample Question Paper 03

History & Civics 10th (Code 50)

General Instructions

1. Attempt all questions from Part I (Compulsory).
2. A total of 5 questions are to be attempted from Part II, 2 out of 3 questions from Section A and 3 out of 5 questions from Section B.
3. The intended marks for questions or parts of questions are given in brackets ( ).

Time : 2 Hrs.
Max. Marks : 80

Part-I Attempt all questions from this part

Que 1.

Choose the correct option. (16)

(i) For choosing the presidential candidate, the name of the candidate should be proposed by 50 members of the Electoral College and has to be agreed by another 50 members. Who among the following is not a part of Electoral College? [Application] (1)

(a) The elected members of the Lok Sabha and the Rajya Sabha
(b) The nominated members of State Legislative Assemblies
(c) Nominated members of the Parliament
(d) Both (b) and (c)

(ii) The below picture shows the current Vice-President of India, Jagdeep Dhankar, which among the following do not came under the Electoral College of Vice-President? [Understanding] (1)

(a) Elected members of the Lok Sabha
(b) Elected member of the Rajya Sabha
(c) Nominated members of the Legislature Council
(d) Elected member of Legislative Assembly of Delhi

(iii) Consider the following details. [Understanding] (1)

Person	Age	Description
P	30	Police Officer
Y	33	Farmer
S	25	Teacher
T	35	Ex-officio Chairman of the Rajya Sabha

Select the person who fulfils the eligibility criteria to become the Vice-President of India.

(a) P　(b) Y　(c) S　(d) T

(iv) Mr. X is 24 years old and has been voting for Mr. Y who is 35 years old MP from his area. Mr. Z is a 20 years old businessman and a neighbour of Mr. X. [Application] (1)

Who amongst X, Y and Z is eligible to become the President of India? [Recall] (1)

(a) X　(b) X and Y
(c) Y　(d) X and Z

(v) Identify the officials who form the Electoral College for the election of Vice- President.

P. Members of Lok Sabha [Recall] (1)
Q. Members of Rajya Sabha

R. Members of State Legislative Councils
S. Nominated members of Vidhan Sabha
(a) P and Q (b) R and S
(c) P and S (d) P and R

(vi) Identify the odd one out of the following functions of Rajya Sabha. [Analyse] (1)
(a) To vote on annual financial statement.
(b) To check hasty and ill-thought bills passed by the Lok Sabha
(c) Rajya Sabha can create or abolish All India Services
(d) Take part in the election of the President.

(vii) Read the two statements below about Fascism and select the option that shows the correct relationship between A and R.
Assertion (A) Benito Mussolini was a socialist in the beginning.
Reason (R) Mussolini formed different groups known as Fascios, who organised violence against the socialists and the communists. [Analyse] (1)

Codes
(a) R contradicts A
(b) R is the reason for A
(c) A is true, but R is false
(d) A and R are independent of each other

(viii) Read the two statements below and select the option that shows the correct relationship between A and R.
Assertion (A) Mahatma Gandhi postponed the Non-Cooperation Movement in 1922.
Reason (R) The postponement was opposed by CR Das and Motilal Nehru. [Analyse] (1)
(a) R contradicts A
(b) R is the reason for A
(c) A is true, but R is false
(d) A and R are independent of each other

(ix) Which of the following is not a function of International Court of Justice? [Application] (1)
(a) It may recommend appropriate procedures of settlement during or at the end of the case.
(b) To settle legal disputes submitted by states in accordance with International Law.
(c) To take military action against an aggressor state.
(d) It plays a significant role in the codification of International Laws.

(x) The person in the below image was a notable commander in the Indian Rebellion of 1857. Identify this personality. [Recall] (1)

(a) Bal Gangadhar Tilak
(b) Kunwar Singh
(c) Tantya Tope
(d) Gopal Krishna Gokhale

(xi) Sakshi is doing a project on a freedom fighter who formed the Forward Bloc and announced that the party would work within the Congress. She is researching on which of the following personalities? [Understanding] (1)
(a) RC Dutt
(b) Bal Gangadhar Tilak
(c) Subhash Chandra Bose
(d) Rashebihari Bose

(xii) Triple Alliance : Britain, France, Russia :: Triple Entente : .... [Recall] (1)
(a) Germany, India, United States
(b) Germany, Italy, Austria-Hungary
(c) Belgium, Norway, United States
(d) Italy, United States, Austria-Hungary

(xiii) Which of the following was not a method adopted by Radicals? [Understanding] (1)
(a) Passive Resistance
(b) Non-Cooperation with Britishers
(c) Promotion of Swadeshi goods
(d) Relying on constitutional and peaceful methods

(xiv) Which of the following is/are the impacts of the Civil Disobedience Movement?
(a) It shattered people's faith in the British government. [Understanding] (1)
(b) It ended the monopoly of the British over salt manufacturing.
(c) It fostered Hindu-Muslim unity
(d) Both (a) and (b)

SP-03

(xv) The First NAM Summit took place at .... [Recall] (1)

(a) Jakarta, Indonesia (b) Belgrade, Serbia
(c) Manila, Philippines (d) New Delhi, India

(xvi) Identify the founder of Bombay Association. [Recall] (1)

(a) Raja Ram Mohan Roy
(b) Gopal Krishna Gokhale
(c) Dadabhai Naoroji
(d) Surendranath Banerjee

Que 2.

(i) Read the extract given below and answer the question which follows.

Headline : Access to Internet is a Fundamental Right: SC

'We consider the restriction on fundamental rights cannot be in the exercise of arbitrary powers,' Justice NV Ramana said. The test of proportionality needs to be satisfied. This freedom can only be restricted after relevant factors are considered and only if there is no other option, he said.

Source: Hindustan Times. 11th January, 2020

Imagine you are a victim of this incident and you approach Supreme Court. Through which instruments will it restore your fundamental rights. [Understanding] (2)

(ii) Explain the role of speaker in maintaining the decorum of the house. [Recall] (2)

(iii) Mention two economic factors of the First War of Independence, 1857. [Recall] (2)

(iv) Mention any two provisions of the Indian Independence Act, 1947. [Recall] (2)

(v) What are the official languages of the United Nations? [Recall] (2)

(vi) Mention any two methods used by the Moderates. [Recall] (2)

(vii) State the power of UN General Assembly to elect members of other principal organs. [Recall] (2)

Part-II Section A (Civics) Attempt any two questions from this section

Que 3.

With reference to the Union Parliament, answer the following questions.

(i) State three conditions on which a person cannot qualify to become a member of Parliament. [Recall] (3)

(ii) The two Houses of the Parliament enjoy co-equal powers in many spheres. Explain it by giving any three examples. [Application & Recall] (3)

(iii) Explain any four powers of Rajya Sabha in India's federal set up. [Recall] (4)

Que 4.

The President of India is a nominal and constitutional head of the nation. In this context, answer the following questions.

(i) (a) Why is the President of India referred to as nominal head of the state? [Analyse]

(b) State two examples of his legislative powers that suggest his nominal status. [Recall] (2+2)

(ii) What are the diplomatic powers of the President? [Recall] (3)

(iii) Explain two discretionary powers of the President. [Recall] (1+2)

Que 5.

With reference to the Judiciary system at state level, answer the following questions.

(i) Mention the three cases in which the High Court enjoys Original Jurisdiction. [Recall] (3)

(ii) Explain any three conditions of service of a Judge of a High Court. [Analyse] (3)

(iii) (a) Under which jurisdiction can a High Court accept an appeal against the decisions of the District Courts? [Analyse]

(b) Mention any two advantages of resolving disputes through the Lok Adalat. [Recall] (2+2)

SP-03

Section B (History) Attempt any three questions from this section

Que 6.

The establishment of the Indian National Congress led to the development of National Movement in India. In this context, answer the following questions.

(i) When did Indian National Congress come into existence? Mention any two roles of AO Hume for laying foundation of Indian National Congress. [Recall] (1+2)

(ii) What circumstances led to the formation of Congress? [Recall] (3)

(iii) How did the British react when the Indian National Congress was founded? Why did their attitude change later? [Analyse] (4)

Que 7.

In the Nagpur Session, 1920, the Congress ratified the resolution to launch the Non-Cooperation Movement under the leadership of Gandhiji. In this context, answer the following questions.

(i) What do you understand by the term Non-Cooperation? [Understanding] (3)

(ii) Explain the impact of Non-Cooperation Movement on India's struggle for freedom. [Recall] (4)

(iii) What were the objectives which the Non-Cooperation Movement sought to achieve? [Recall] (3)

Que 8.

Read the excerpt given below and answer the questions that follow.

India criticises further delay over UNSC reforms, says process could go on for another 75 years.

As the UN General Assembly decided to roll over the Inter-Governmental Negotiations on Security Council reform to its next session, India has termed it as "yet another wasted opportunity" and said the process could well go on for another 75 years.

(i) Discuss the composition of Security Council. [Application] (3)

(ii) Discuss the powers and functions of Security Council. [Application] (3)

(iii) Discuss the role of Security Council in International Affairs. Explain its veto power. [Application] (2+2)

Que 9.

With reference to the picture given below, answer the following questions.

(i) Identify the Viceroy in the picture. Mention any two main points of June plan. [Recall] (1+2)

(ii) Why was he sent to India? How did he plan to solve the communal problem existing in India? [Analyse] (1+2)

(iii) Why did the Congress accept Mountbatten's plan? State three reasons to justify its acceptance. [Analyse & Recall] (1+3)

Que 10.

The Second World War is considered as the most disastrous war. In this context, state how each of the following factors was the cause of the Second World War.

(i) The failure of the League of Nations. [Recall] (3)

(ii) The Aggressive Nationalism of Germany. [Recall] (3)

(iii) State in brief any four similarities between the ideologies of Fascism and Nazism that emerged during the Second World War. [Analyse] (4)

Answers in Topper's Style

My Commitment *I affirm that I am reviewing these answers only after I have solved the Sample Question Paper 3 on my own. My purpose of looking the answers is solely to verify whether my answers were correct or not and to identify my mistakes in case my answers were wrong or I could not answer that.*

1. (i) (d) Both (b) and (c)
(ii) (c) Nominated members of the Legislature Council
(iii) (d) T
(iv) (c) Y
(v) (a) P and Q
(vi) (a) To vote on annual financial statement.
(vii) (d) A and R are independent of each other
(viii) (b) R is the reason for A
(ix) (c) To take military action against an aggressor state.
(x) (c) Tantya Tope
(xi) (c) Subhash Chandra Bose
(xii) (b) Germany, Italy, Austria-Hungary
(xiii) (d) Relying on constitutional and peaceful methods
(xiv) (d) Both (a) and (b)
(xv) (b) Belgrade, Serbia
(xvi) (c) Dadabhai Naoroji

2. (i) Any citizen whose fundamental rights have been violated can directly approach the Supreme Court and the latter can issue writs such as habeas corpus, mandamus, quo warranto, etc for the enforcement of fundamental rights.
The Supreme Court can declare any law made by the Government as null and void if it violates the fundamental rights of any individual.

(ii) The role of the Speaker is as follows
- The speaker is responsible to chairs the sessions of the Lok Sabha ensuring that the debates and discussion is being conducted in an orderly manner.
- Speaker maintains impartiality and transparency in the house.

(iii) Two economic factors of the First War of Independence, 1857 were as follows
(a) The East India Company made huge profit by purchasing textiles, indigo, spices, foodgrains in a low price from India and sold them abroad at very high prices.
(b) As a result of the East India Company's policy of making India a raw material producing country, Indian handicrafts and cottage industries died out.

(iv) The two main provisions of the Indian Independence Act, 1947 were
(a) It provided for the creation of two independent dominions from 15th August, 1947, to be known as India and Pakistan.
(b) Princely States would become independent, all powers and authority of the British Empire will be terminated.

(v) The official languages of the United Nations are Arabic, Chinese, English, French, Russian and Spanish. Any speech made in any one of these languages are immediately translated into the other five languages.

(vi) Two methods used by the Moderates were
(a) Arouse political consciousness by creating a public opinion.
(b) Sending petitions to government officials and the British Parliament.

(vii) The General Assembly elects the members of other principal organs of the United Nations, namely; the Non-permanent members of the Security Council, members of the Economic and Social Council and judges of the International Court of Justice. The assembly also elects members to its subsidiary organs and to the executive boards and governing councils of the United Nations agencies, funds and programmes.

3. (i) A person cannot qualify for being chosen as, or for being, a member of the Parliament by following
(a) If he holds any office of profit under the Government of India or the government of any state, or local authority.
(b) If he is of unsound mind and stands so declared by a competent court.
(c) If he is so disqualified by or under any law made by Parliament.

(ii) The Lok Sabha and Rajya Sabha have many co-equal powers in many spheres.
The examples are
(a) All bills other than Money Bill can be introduced in either house and follow the same procedure.
(b) Both Lok Sabha and Rajya Sabha have co-equal powers with respect to the election of the President and Vice-President.
(c) In the matter of amendment to the Constitution, the authorities of the two houses are equal. Amendments have to be passed by two-third majority in each house according to Article 368.

(iii) Rajya Sabha's powers in India's federal set up are as follows
(a) Any non-Money Bill can originate in the Rajya Sabha and if a non-Money Bill has been initiated

and approved by the Lok Sabha, it has to be approved by the Rajya Sabha also, before it becomes an act.

(b) The Rajya Sabha shares the power with the Lok Sabha to amend the Constitution.

(c) With two-third majority vote of the members present and voting, the Rajya Sabha can empower the Parliament to make law on any matter contained in the State List on the ground of national interest.

(d) The Rajya Sabha takes part in the election of the President as well as of the Vice-President of India.

4. (i) (a) The President of India is referred as the nominal head because India obeys the parliamentary system of the Government. In reality, the power is exercised by the Council of Ministers and it is headed by the Prime Minister of India. The President of India takes decisions on the behalf of the Prime Minister (PM). Constitution, the President is bound to follow the advice given by the Prime Minister and the Council of Ministers.

(b) The legislative powers of the President which suggest his nominal status are as follows

- The President issues ordinances during the recess of the Parliament only on the advice of the Council of Ministers.
- The nomination of members in Lok Sabha and Rajya Sabha is done by the President on the advice of Prime Minister and the Council of Ministers.

(ii) The diplomatic powers of the President are as follows

- As the executive head of the Union, he can appoint and send ambassadors, High Commissioners and other diplomats.
- He can also ask foreign diplomats to leave India by declaring them 'persona non grata', means person not acceptable.
- All international treaties and agreements concluded by India, are on behalf of the President.

(iii) Two discretionary powers of the President are as follows

- The President appoints the Prime Minister in a situation where no single party secures the majority of the Lok Sabha.
- After the vote of no confidence is passed against the prevailing government, the President may dissolve the Parliament or ask leader of alternate party to prove its majority on the floor of the house.

5. (i) The High Court has Original Jurisdiction in the following cases

(a) Along with the Supreme Court, it enjoys original jurisdiction for the enforcement of the Fundamental Rights guaranteed by the Constitution. It can also issue writs.

(b) In regard to the state revenue and its collection.

(c) In regard to admiralty, wills, marriage laws, company laws and contempt of court.

(ii) Three conditions of service of a Judge of a High Court are as follows

(a) The Chief Justice and other Judges of the High Court are appointed by the President in consultation with the Chief Justice of the Supreme Court, Governor of the concerned state and also the Chief Justice of High Court in case of the other judges.

(b) The Chief Justice and other judges of the High Courts once appointed, hold office till they retire at the age of 62 years or they themselves resign from their offices.

(c) It is very difficult to remove a judge. The method is the same as one to remove Judges of the Supreme Court.

(iii) (a) Under Appellate Jurisdiction, a High Court can accept an appeal against the decisions of the District Courts in respect of civil as well as criminal matters. Only those civil cases which have been decided by Subordinate Courts under the jurisdiction of the High Court concerned, can be brought to the High Court.

(b) Two advantages of resolving disputes through the Lok Adalat are as follows

- It is a much cheaper method to arrive at a solution and also promotes social justice.
- It works with a spirit for compromise and understanding. As a result, both the parties feel satisfied.

6. (i) The Indian National Congress come into existence in 1885, with the numerous efforts of AO Hume.

The role of AO Hume for laying foundation of National Congress were as follows

(a) He wanted to-set up an organisation that would draw the attention of the government towards the drawbacks of administration and also suggest the means to remove them.

(b) Besides, he also declared openly to help the Indians to develop themselves intellectually, socially and politically, to promote the cause of nationalism and create an all Indian platform to fight for the rights of the Indians.

(ii) Following were the circumstances which led to the formation of Congress

- Many political organisations came into existence during the second half of the 19th century as a result of the growth of national consciousness.

- The gulf between the educated Indians and British Indians was widening. There was an urgent need for an organisation which could train and organise public opinion and present them before the government.

Thus, this paved a way for the formation of an organisation which became a channel between public and British government. This organisation came to be known as Congress.

(iii) When the Indian National Congress was founded, the attitude of the British Government was very friendly and sympathetic. Lord Dufferin, the Viceroy also favoured the foundation of the Congress because he felt that this All India Party (Indian National Congress) would act as a safety valve for release of popular discontentment to safeguard the British interest in India.

The sympathetic attitude of the British Government changed later when the Congress began to demand more rights for the people and also when they saw the growth of Nationalism. The Britishers began to criticise the Congress leaders and branded them as 'Disloyal Babus, Seditious Brahmins and Violent Villians'.

7. (i) Non-Cooperation means Boycott of Civil Services, Army, Police, Courts, Legislative Councils, Schools, Foreign goods etc everything related to the British Government. In his book, 'Hind Swaraj', Mahatma Gandhi declared that British rule was established in India with the cooperation of Indians and had survived only because of this cooperation.

Gandhiji asked his countrymen not to assist British Government to rule over them. He believed that if Indians will refuse to cooperate with the British rule in India and it would lead to collapse of British government within a year and Swaraj would be achieved.

(ii) The impact of Non-Cooperation Movement on India's struggle for freedom were as follows

- This movement brought Gandhiji into close contact with the masses. Earlier, the National Movement had remained the concern of the middle class and intellectuals. This was the first time, masses joined the National Movement and Mahatma Gandhi became the symbol of poor and downtrodden.
- The movement improved about Hindu-Muslim unity by combining Khilafat Movement with it. No movement received the willing support of Hindus and Muslims like this before. The movement undermined the British authority and instilled confidence in the people of India.
- For the first time, Indians realised that passive resistance was more powerful than any weapon used by the British. Repression by the British failed to crush the spirit of Indians.
- This movement provided a national base to the Congress making it a genuine, nationalistic organisation. The Congress received the support of common masses.

(iii) Objectives of the Non-Cooperation Movement were

- To attain Swaraj or Self-Government by peaceful and legitimate means.
- To restore the old status of 'Khalifa', the Non-Cooperation and Khilafat Movement started in 1921.
- To strengthen national feeling and Hindu-Muslim unity, the Congress at its Nagpur Session (1920) passed a resolution for launching the Non-Cooperation Movement.

8. (i) Security Council is an executive body of the United Nations. It consists of 15 members. It has five permanent members–China, France, Russia, Britain and the United States of America. Ten other non-permanent members consist of 5 members from the Afro-Asian countries, 2 members from the Latin American countries, 2 members from the West European countries and 1 member from the East European countries.

(ii) Functions and powers of the Security Council are

- To maintain international peace and security.
- To investigate any dispute or situation which might lead to international tension or conflicts.
- To establish plans for the establishment of a system to regulate armaments.
- To take military action against an aggressor.

(iii) Role of Security Council in International Affairs are

The Security Council aims to peacefully resolve international disputes in accordance with Chapter VI of the UN Charter, which authorises the Security Council to call on parties to seek solutions via negotiation, arbitration, or other peaceful means.

Each of the 5 permanent members of the Security Council has the power to veto a decision. The negative vote of a permanent member is called a veto. By application of this right, a permanent member may reject any decision at the Security Council. The Council is unable to act further if any of the permanent member uses the veto power. However, if a member refused to vote, then it will not be counted as a negative vote.

9. (i) The picture belongs to Viceroy Lord Mountbatten who arrived in India on 22nd March, 1947.

The two main points of this plan were as follows

(a) **Partition** The British India would be divided into two Dominions. i.e. India and Pakistan.

(b) **A Boundary Commission** The plan provided for creation of a Boundary Commission to settle the boundaries of the two Dominions in case partition was decided upon.

(ii) Lord Mountbatten was sent to India to solve the disputes of Muslim League and the Congress. Further, Clement Attlee, the Prime Minister of England made an announcement that the British would leave India by June, 1948. Thus, power would be handed over to one or more Central Government. This was a clear indication for the partition of the country. To take necessary steps for the transfer of power, Mountbatten was appointed the Viceroy of India.

Riots broke out in Calcutta, Punjab, Assam and North-West Frontier province. To handle the situation of communal riots, Mountbatten consulted with different political personalities, like Jawaharlal Nehru, Sardar Patel, Maulana Azad, M Ali Jinnah, Liaqat Ali, etc. After meeting leaders of different parties and communities, Mountbatten came to the conclusion that he could not unite the two major parties and partition of the country was inevitable.

(iii) The Congress reluctantly accepted Mountbatten's Plan. The reasons behind its acceptance were

(a) Communal riots all over the country had taken a serious turn as a result of the conflict between the Congress and Muslim League. Partition would offer a new solution as a smaller united India was better than a bigger disorganised country.

(b) Extension of the British rule would be harmful for the country. 'The Divide and Rule' policy of the British had already damaged largely the Hindu-Muslim unity. To control further damage, the Congress admitted to accept the plan.

(c) The Congress realised that it could not have a joint administration. The Congress had bitter experience with the league when the latter joined the Interim Government in 1946.

10. (i) Main reasons for the failure of the League of Nations were

- **Absence of the United States** The League of Nations was significantly weakened by the absence of the United States, the most powerful nation in the world. Its non-membership undermined the League's effectiveness from the outset.
- **Self-Interest of Major Powers** The major powers in the League, being the dominant nations of the world, were often driven by their own interests. This self-serving approach obstructed the development of a spirit of cooperation and mutual respect among member states.
- **Ineffectiveness of the League** The League of Nations lacked the authority and mechanisms to enforce its decisions and mandates. This powerlessness severely limited its ability to maintain peace and resolve international conflicts.
- **Aggressive Actions of Hitler** Hitler's aggressive policies and expansionist actions, such as the invasions of Czechoslovakia, Austria and the subsequent invasion of Poland, demonstrated his disregard for the League's goals.

(ii) Germany, under the Nazi Government of Hitler wanted to revive its past glory and also to avenge the humiliating Treaty of Versailles. Hitler declared rearmament in 1936 and started regaining its lost territories on all frontiers. He annexed Austria, occupied Rhineland, Czechoslovakia. He demanded the port of Danzig from Poland. Russia also wanted Poland as a buffer state between Germany and itself, so on 23rd, August, 1939, the Nazi-Soviet Non-Aggression Pact was signed for a duration of 10 years. But Germany attacked Poland on 1st September, 1939. After this, Britain and France declared war on Germany and the Second World War started.

(iii) Four similarities between the ideologies of Fascism and Nazism that emerged during the Second World War were

(a) Both Fascism and Nazism favoured totalitarian rule.

(b) They both were against democratic political system.

(c) Both believed in the state supremacy, which could suppress Fundamental Rights and individual freedom.

(d) Both the parties were held by one party and leader for a state and believed in aggressive nationalism and imperialism.

SQP Code : **PB-4/15** Series ***i*-Succeed 4-25/15** Roll No. | | | | | | | | |

Sample Question Paper 04

History & Civics 10th (Code 50)

General Instructions

1. Attempt all questions from Part I (Compulsory).
2. A total of 5 questions are to be attempted from Part II, 2 out of 3 questions from Section A and 3 out of 5 questions from Section B.
3. The intended marks for questions or parts of questions are given in brackets ( ).

Time : 2 Hrs.

Max. Marks : 80

Part-I Attempt all questions from this part

Que 1.

Choose the correct option. (16)

(i) 'In India, President's (or Governor's) rule is the suspension of state government and imposition of direct union government rule in the state'. Which of the following articles corresponds to President's rule in a state?

(a) 352 (b) 360 [Application]

(c) 356 (d) 386

(ii) Given below are details of our Constitution list. (1)

	Terms	Details
1.	Union List	Defence
2.	State List	?
3.	Concurrent List	Forests

Select from the following options related to the State list. [Understanding]

(a) Criminal Law

(b) Communication

(c) Foreign Affairs

(d) Education

(iii) In some cases, the President neither gives assent to the bill nor reject or return the bill, but simply keeps the bill pending for indefinite period of time, which of the following veto, can be seen in the image below? [Understanding] (1)

(a) Qualified Veto (b) Pocket Veto

(c) Suspensive Veto (d) Absolute Veto

(iv) Regarding the qualifications for membership in the Lok Sabha, which of the following is not a correct criterion? [Analyse] (1)

(a) The member must be at least 25 years old.

(b) The member must be a member of a political party.

(c) The member must be an Indian citizen.

(d) The member must not be declared bankrupt.

(v) Which among the following are the federal features of Constitution of India? [Recall] (1)

P. Dual Government

Q. Bicameralism

R. Consolidation of powers

S. Combined Judiciary

Codes

(a) P and Q (b) R and S

(c) P and R (d) Q and S

(vi) Read the two statements given below and select the option that shows the correct relationship between A and R. [Analyse]

Assertion (A) The Congress boycotted the Simon Commission.

Reason (R) The Simon Commission did not have a single Indian member. (1)

(a) R contradicts A

(b) R is the reason for A

(c) A is true, but R is false

(d) A and R are independent of each other

(vii) Read the two statements given below regarding Swadeshi Movement and select the option that shows the correct relationship between A and R. [Analyse] (1)

Assertion (A) Radicals asked people to use only Swadeshi Goods.

Reason (R) Use of Swadeshi Goods was promoted to encourage Indian Industries.

(a) R contradicts A

(b) R is the reason for A

(c) A is true, but R is false

(d) A and R are independent of each other

(viii) Early nationalists of Country A used similar methods of raising demands as used by Indian Nationalists.

Which methods of demands must have been used by them? [Application] (1)

(a) Prayer

(b) Petitions

(c) Protests

(d) All of the above

(ix) Identify, the odd one out from the countries that were part of 'Axis power' bloc in World War II. [Analyse] (1)

(a) Germany

(b) Italy

(c) Japan

(d) Russia

(x) The person in the below image played a crucial role in beginning of Revolt of 1857. Identify the personality. [Recall] (1)

(a) Mangal Pandey (b) Nana Saheb

(c) Tantya Tope (d) Kunwar Singh

(xi) The country which emerged as a world power, militarily and economically after the First World War is .... [Recall] (1)

(a) Great Britain

(b) United States of America

(c) France

(d) Italy

(xii) Aditya is enacting a play where he is acting a role of Sher-e-Punjab. Whose role is he enacting? [Understanding] (1)

(a) Bipin Chandra Pal (b) Lala Lajpat Rai

(c) Lokmanya Tilak (d) RC Dutt

(xiii) Which of the following aspect is not correct with respect to Simon Commission? [Application] (1)

(a) The commission was constituted under Sir John Simon.

(b) It was constituted to review the functioning of the Constitutional system in India.

(c) A vague offer for dominion status was offered by this commission.

(d) This commission was opposed by the Indians as there were no Indians in it.

(xiv) Which specialised agency of UNO lists World Heritage Sites? [Understanding] (1)

(a) UNESCO (b) UNICEF

(c) WHO (d) WTO

(xv) In 2011, Anna Hazare took an oath of "fast unto death, persuading the government to bring stronger anti-corruption Lokpal Bill. This satyagraha was equated with the satyagraha done by Mahatma Gandhi.

Which among the following was the first satyagraha movement led by Mahatma Gandhi in India? [Application] (1)

(a) Kheda Satyagraha

(b) Bardoli Satyagraha

(c) Champaran Satyagraha

(d) Ahmedabad Mill Strike

(xvi) Welby Commission : 1895 :: Indian Council Act :: .... [Recall] (1)

(a) 1890 (b) 1892 (c) 1893 (d) 1894

Que 2.

(i) Read the extract given below and answer the question which follows.

Headline : President Draupadi Murmu on 3-day visit to Vidarbha from 4th July.

President Murmu will arrive at Nagpur airport from Hyderabad on 4th July evening. She will travel to Maharashtra's tribal district of Gadchiroli on 5th July morning. She will be the chief guest at the convocation ceremony of Gondwana University in Gadchiroli.

Source: Hindustan Times, 1st July

On the basis of above news, discuss any two executive powers of President. [Understanding] (2)

(ii) Enumerate the cases in which Vice-President will act as the President of India? [Analyse] (2)

(iii) Mention two ways by which Britishers tried to increase racial bitterness after 1857. [Recall] (2)

(iv) State two methods of political struggle evolved by Mahatma Gandhi as a part of the National Movement. [Recall] (2)

(v) Mention any two differences of ideology between Gandhiji and Subhash Chandra Bose. [Recall] (2)

(vi) Mention any two objectives of the Congress which was enumerated by WC Bonnerjee. [Recall] (2)

(vii) State any two underlying principles of Fascism. [Recall] (2)

Part-II Section A (Civics) Attempt any two questions from this section

Que 3.

Legislative proposals are brought before the Houses of the Parliament in the form of a Bill. In this context, answer the following questions.

SP-04

(i) What is a Bill? Which kinds of Bills are introduced in the Parliament? [Analyse] (3)

(ii) (a) Money bill can be initiated in which house of the Parliament? [Recall] (1+2)

(b) Who has final decision-making power regarding nature of bill; whether it is Money Bill or not? [Analyse]

(iii) What is the procedure to be followed by the Union Parliament for passing a Money Bill? [Application] (4)

Que 4.

The Prime Minister is *de facto* executive of the government. In this context, answer the following questions.

(i) What is the role of the Prime Minister in foreign affairs? [Analyse] (3)

(ii) Mention any three relations of Prime Minister with the Parliament. [Recall] (3)

(iii) Can the Prime Minister become a Dictator? Discuss [Understanding] (4)

Que 5.

The Supreme Court is placed at the apex of the entire judicial system in India. In this context, answer the following questions

(i) State the composition and the procedure of appointment of Supreme Court Judges. [Recall] (3)

(ii) Mention the two important powers of Supreme Court as a Court of Record. [Recall] (3)

(iii) State the power of Judicial Review of the Supreme Court. Give reasons why it is necessary. [Application & Recall] (1+3)

Section B (History) Attempt any three questions from this section

Que 6.

The Uprising of 1857 AD was an outburst of nationalist sentiments. In this context answer the following questions.

(i) What was the intention behind the annexation of states of Dalhousie's Plan of annexation? [Analyse] (3)

(ii) What were the political causes of uprising of 1857? Mention any three. [Analyse & Recall] (3)

(iii) Mention any two uprising spread at the time of 1857. [Recall] (4)

Que 7.

The Non-Aligned Movement is a forum of 120 countries that are not formally aligned with or against any major power bloc. It was founded with the view to advancing interests of developing countries in the context of Cold War confrontation. In the view of the statement, answer the following questions

(i) What was the primary purpose of the Non-Aligned Movement (NAM) when it was founded during the Cold War? [Recall] (3)

(ii) What were the objectives of the Non-Aligned Movement as envisioned by its co-founder Jawaharlal Nehru? [Recall] (3)

(iii) State five principles of Panchsheel Agreement. [Recall] (4)

Que 8.

Read the excerpt given below and answer the questions that follows.

From the perspective of Indian nationalists, however, the partition was viewed as a deliberate attempt by the British to divide and rule by splitting Bengal on religious lines. Nationalists believed that the real motive behind this move was to weaken the burgeoning nationalist movement in Bengal, one of the most politically active regions, by curbing its influence and sowing seeds of division between Hindu and Muslim communities. This led to widespread protests, demonstrations, and eventually the Swadeshi movement, advocating for self-sufficiency and the boycott of British goods.

(i) What were the official reasons given by the British government for the Partition of Bengal in 1905? [Recall] (3)

(ii) How did the geographical distribution of religions play a role in the decision to partition Bengal? [Analyse] (3)

(iii) What were the perspectives of Indian Nationalists on the decision of partition of Bengal? [Recall] (4)

Que 9.

Look at the picture given below carefully.

The ideology of the Mahatma Gandhi and his direction led the movement towards the country's independence.
In this context answer the following questions.

(i) In the term of Gandhiji, what is the meaning of Swadeshi? [Analyse] (3)

(ii) Why did Gandhiji launch Rowlatt Satyagraha? [Understanding] (3)

(iii) Mention and explain first two Satyagrahas of Gandhiji. [Recall] (4)

Que 10.

24th October, since 1945 has been celebrated every year as the United Nations Day. With respect to the above statement, answer the following questions.

(i) Objective of the United Nations. [Recall] (3)

(ii) Composition of any three organs of the UN. [Recall] (3)

(iii) Powers and functions of General Assembly. [Recall] (4)

SP-04

Answers *in Topper's Style*

My Commitment *I affirm that I am reviewing these answers only after I have solved the Sample Question Paper 4 on my own. My purpose of looking the answers is solely to verify whether my answers were correct or not and to identify my mistakes in case my answers were wrong or I could not answer that.*

1. (i) (c) 356
(ii) (d) Education
(iii) (b) Pocket Veto
(iv) (b) The member must be a member of a political party.
(v) (a) P and Q
(vi) (b) R is the reason for A
(vii) (d) R is the reason for A
(viii) (d) All of the above
(ix) (d) Russia
(x) (a) Mangal Pandey
(xi) (b) United States of America
(xii) (b) Lala Lajpat Rai
(xiii) (c) A vague offer for dominion status was offered by this commission.
(xiv) (a) UNESCO
(xv) (c) Champaran Satyagraha
(xvi) (b) 1892

2. (i) Two executive powers of President of India are

(a) The President is the head of the Indian Union. All executive orders are issued by the Prime Minister and his cabinet on the name of the President.

(b) All key appointments are made on the name of the President on the advice of the Prime Minister and his cabinet.

(ii) The Vice-President act as the President when there is vacancy due to death, absence of the President or he/she resigns from their post or due to impeachment or due to any other unforseen situation.

(iii) Britishers followed the policy of Divide and Rule to increase racial bitterness. The ways adopted were

(a) After 1857, Britishers started favouring Hindus and when the activities of the Congress grew against them, then they started favouring Muslims.

(b) They carried discrimination on the basis of caste and community and gave high ranking in administration and army on that basis.

(iv) The two methods of political struggle evolved by Mahatma Gandhi as a part of the National Movement were

(a) Gandhiji promoted the use of Satyagraha which was the moral force of truth and non-violence. The Satyagraha Movement of Gandhiji was directed against the British system of exploitation and not the British people individually.

(b) Gandhiji advocated the Non-Violence Movement. According to him, non-violence was a peaceful way of attaining goals.

(v) The two differences of ideology between Gandhiji and Subhash Chandra Bose were

(a) Bose was in favour of armed struggle against the British for which he organised INA with Japanese assistance. Gandhiji was in favour of Satyagraha and non-violence to overthrow the British rule.

(b) In 1939, Bose launched the National Planning Committee for drawing up a comprehensive plan of industrialisation. However, Gandhiji opposed it. He favoured small scale industries to make the villages self-sufficient.

(vi) The two objectives of Indian National Congress, which were declared by the WC Bonnerjee in December 1885, were

(a) To promote friendly relations of nationalist with political workers from various parts of the country.

(b) To develop and consolidate the feelings of national unity, irrespective of caste, religion or province.

(vii) The two principles of Fascism were

(a) Fascism was an antithesis of democracy. Fascists believed that democracy was not suitable for the country because it widens the gulf between the poor and the rich.

(b) Fascists favoured tight control over all sections of society. They wanted to control capitalists, industrialists, labourers, landlords, peasants, artisans and all other productive groups.

3. (i) A bill is a written proposal for legislation that is submitted to one of the two Houses of Parliament. It must be passed by both houses and obtain the president's approval to become law. Legislative ideas are introduced in the form of bills.

The Bills introduced in the Parliament can be classified into four categories

(a) Ordinary Bills, which are concerned with any matter other than financial subjects.

(b) Money Bills, which are concerned with the financial matters.

(c) Financial Bills; which are also concerned with financial matters but are different from Money Bills.

(d) Constitutional Amendment Bills, which are concerned with the amendment of the provisions of the Constitution.

(ii) (a) The Money Bill can be initiated only in the Lok Sabha.

(b) The decision of the Speaker whether a Bill is a Money Bill or an Ordinary Bill is final. This means that the nature of a Bill which is certified by the Speaker as a Money Bill shall not be open to question either in a Court of Law or in the either House or even by the President. When a Bill is transmitted to the Council of States, or Rajya Sabha or is presented for the assent of the President, it shall bear the endorsement of the Speaker that it is a Money Bill.

(iii) A Money Bill can only originate in the Lok Sabha.

The procedure is as follows

- After its introduction in the Lok Sabha, the bill is discussed, debated and voted in the house.
- After being passed by the Lok Sabha, the bill is then sent to the Rajya Sabha for recommendations.
- The Rajya Sabha must return the bill within 14 days with or without recommendations.
- The bill then comes to the Lok Sabha, which may accept or reject any or all of the recommendations of the Rajya Sabha.
- After 14 days, if the bill is not returned, it is deemed to have been passed by both the houses in its original form.

4. (i) The role of the Prime Minister in foreign affairs is as follows

- The Prime Minister represents India in international conferences. He attends the world organisations' meetings and puts forward India's view before the world leaders.
- The Prime Minister may visit any country to improve the relations of India and to solve outstanding issues.
- The Prime Minister is the Chief Architect of foreign policy of India. Usually the Foreign Minister accompanies the Prime Minister in all conferences.

(ii) The three relations of the Prime Minister with the Parliament are as follows

(a) The President summons and prorogues the Houses of the Parliament and dissolve the Lok Sabha on the advice of the Prime Minister.

(b) The Prime Minister is chief spokeman of the Government in the Parliament and makes all important announcements of the government policies on the floor of the House.

(c) The Prime Minister makes a concluding speech in all matters of discussion and debate in the House.

(iii) No, the Prime Minister cannot become a dictator because there are so many checks on his authority as given below

- The presence of the opposition in the Parliament with its leaders keep Prime Minister under check.
- The Prime Minister's responsibility to the Parliament prevents him from becoming a dictator.
- Regular and periodic free and fair elections in the country ensures the democratic set up of India.
- There may be differences within the ruling party itself. The Prime Minister has to secure the willing cooperation of all important persons of his party. This cannot be done by a dictator.

5. (i) Under Article 124 of Indian Constitution the Supreme Court consists of 34 judges in which there is one Chief Justice and 33 other judges.

The President of India appoints the Judges of the Supreme Court through the following procedure

- When the President appoints the Chief Justice, he/she may consult with judges of the Supreme Court and the High Court.
- When the President appoints other judges of the Supreme Court, he/she consults with the Chief Justice of India.
- Usually, the senior most judge of the Supreme Court is appointed as the Chief Justice of India.

(ii) As a Court of Record, the Supreme Court has two important powers. These are as follows

(a) The judgements, proceedings and acts of the Supreme Court are recorded for perpetual memory and testimony. These records cannot be questioned when produced before any court. The judgements are in nature of precedents i.e. the High Courts and other courts are bound to give a similar decision in a similar case.

(b) It has power to punish for the contempt of court (which is of two types i.e. civil contempt and criminal contempt) either with simple imprisonment for a term of six months or fine upto ₹ 2000 or with both.

(iii) The Supreme Court is the sole interpreter of the Constitution. It has the power to review any laws passed by the Union or State Legislature. If any law passed by the Legislature is against the spirit of the Constitution or contravenes any provision of the Constitution, the Supreme Court can declare such law as null and void.

Judicial review is necessary for the following reasons

- The Constitution is in written form. So, whenever the question of interpretation arises, the Supreme Court acts as an interpreter.
- To uphold the principle of supremacy of the Constitution.
- To maintain the Fundamental Rights of citizens.

- The legislature may lack the wisdom, experience and impartiality to interpret the law effectively. This function is best performed by the Supreme Court.

6. (i) The intention behind the annexation of states of Dalhousie's Plan of annexation was
- to expand the British Empire, by constantly adding new states to it.
- to rule over India for a longer time or to keep themselves in power.
- to further exploit India's resources and carry its wealth to England thereby making their country prosperous.

(ii) The political causes that led the uprising of 1857 were

(a) **Territorial Expansion** Since Battle of Plassey (1757) the Company's territorial expansion had been rapid. By 1818 AD when the last Peshwa was dethroned, all Princely States had either been annexed or compelled to sign Treaties or Subsidiary Alliances with the Company.

(b) **Unpopular Administration** The British officers were very arrogant and had contempt for the Indians and they were not easily approachable. Therefore, people were not in favour of British administration.

(c) **Absentee Rule** Indians did not like the idea that their country was ruled from Britain. This was unlike Mughals who settled here and made India their own country. Thus, Indians resented the British rule.

(iii) The two uprising spread at the time of 1857 were

(a) **Lucknow** The uprising broke out at Lucknow on 14th June, 1857. British Resident Henry Lawrence was killed during the seige of the residency by the Patriotic rebels. In March 1858, the city of Lucknow was recaptured by the British. Begum Hazrat Mahal fled to Nepal.

(b) **Kanpur** Nana Sahib was proclaimed as the Peshwa on 5th June, 1857. He led the uprising in Kanpur along with Tantia Tope. General Sir Hugh Wheeler surrendered on 27th June, 1857. But General James O'Neil and General Campbell recaptured Kanpur. Nana Sahib fled to Nepal. Tantia Tope escaped and joined the Rani of Jhansi, Rani Lakshmi Bai.

7. (i) The purpose of the Non-Aligned Movement was
- The Non-Aligned Movement (NAM), was established in 1961 during the height of the Cold War.
- It aimed to create a path of neutrality and collective self-reliance among its member countries, and preventing them from falling under the influence of the two dominant superpowers, the United States and the Soviet Union.
- NAM aimed to support these newly independent countries in their efforts to avoid being coerced into military or ideological alliances.
- By maintaining a non-aligned stance, member states hoped to focus on internal development, advocate for equitable international relations, and promote world peace.
- The founding of NAM represented a significant assertion of sovereignty and a refusal to participate in power politics that could potentially compromise their political and economic independence.

(ii) Jawaharlal Nehru, one of the principal founders of the Non-Aligned Movement, envisioned several key objectives for the movement that were deeply influenced by the principles of Panchsheel. These objectives included
- **Maintaining National Independence** Nehru emphasised the importance of countries maintaining their sovereignty without succumbing to the influence of either the Western or Eastern blocs during the Cold War.
- **Promoting Peaceful Coexistence** Nehru advocated for mutual respect for each other's territorial integrity and sovereignty, mutual non-aggression, mutual non-interference in internal affairs, etc.
- **Economic Cooperation and Development** Nehru also supported the idea of economic collaboration among non-aligned countries to promote development and reduce dependence on the major powers.
- **Cultural Exchange and Solidarity** Nehru saw the Non-Aligned Movement as a platform for cultural exchange and solidarity among developing nations, helping to strengthen cultural ties and mutual understanding across diverse global cultures. This was seen as a way to foster unity among nations with different social and political systems.

(iii) The Five Principles of Panchsheel, or the Panchsheel Agreement, were jointly enunciated by Indian Prime Minister Jawaharlal Nehru and Chinese Premier Zhou Enlai in 1954. The five principles were

(a) **Mutual respect for each other's territorial integrity and sovereignty** This principle emphasises that each nation should respect the other's sovereignty and geographical boundaries without interference, fostering a relationship based on mutual trust.

(b) **Mutual non-aggression** Both countries agreed to refrain from aggression against each other, ensuring a peaceful and stable relationship without military conflict.

(c) **Mutual non-interference in each other's internal affairs** This principle advocates that each country should avoid involvement in the internal politics, development, and administration of the other, which helps in maintaining each country's independence and reduces conflicts.

(d) **Equality and mutual benefit** This principle emphasises equal partnership and cooperation that leads to mutual benefits for both countries, promoting a balanced and fair relationship.

(e) **Peaceful co-existence** This overarching principle encompasses the essence of the Panchsheel agreement, promoting the idea that nations can coexist in peace regardless of ideological differences.

8. (i) The British government presented several justifications for the Partition of Bengal in 1905, emphasising the administrative challenges posed by the region's size and population.

Officially, they argued that Bengal, as it stood, was too large for effective administration and that its division would lead to better governance.

The British claimed that the eastern part of Bengal was underdeveloped and neglected, and that the partition would facilitate focused administrative attention and economic development.

Additionally, they suggested that a smaller administrative unit would enable more efficient tax collection and law enforcement, which were becoming increasingly difficult due to the vastness and diverse needs of the large population.

By portraying the partition as a move towards better governance, the British aimed to rationalise their decision in terms of administrative necessity rather than political strategy.

(ii) The geographical distribution of religious communities was a crucial factor in the British decision to partition Bengal. The partition line was drawn in such a way that it divided the predominantly Muslim eastern areas from the predominantly Hindu Western areas.

This division appeared strategic, aiming to dilute the strong nationalist sentiments that were prominent in Bengal at the time.

By segregating the populations based on religion, the British hoped to curb the growing strength of the nationalist movements that were gaining momentum across Hindu and Muslim communities. This tactic was reflective of the broader British colonial policy of 'divide and rule,' where fostering divisions among key groups weakened unified resistance against British authority.

The impact of this partition on communal lines sowed the seeds of long-term religious strife, which altered the course of regional politics and community relationships in Bengal.

(iii) Indian nationalists strongly opposed the decision of the Partition of Bengal in 1905, viewing it as a strategic move by the British colonial rulers to divide and weaken the unity of Bengal on the basis of religion. Here are some key perspectives held by Indian nationalists regarding the partition

- **Divide and Rule Strategy** Nationalists believed that the primary motive behind the partition was the British policy of 'divide and rule.' By splitting Bengal into a predominantly Hindu West Bengal and a predominantly Muslim East Bengal, the British aimed to create religious divisions and thereby weaken the strong nationalist movements in the region.
- **Disruption of National Unity** The partition was seen as a direct attack on the growing unity among Indians that transcended religious lines. Bengal was a hub of intellectual and political activities against British rule, and dividing it was perceived as an attempt to fragment this unity and dilute the nationalist fervor.
- **Economic Motivations** Some nationalists argued that the partition was also economically motivated. They believed it was designed to break the economic backbone of Bengal, which was one of the most economically vibrant regions of India, thereby making it easier to control.
- **Cultural and Social Impact** The decision was viewed as an assault on the rich cultural and social fabric of Bengal. The region had a long history of communal harmony and intellectual exchange, and the partition threatened to disrupt these deep-rooted connections.

The response to the Partition of Bengal was one of the first major nationwide agitations against British rule and marked a significant shift in Indian nationalism from moderate to more assertive forms of protest.

9. (i) According to Gandhiji, the term Swadeshi means producing necessary items in one's own country and using them for one's use without being dependent on imported goods. The Swadeshi Movement was mainly directed towards social and economic upliftment of the society, especially of the rural workers. Gandhiji was in favour of using Swadeshi goods and boycott of foreign goods to harm the English trade. He emphasised the use of 'Charkha' and 'Khadi' to improve the economic condition of the Indian workers. He was in favour of establishing cottage industries in rural areas to uplift the rural people.

Gandhiji launched the Swadeshi Movement to get rid of the problem of poverty and unemployment, to arouse self-respect and moral courage to fight against the wrong.

(ii) Gandhiji launched Rowlatt Satyagraha on April 6, 1919 against the laws of Rowlatt Act passed in March 1919.

The Rowlatt Act gave

- enormous powers to the government to suppress political activities.
- power to police to search any place and arrest any person without warrant.

According to Gandhi, the Rowlatt Act was 'destructive to the elementary rights of an individual'. He called upon the people to do Satyagraha. Gandhiji asked the people to fast, pray and hold public meeting against the Black Act, and also made an appeal to observe hartal for a day.

(iii) The first two Satyagrahas of the Gandhiji were Champaran Satyagraha (1917) and Ahmedabad Satyagraha (1918-19).

(a) **Champaran Satyagraha** The indigo cultivators of Champaran district of Bihar were greatly exploited by the European planters. They were bound by law to grow indigo on 3/20th (Tinkathia) of their land and sell it to the British planters at prices fixed by them.

The cultivators invited Gandhiji to take up their cause. He fought for the rights of the cultivators and forced the government to pass an Act for the welfare of the peasants.

(b) **Ahmedabad Satyagraha** Gandhiji organised his Satyagraha movement in Ahmedabad in 1918, using Satyagraha tactics and a hunger strike to address an industrial dispute between cotton mill workers and the mill owners. The workers sought a 35 per cent increase in wages, while the owners were aiming to withdraw the plague bonus. The movement was successful, leading to the workers achieving their wage increase.

10. (i) Objectives of the United Nations are as follows

- To maintain international peace and security.
- To develop friendly relations among nations, based on the respect for the principle of equal rights and self-determination of people.
- To achieve international co-operation in solving various international, economic, social, cultural or humanitarian problems.

(ii) Composition of three organ of the UN as follows

(a) **General Assembly** The Composition of the General Assembly consists of 5 members of each country that are members of the UN. There is a President, 21 Vice-Presidents and Chairmen of the committees. The assembly consist of 6 main committees.

(b) **The Security Council** It consist of 15 members, out of which there are 5 permanent members (US, Britain, France, Russia, China) and 10 non-Permanent members i.e. 5 from Afro-Asian countries, 2 from Latin America, 2 from West-Europe and 1 from East Europe.

(c) **International Court of Justice** The court consist of 15 judges that are elected for a term of 9 years. The President and Vice-President are also elected from among them for 3 years.

(iii) The powers and functions of the General Assembly are as follows

- To consider and make recommendations on the principles of co-operation, in the maintenance of international peace and security.
- To discuss any question relating to international peace and security and to make recommendations on it.
- To make recommendations for the peaceful settlements of disputes.
- To receive and consider reports from the Security Council and other organs of the UN.
- To review and approve the United Nations budget and allocate financial contributions among member states.

SQP Code : **PB-5/15** Series ***i*-Succeed 5-25/15** Roll No. [ ]

Sample Question Paper 05

History & Civics 10th (Code 50)

General Instructions

1. Attempt all questions from Part I (Compulsory).
2. A total of 5 questions are to be attempted from Part II, 2 out of 3 questions from Section A and 3 out of 5 questions from Section B.
3. The intended marks for questions or parts of questions are given in brackets ( ).

Time : 2 Hrs.

Max. Marks : 80

Part-I Attempt all questions from this part

Que 1.

Choose the correct option. (16)

(i) Comptroller and Auditor General's report is examined by a government organ. Who among the following examines this report? [Application] (1)

(a) Parliament (b) President
(c) Election Commission (d) Lok Sabha

(ii) Given below are few details. [Understanding] (1)

Post	Details
Prime Minister	Head of the Cabinet
President	Head of the Union
?	Supreme decision-making body in India.

(a) Cabinet (b) Council of Ministers
(c) Lok Sabha (d) Rajya Sabha

(iii) An ordinance is passed by the President on the advice of which of the following? [Understanding] (1)

(a) Speaker (b) Council of Ministers
(c) Vice-President (d) Chief Justice of India

(iv) In a village, a person named X went to a nearby police station to complaint about a theft that took place last night, but the policeman Y refused to file an FIR. [Application] (1)

In the above scenario which of the following writ can be issued against the person Y?

(a) Mandamus (b) Quo Warranto
(c) Habeas Corpus (d) Certiorari

(v) Which among the following is an original jurisdiction of High Court? [Recall] (1)

P. Election of Members of Parliament
Q. Revenue Collection
R. Disputes between States
S. Disputes between Centre and States

Codes

(a) P and Q (b) R and S
(c) P and R (d) Q and S

(vi) Read the two statements given below and select the option that shows the correct relationship between A and R. [Analyse] (1)

Assertion (A) The President or a Governor cannot be sued in a Court of law for any act.

Reason (R) The President can be impeached, by passing a resolution in any house.

Codes

(a) R contradicts A
(b) R is the reason for A
(c) A is true, but R is false
(d) A and R are independent of each other

(vii) Read the two statements below regarding INA and select the option that shows the correct relationship between A and R.

Assertion (A) Interim Government of Free India was recognised by World Powers. [Analyse] (1)

Reason (R) The objective of Azad Hind was to establish its permanent National Government.

(a) R contradicts A
(b) R is the reason for A
(c) A is true, but R is false
(d) A and R are independent of each other

(viii) Who helped Gandhiji in his fight against discrimination in South Africa? [Recall] (1)

(a) RC Dutt
(b) Surendranath Banerjee
(c) M A Jinnah
(d) Gopal Krishna Gokhale

(ix) Which of these is not correct about Lala Lajpat Rai? [Analyse] (1)

(a) He started newspapers like Young India.
(b) He was known as 'Father of Revolutionary Thought in India'.
(c) He boycotted the Simon Commission and demonstrated against it in Lahore.
(d) He founded the National School of Lahore.

(x) The below personality established which educational institutions? [Recall] (1)

(a) BHU (b) DAV
(c) Jamia Milia Islamia
(d) Fergusson College

(xi) The Treaty of Versailles was signed on .... in the Hall of Mirrors at Versailles in France. [Recall] (1)

(a) 28th June, 1919
(b) 25th June, 1919
(c) 30th June, 1919
(d) 29th June, 1919

(xii) Bindu is studying about a personality who edited the newspaper 'Bengalee' and set up Ripon College. Whom is she referring to? [Application] (1)

(a) Surendranath Banerjee
(b) Dadabhai Naoroji
(c) Lokmanya Tilak
(d) Justice Ranade

(xiii) Identify the odd one out, which do not form part of Indian Independence Act. [Analyse] (1)

(a) Creation of Boundary Commission to decide the boundary of two dominions.
(b) India would be partitioned and two independent Dominions i.e. India and Pakistan.
(c) India was to compromise the remaining territories included in the British India.
(d) A plebiscite would be held in North-West Frontier Province as well as in Sylet district in East Bengal.

(xiv) Simon Commission: 1927 :: Gandhi-Irwin Pact: .... [Recall] (1)

(a) 1928 (b) 1929
(c) 1930 (d) 1931

(xv) The reason due to which Hitler attacked Poland was to .... [Recall] (1)

(a) control trade activities
(b) regain the Dansing Port
(c) seize the Coal mines
(d) militarise the Rhine Valley area

(xvi) Identify which UN specialised agency organises conferences to bring scientists together. [Recall] (1)

(a) World Health Organisation
(b) UNICEF
(c) UNESCO
(d) International Labour Organisation

Que 2.

Read the extract given below and answer the question which follows.

Headline President Murmu approves 412 Gallantry Awards to Armed Forces Personnel, The 412 Gallantry Awards include six Kirti Chakras and 15 Shaurya Chakras for Armed Forces personnel and others.

Source: *India Today 26th January, 2023*

(i) On the basis of above news, discuss the military powers of President of India. [Understanding] (2)

(ii) What are the similarities between Supreme Court and the High Court? Mention any two such similarities. [Analyse & Recall] (2)

(iii) What was Queen Victoria's proclamation? Who read it? [Recall] (2)

(iv) Wahabi Revolt was one of the factor which promoted Nationalism. Mention any two facts about the Revolt. [Recall] (2)

(v) Mention any two impacts of revolutionary movement after partition of Bengal. [Recall] (2)

(vi) Write any two important objectives of the Indian National Army. [Recall] (2)

(vii) Mention any two reasons, why USA entered into the First World War? [Recall] (2)

Part-II Section A (Civics) Attempt any two questions from this section

Que 3.

The Parliament is the legislative organ of the Union Government and occupies a pre-eminent and central position in Indian democracy.

In this context, answer the following questions.

(i) Briefly describe organisation of the Parliament. [Recall] (3)

(ii) Mention any three differences between adjournment and prorogation of the session of the Parliament. [Recall] (3)

(iii) Write four differences between censure motion and no-confidence motion. [Understanding] (4)

Que 4.

The President of India enjoys the Veto Power regarding a Bill because he is an integral part of the Parliament. With reference to the Veto Power of the President, answer the following questions.

(i) What are the three alternatives, when a Bill is presented to the President for his assent? [Analyse] (3)

(ii) What do you mean by Absolute Veto? Mention any two cases when it is exercised? [Understanding & Recall] (1+2)

(iii) Explain the Pocket Veto Power of the President with a suitable example. [Recall] (4)

Que 5.

Under the Single integrated Judicial system, there are no seperate sets of law and Supreme Court stands at the apex of the system. In this context answer the following questions

(i) Mention any three cases, where the Original Jurisdiction of the Supreme Court does not extend. [Recall] (3)

(ii) How does the Supreme Court maintain the sanctity of the Constitution of India? [Recall] (3)

(iii) Mention any four administrative powers of the High Court. [Recall] (4)

Section B (History) Attempt any three questions from this section

Que 6.

The Revolt of 1857 was outburst of nationalist sentiments. In this context, explain the following

(i) Ill treatment of indigo cultivators. [Recall] (3)

(ii) The laws that interfered with the religious customs. [Recall] (3)

(iii) Annexation of Awadh and Berar. [Recall] (4)

Que 7.

(i) Mention any three functions of the General Assembly. [Recall] (3)

(ii) What does UNICEF stands for and what is the source of finance of the UNICEF? [Understanding & Recall] (3)

(iii) State the functions of the Security Council of United Nations. [Recall] (4)

Que 8.

Read the excerpt given below and answer the questions that follow.

The Swadeshi Movement has been the core of the Independence movement as well and has contributed a lot to the development of Indian nationalism. This Swadeshi Movement has got much wider support from the masses since 1906 against the erstwhile partition of Bengal and ultimately turned into a full-blown Independence movement in the early 20th century till we attained independence.

(i) Name the major cause of this movement. Give any two reasons for partition of Bengal. [Application & Recall] (1+2)

(ii) Discuss any three programmes of this movement. [Application] (3)

(iii) Mention any four impacts of Swadeshi Movement. [Recall] (4)

Que 9.

Look the picture carefully. Explain the following related questions.

(i) Identify the event in the above picture and explain the main cause of this event. [Recall] (4)

(ii) Explain the impact of the event. [Recall] (3)

(iii) Explain the course of the event. [Recall] (3)

Que 10.

Post-Second World War, the world stood divided into two power blocs i.e. American Bloc and Soviet Bloc. These Blocs led to Cold War. In this context, answer the following questions

(i) What is meant by Cold War? Name some international crises during the Cold War period. [Analyse & Recall] (2+1)

(ii) Mention any three specific causes of Cold War. [Recall] (3)

(iii) What were the consequences of the Cold War? Explain four causes. [Analyse & Recall] (2+2)

Answers in Topper's Style

My Commitment *I affirm that I am reviewing these answers only after I have solved the Sample Question Paper 5 on my own. My purpose of looking the answers is solely to verify whether my answers were correct or not and to identify my mistakes in case my answers were wrong or I could not answer that.*

1. (i) (a) Parliament
   (ii) (a) Cabinet
   (iii) (b) Council of Ministers
   (iv) (a) Mandamus
   (v) (a) P and Q
   (vi) (d) A and R are independent of each other
   (vii) (d) A and R are independent of each other
   (viii) (d) Gopal Krishna Gokhale
   (ix) (b) He was known as 'Father of Revolutionary Thought in India'.
   (x) (b) DAV
   (xi) (a) 28th June, 1919
   (xii) (a) Surendranath Banerjee
   (xiii) (a) Creation of Boundary Commission to decide the boundary of two dominions.
   (xiv) (d) 1931
   (xv) (b) regain the Dansing Port
   (xvi) (c) UNESCO

2. (i) Military powers of the President are
   - The President is the Supreme Commander of the armed forces in India.
   - He appoints the Chiefs of all the three wings of the Armed Forces on the recommendations of the Prime Minister and his Council of Ministers, the Parliament and the Military Secretary.

   (ii) The similarities between Supreme Court and High Court are as follows
   (i) Supreme Court has superintendence over all laws and tribunals of the country whereas High Court has superintendence over all the courts under its jurisdiction.
   (ii) Both of them can make decision on civil and criminal cases and ensure the enforcement of fundamental rights.

   (iii) Queen Victoria's Proclamation was a promise to Indian people and the Princes that the British Government would not annex the Indian states, and all the treaties that the Princes had concluded with the East India Company would be honoured.
   The first Viceroy of India Lord Canning read the Queen Victoria's proclamation on 1st November, 1858.

   (iv) The two facts about the Wahabi Revolt were
   (a) Syed Ahmad of Rae Bareli was the Leader of the Wahabi Movement.
   (b) The Wahabis were the followers of a Muslim sect and they urged the people to join in a holy war to overthrow the British Rule.

   (v) The two impacts of Revolutionary Movement after partition of Bengal were
   (a) The revolutionaries made the people realise that death for the sake of independence of the country was much better than the life in the slavery.
   (b) The revolutionaries forced the British Government to pass the Morley-Minto reforms, 1909 and to annual the partition of Bengal.

   (vi) The two objectives of the Indian National Army are as follows
   (a) To organise an armed revolution.
   (b) To organise a Provisional Government of Free India in order to mobilise all the forces effectively.

   (vii) On 6th April, 1917, USA declared war thus entering into the First World War. The reasons were
   (a) In 1915, the German U-Boats had sunk, a British ship Lusitania sailing from New York for Liverpool in which 128 Americans were killed.
   (b) America also feared if Germany won the war, it would become a serious rival of USA.

3. (i) Under the Constitution of India, the Parliament consists of the President, the Council of States (Rajya Sabha) and the House of People (Lok Sabha).
   - The Rajya Sabha is the Upper House or Second Chamber or House of Elders whereas the Lok Sabha is Lower House or First Chamber or popular house of the Parliament.
   - The Rajya Sabha represents the States and Union Territories of the Indian Union, while the Lok Sabha represents the people of India as a whole.
   - The third part i.e. the President of India is not a member of either House of the Parliament and does not attend its meetings, yet he is an integral part of the Parliament. This is because a Bill cannot become a law without the President's assent. The President summons and prorogues both the Houses, dissolves the Lok Sabha, address both the Houses and so on.

(ii) The differences between adjournment and prorogation of the session of the Parliament are

Adjournment	Prorogation
It only terminates a sitting and not a session of the House.	It not only terminates a sitting but also a session of the House.
It is done by presiding officer of the House.	It is done by the President of India.
It does not affect the bills or any other business pending before the House.	It also does not affect the Bills or any other business pending before the House but all pending notices lapse on prorogation and fresh notices have to be given for the next session.

(iii) The differences between censure and no-confidence motion are given below

Censure Motion	No-Confidence Motion
It should state the reasons for its adoption in the Lok Sabha.	It does not need to state the reasons for its adoption in the Lok Sabha.
It can be moved against an individual Minister or a group of Ministers or the entire Council of Ministers.	It can be moved against the entire council of Ministers only.
It is moved for censuring the Council of Ministers for specific policies and actions.	It is moved for ascertaining the confidence of Lok Sabha in the Council of Ministers.
If it is passed in the Lok Sabha, the Council of Ministers does not need to resign from the office.	If it is passed in the Lok Sabha, the Council of Ministers must resign from offices.

4. (i) When a Bill is presented to the President for his assent, then he has three alternatives, they are as follows

(a) He may give his assent to the Bill.

(b) He may withhold his assent to the Bill.

(c) He may return the Bill for reconsideration of the Parliament, (Except Money Bill). However, if the Bill passes again with or without amendment, then the President must give his assent.

(ii) Absolute Veto means, President withholds his assent to the Bill which is passed by the Parliament. The Bill then ends and does not become an act.

Usually, this veto is exercised in the following two cases

(a) With respect to private member's Bills, that is Bills introduced by any MP who is not a Minister.

(b) With respect to the government Bills when the cabinet resigns and the new cabinet advises the President not to give his assent to such Bills.

(iii) In power of Pocket Veto, the President neither ratifies nor rejects nor returns the Bill, but simply keeps the Bill pending for an indefinite period. It literally means that the President does not take any action either positive or negative on the Bill. The President can exercise this Veto Power as the Constitution does not prescribe any time limit within which he has to take decision with respect to a Bill presented to him.

For example

In 1986, President Zail Singh exercised the Pocket Veto with respect to the Indian post office Amendment Bill.

The Bill was passed by Rajiv Gandhi Government which imposed restrictions on the freedom of press and hence, was widely criticised.

After three year in 1989 the next President R Venkataraman sent the Bill back for reconsideration, but the new National Front Government decided to drop the Bill.

5. (i) The Original Jurisdiction of the Supreme Court does not extend to the following three cases

(a) A dispute arising out of any pre-Constitution treaty, agreement, covenant, engagement, covenant or other similar instrument.

(b) Adjustment of certain expenses and pensions between the centre and the states.

(c) Inter-state water disputes.

(ii) The Supreme Court maintains the sanctity of the Constitution of India in the following ways

(a) The Supreme Court has the power of exclusive jurisdiction in regard to questions as to constitutional validity of Central laws.

(b) The Supreme Court is the interpreter of the Constitution and its decisions is final.

(c) It has the power to review laws passed by the Union or State legislatures.

(iii) The four administrative powers of the High Court are

(a) Sending for a detailed report on the working of lower courts.

(b) Making and issuing, general rules and prescribe forms for regulating the practice and proceedings of lower courts.

(c) Transfering and recall a District judge.

(d) Prescribing forms in which books, entries and accounts are to be kept by lower courts.

6. (i) A new indigo plantation system introduced in 1833 brought incalculable misery for the Indian peasants. Indigo was required by cloth manufacturers to dye cloth.

As the indigo trade grew, commercial agents and officials of the company began investing in indigo production. They forced the peasants to produce only indigo. The condition of Indigo cultivators was miserable and most of them were in a debt trap. The peasants who were initially tempted by the loans soon realised how harsh the system was. The price they got for the indigo they produced was very low and the cycle of loans never ended.

(ii) There are many laws that interfered with the religious customs of the people. They were

- **The Religious Incompetence Law** According to this law, if a person belonging to the Hindu religion changed his religion, he could remain an heir of his ancestral property. The people reacted that it was enacted to promote the conversion of Hindu to Christianity.
- **Widow Remarriage Act** Widow Remarriage Act, 1856 legalised widow to remarriage. This was also not liked by the orthodox Hindus.
- **General Service Enlistment Act** Under this Act new recruits were required to serve anywhere in India or overseas. According to the Hindu customs, crossing the sea was contrary to their religion.

(iii) **Annexation of Awadh** Awadh was a protected feudatory state with control over internal administration only. On 13th February, 1856, Lord Dalhousie annexed Awadh on the pretext of maladministration by Nawab Wajid Ali Shah. Nawab was sent to Calcutta on a pension of ₹ 12 Lakh per annum. Consequently, a number of taluqdars or nobles, officials and the soldiers were deprived of their status and rendered jobless.

Annexation of Berar Unable to pay the debt, Lord Dalhousie annexed Berar in 1853. The Nizam owed a lot of money to the English Company on account of the contingent forces.

As the Nizam was unable to pay, the debt reached to about 1,80,000 pounds. A new treaty was signed by which Nizam gave Berar to the British for maintenance of the contingent.

Thus, Dalhousie's annexation of Awadh and Berar to the British Empire was illegal and the people of Awadh and Berar were displeased with the British.

7. (i) The three functions of the General Assembly are

(a) Consider and make recommendations on the general principles of co-operation for maintaining international peace and security, including disarmament.

(b) Discuss any question relating to international peace and security except where a dispute or situation is currently being discussed by the Security Council and make recommendations on it.

(c) Discuss and make recommendations on any questions within the scope of the charter or affecting the powers and functions of any organ of the United Nations.

(ii) UNICEF stand for United Nations International Children's Emergency Fund was established on 11th December, 1946 by the UN Relief and Rehabilitation Administration to offer urgent assistance to children and mothers impacted by World War II.

The UNICEF is financed by voluntary contributions from Governments, Organisations and Individual.Fund raising campaigns are carried on by organisations and individuals which include selling of UNICEF cards.

(iii) Functions of the Security Council are as follows

- To maintain international peace and security in accordance with the principles and purposes of the UN.
- To investigate any dispute or situation, to take military action against an aggressor, and to recommend terms of settling disputes and any methods of adjusting them.
- To call on members to apply economic sanctions and measures other than force, to prevent or stop aggression.
- To recommend to the General Assembly for the appointment of the Secretary-General and to elect the Judges of the International Court of Justice together with the General Assembly.
- To determine existence of threats and to recommend actions of the same.

8. (i) The immediate cause of the Swadeshi Movement was the British decision to partition Bengal in 1905, a move seen as an effort to weaken Indian nationalism through the creation of religious discord. This decision sparked widespread outrage and prompted a movement to boycott British products.

Two reasons for the partition of Bengal were

(a) Bengal was an important centre of Indian nationalism. The British hoped that by dividing the province on communal lines, they would be able to stop the rising wave of nationalism.

(b) The partition also aimed at curbing the influence of Bengal by reducing Bengalis in minority in their own home state.

(ii) The programmes of this movement were

(a) Boycotting of British-made cloth and imported sugar and salt.

(b) To give up government posts and seats in the Legislative Council.

(c) To promote Hindi and vernacular languages.

(iii) The impacts of Swadeshi Movement were

- The movement brought people belonging to different sections of society closer to each other. The movement saw the participation of students and women in large numbers.

- The movement gave huge impetus to the indigenous industries. Many industries ranging from textile mills, soap and match factories to large-scale enterprises were opened and there was an increase in production of indigenous goods.
- The Swadeshi Movement gave employment opportunities to many craftsmen and weavers working in handloom and handicraft industries.
- The movement saw the flowering of nationalist poetry, prose and journalism. Poets such as Tagore and Syed Abu Mohammed wrote many inspirational poets and songs.

9. (i) The event in the given picture depicts the demonstration against the Simon Commission. In 1927, the British Government appointed the Indian Statuatory Commission, known as Simon Commission, to investigate the need for further constitutional reforms.

One of the main cause of this event was that it had only British members. For a commission that wanted to understand the administration and how it affected the Indian masses, it lacked Indian representation, which is why the commission was severly criticised. Many protests were carried out individually as well as in groups, urging the British administration to review the Constitution of the commission. Thus, the commission was seen as a deliberate insult to the self-respect of Indians.

(ii) **Impact of the Event**

The government used brutal suppression and police attacks to break the popular opposition.

Lala Lajpat Rai was beaten up mercilessly and lost his life as a result of the lathi blows. After his death, the extremists followed more aggressive paths. In spite of all the protests, the Simon Commission travelled to different parts of the country, met people and made their recommendations.

(iii) **Course of the Event**

At the Madras Session of Congress in 1927, presided over by Dr Ansari, the Congress decided to boycott the commission at every stage and in every form. The Muslim League and the Hindu Mahasabha decided to support the Congress decision on 3rd February. This day the commission reached Bombay, an All India Hartal was organised. Wherever the commission went, it was greeted with hartals and black flag demonstrations.

10. (i) The term Cold War describes Post-World War-II as geo-political tensions between the Soviet Union and the USA and their allies from the mid-1940s to the early 1990s.

Throughout this period, rivalry between the two superpowers was expressed through military coalitions, propaganda, espionage, weapons development, industrial advances, and competitive technological development. During the next few decades, the Cold War spread beyond Europe to every region of the world.

The Cold War period was characterised by international crises such as

- The Berlin Blockade (1948-49)
- The Korean War (1950-53)
- The Berlin Crisis (1961)
- The Vietnam War (1959-75)
- The Soviet-Afghan War (1979-89)
- The Cuban Missile Crisis (1962)

(ii) The following may be considered as the specific causes of the origin of the Cold War

(a) **Ideological Confrontation** The Cold War was rooted in the opposite ideologies of the USA and the Soviet Union. The US Bloc considered communism as a potential danger to freedom liberty, democracy and open society. On the other hand USSR branded USA as capitalist nation and an imperialist.

(b) **Mutual Distrust** USA dropped atom bombs on Japan during Second World War without taking Soviet Union into confidence. Soviet Union wanted to impose heavy penalaties on Germany, but Britain and USA opposed this.

(c) **The US Marshall Plan Vs Soviet Molotov Plan** The US secretary of State George C Marshall announced the European Recovery Plan (ERP) in June 1947 to increase financial aid to European countries so that they could be saved from coming under communist influence.

To counter the plan, USSR announced the Molotov Plan to provide economic aid to rebuild the countries in Eastern Europe that were aligned to the Soviet Union.

(iii) The consequences of the Cold War were as follows

- **Arm Race and Militarisation** The Cold War set in motion a mad race for armaments. Both the Blocs spent huge sums on arm and amassed deadly weapons.
- **Formation of Military Alliance** The Cold War led to the formation of various alliance such as NATO, SEATO, CENTO, The Warsaw Pact, etc.
- **Setback to the United Nations** The Cold War gave a major setback to the working of the United Nations. The rivalry between the Blocs barred admission of certain nations to the UNO.
- **Emergence of Non-Aligned Movement** The concept of NAM emerged during the Cold War. During this period many countries became independent from colonial rule. They decided not to join the two Blocs and to remain non-aligned. The NAM was the Chief characteristic of awakening of Asia and Africa.

SQP Code : **PB-6/15** Series ***i*-Succeed 6-25/15** Roll No. | | | | | | | | |

Sample Question Paper 06

History & Civics 10th (Code 50)

General Instructions

1. Attempt all questions from Part I (Compulsory).
2. A total of 5 questions are to be attempted from Part II, 2 out of 3 questions from Section A and 3 out of 5 questions from Section B.
3. The intended marks for questions or parts of questions are given in brackets ( ).

Time : 2 Hrs.

Max. Marks : 80

Part-I Attempt all questions from this part

Que 1.

Choose the correct option. (16)

(i) The executive power of the Union is vested in the President, who exercises this authority either directly or through officer's subordinate to him, in accordance with the Constitution. Additionally, the President holds the supreme command of the Union's defense forces. In what situation can the President assume the functions of a state government? [Application] (1)

(a) When there is a failure of the constitutional machinery in that state.
(b) When the state government requests assistance.
(c) When the President disagrees with the state policies.
(d) During a state election.

(ii) Given below are the few details.

Terms	Details
De Facto	Prime Minister
De Jure	?
Members of Union Cabinet	Article 352
Money Bills	Lok Sabha

Fill in the blanks with the help of correct options given below. [Understanding] (1)

(a) President (b) Cabinet
(c) Council of Ministers (d) None of these

(iii) He/She is chosen from the members of opposition. Who is he/she referred to? [Application] (1)

(a) Speaker (b) Deputy Speaker
(c) CAG (d) Chairman of Rajya Sabha

(iv) Fundamental Rights are a part of justiciable laws mentioned in the constitution of country X. These rights have been sourced from a country Y. Identify the country X and the country Y. [Application] (1)

(a) India and USA (b) India and Ireland
(c) India and UK (d) India and Australia

(v) Identify the financial powers of the President from the given options. [Recall] (1)

P. Introduce annual budget
Q. Promulgate Ordinance
R. Permission for Demand for Grants
S. Appointment of Finance Minister

(a) P and Q (b) P and R (c) R and S (d) Q and S

(vi) Read the two statements given below and select the options that shows the correct relationship between A and R. [Analyse] (1)

Assertion (A) The Lok Sabha has the exclusive power to initiate money bills.

Reason (R) According to the Indian Constitution, the Speaker of the Lok Sabha certifies a bill as a money bill.

Codes

(a) R contradicts A
(b) R is the reason for A
(c) A is true, but R is false
(d) A and R are independent of each other

(vii) Read the statements given below regarding Early Nationalist and select the option that show the correct relationship between A and R.

Assertion (A) Objective of Early Nationalists was to influence British Government and British Public.

Reason (R) They used Print Media to criticise British Policies. [Recall] (1)

(a) R contradicts A
(b) R is the reason for A
(c) A is true, but R is false
(d) A and R are independent of each other

(viii) Identify the International causes that led to rise of Assertive Nationalism in India. [Recall] (1)

(a) Boer War
(b) Defeat of Russia by Japanese
(c) First World War
(d) Both (a) and (b)

(ix) Which of the following aspect is not correct about Cold War? [Understanding] (1)

(a) Ideological differences emerged between USA and USSR.
(b) A state of extreme political tension emerged during this period.
(c) Cold War emerged immediately after the First World War.
(d) An atmosphere with no armed struggle.

(x) The personality in the image given below opposed Arms Act. Identify the personality. [Recall] (1)

(a) Bipin Chandra Pal
(b) Lala Lajpat Rai
(c) Rajendra Prasad
(d) R C Dutt

(xi) Which among the following was not a part of strategy followed by the extremist? [Understanding] (1)

(a) Involving masses in their campaigns
(b) Using religious symbols and culture for mass awakening
(c) Prayer and petition
(d) Aiming for 'Swaraj' which meant self independent rule

(xii) Chitra is studying about a movement that was popular among Muslim community. Which movement is she referring to? [Application] (1)

(a) Warkari Movement
(b) Bhoodan Movement
(c) Wahabi Movement
(d) Nirankari Movement

(xiii) Which among the following countries do not enjoy Veto Power in United Nation Security council [Understanding] (1)

(a) USA (b) Canada (c) France (d) China

(xiv) Hiroshima Attack: 6 August, 1945 : : Nagasaki Attack: .... [Recall] (1)

(a) 7th August, 1945 (b) 8th August, 1945
(c) 9th August, 1945 (d) 10th August, 1945

(xv) .... invaded China as a part of a mass campaign of territorial expansion before the Second World War. [Recall] (1)

(a) Germany (b) Italy (c) Russia (d) Japan

(xvi) Identify the personalities who played significant roles in bringing Congress and Muslim League closer after the Lucknow Pact. [Recall] (1)

(a) Annie Besant and Bal Gangadhar Tilak
(b) Abdul Kalam Azad and Ali Brothers
(c) Mahatma Gandhi and Bal Gangadhar Tilak
(d) None of the above

Que 2.

Read the extract given below and answer the questions which follow.

Eye on 2047, not 2024: PM Modi at Union Council of Ministers' meeting Prime Minister Narendra Modi chaired a meeting of the Union Council of Ministers at the Pragati Maidan convention centre where he asked the ministers to work with the aim of boosting India's growth in a host of areas by 2047, the 100th year anniversary of the country's independence.

Source : India Today, 3rd July

(i) On the basis of above news discuss any two financial powers of Council of Ministers [Understanding] (2)

(ii) Explain the following terms [Application] (2)
   (a) Habeas Corpus
   (b) Mandamus

(iii) What did the British do to foster the policy of 'Divide and Rule' and why? [Analyse & Recall] (2)

(iv) Describe the impact of the attack on Pearl Harbor during World War II. [Recall] (2)

(v) Who is often referred to as the political Guru of Gandhi and why? [Recall] (2)

(vi) What is the 'Safety Valve Theory' about the formation of the Congress? [Analyse] (2)

(vii) Mention any two recommendations of Simon Commission. [Recall] (2)

Part-II Section A (Civics) Attempt any two questions from this section

Que 3.

The rules and formalities for proper transaction of the business of the Parliament have been termed as 'Parliamentary Procedures'. In this context answer the following questions

(i) What is meant by Motion of Thanks? What is the result of Defeat of Motion? [Understanding & Recall] (1+2)

(ii) How many types of questions can be asked by members in the Parliament? [Recall] (3)

(iii) What do you mean by Cut Motions? Mention its types. [Understanding & Recall] (2+2)

Que 4.

In order of hierarchy of the government, President and Vice-President are on top. In this context, answer the following questions.

(i) Clearly indicate the actual position of the President as mentioned in the Constitution. [Understanding] (3)

(ii) What are the limitations on the President's Powers? [Recall] (3)

(iii) What are the functions of the Vice-President? [Recall] (4)

Que 5.

The High Court stands at the apex of the Judiciary in the state. In this context, answer the following questions.

(i) How are the Chief Justice and other Judges of a High Court appointed? [Recall] (3)

(ii) How and under what conditions are the acting Judges of a High Court appointed? [Analyse & Recall] (3)

(iii) What qualifications are required for a person to be appointed as a Judge of the High Court? How the Constitution maintains the independence of the Judiciary at state level? [Application & Recall] (2+2)

Section B (History) Attempt any three questions from this section

Que 6.

The Partition of Bengal in 1905 was intended to check the rising tide of Indian Nationalism and to break the Hindu-Muslim unity in Bengal.

In this context, answer the following questions.

(i) Reaction of the nationalists to the Partition of Bengal. [Recall] (3)

(ii) Reaction of the British against the agitators. [Recall] (3)

(iii) What were Curzon's two real motives behind the Partition of Bengal? [Recall] (4)

Que 7.

Gandhiji guided the affairs of the Indian National Congress with new techniques. Through various national movements he got the public support to win freedom for India.

In this context, answer the following questions.

(i) What were Gandhiji's methods to achieve Freedom? [Recall] (3)

(ii) State the reasons leading to the Non-Cooperation Movement. [Application] (3)

(iii) What were the methods of the Non-Cooperation Movement adopted by the people? [Recall] (4)

Que 8.

Read the excerpt given below and answer the questions that follows.

The Second World War, spanning from 1939 to 1945, was a global conflict that reshaped the political and social structure of the world. Its causes were complex, including dissatisfaction with the Treaty of Versailles, the rise of Fascism and Nazism, the policy of appeasement, and aggressive expansionist policies by Axis powers. The war concluded with significant consequences, including the defeat of the Axis Powers, the formation of the United Nations aimed at preventing future conflicts, and the beginning of the Cold War between the Soviet Union and the United States.

(i) Explain how the Treaty of Versailles contributed to the outbreak of the Second World War. [Recall] (3)

(ii) Mention any two causes that led to cold war. [Recall] (3)

(iii) Discuss any four consequences of the Second World War. [Recall] (4)

Que 9.

Look at the picture given below carefully and answer the following questions.

(A)

(B)

(i) Identify the persons 'A' and 'B' given above. To which section of the Congress did each belong and what were their ultimate objectives? [Recall] (3)

(ii) Highlight two different methods of struggle adopted by each section of the Congress. [Analyse] (3)

(iii) State the contributions of the person 'B' in the freedom struggle. [Recall] (4)

Que 10.

The aim of the UN is to safeguard the world from the scourge of war. In this context, answer the following questions.

(i) Describe briefly the composition of UN Security Council. [Recall] (3)

(ii) Mention the functions of International Court of Justice. [Recall] (3)

(iii) How does Security Council enforce its recommendations. [Recall] (4)

Answers in Topper's Style

My Commitment *I affirm that I am reviewing these answers only after I have solved the Sample Question Paper 6 on my own. My purpose of looking the answers is solely to verify whether my answers were correct or not and to identify my mistakes in case my answers were wrong or I could not answer that.*

1. (i) (c) When the President disagrees with the state policies.

(ii) (a) President

(iii) (b) Deputy Speaker

(iv) (a) India and USA

(v) (b) P and R

(vi) (a) R contradicts A

(vii) (d) A and R are independent of each other

(viii) (d) Both (a) and (b)

(ix) (c) Cold War emerged immediately after the First World War.

(x) (d) R C Dutt

(xi) (c) Prayer and petition

(xii) (c) Wahabi Movement

(xiii) (b) Canada

(xiv) (c) 9th August, 1945

(xv) (d) Japan

(xvi) (a) Annie Besant and Bal Gangadhar Tilak

2. (i) Two financial powers of Council of Ministers are

(a) **Preparation of Annual Budget** The Finance Minister, the integral part of the Cabinet, prepares the Annual Budget which contains the estimates of the income and expenditure of a financial year.

(b) **Taxation and Fiscal Policy** The Council of Ministers proposes taxation measures and formulates fiscal policies aimed at promoting economic growth and stability.

(ii) (a) Habeas Corpus literally means 'to have a body of'. This writ is issued to enforce the Fundamental Right of individual Liberty against unlawful detention.

(b) The literal meaning of mandamus is 'we command'. This writ is issued against any public body/official who has failed to perform his/her duty or refuse to do his/her duty. For example, it can be issued against a corporation and inferior court, etc.

(iii) Through the policy of 'Divide and Rule', the British Government tried to divide the Muslims and the Hindus and thereby weaken the National Movement led by the Congress. When the Muslim League was founded in 1906, to foster the policy of 'Divide and Rule' the British gave full support to their demands and thus, sowed the seeds of discontent in the political life of India.

(iv) The attack on Pearl Harbor, carried out by the Imperial Japanese Navy on 7th December, 1941, had profound consequences for the United States and the course of World War II. It led directly to the United States' entry into the war, galvanising public opinion and triggering a declaration of war against Japan. This event marked a turning point, shifting American focus from isolationism to active participation in the global conflict, significantly altering the dynamics of the war and hastening the defeat of the Axis Powers.

(v) The moderate leader Gopal Krishna Gokhale is referred to as the political Guru of Mahatma Gandhi. In his autobiography, Gandhi calls him his mentor and guide. Gokhale had great influence on Gandhiji during his formative years. His approach to reform, emphasising negotiation and constitutional methods rather than agitation and protest, strongly influenced Gandhi's political evolution.

In Gandhiji's 'Satyagraha', it was Gokhale who guided his early steps on the path of political activism. For these reasons, Gopal Krishna Gokhale is often referred to as the 'Political Guru' of Mahatma Gandhi.

(vi) The 'Safety Valve Theory' about the formation of the Congress suggested that the Congress was set up to channelise the discontent of the people to a forum where Indians could speak about their grievances and give vent to their feelings and thus, save the British from facing an open revolt.

(vii) The two recommendations of Simon Commission were

(a) Abolition of Dyarchy and grant full provincial autonomy to the provinces with the Governors having some over-riding powers in the matter of internal security.

(b) To recognise a Federal Government in India with the provinces and the Princely States as units.

3. (i) The debate on the President's Address takes the form of a Motion thanking the President for the speech. This speech is known as Motion of Thanks. The Motion of Thanks is moved by some member and backed by other members. It provides an opportunity for the discussion of matters referred to in the Address. At the end of the discussion, the Prime Minister replies to the debate, then motion of thanks is put to vote. Defeat of motion would cause the resignation of the government. Motion of

Thanks is, in reality, a motion of confidence in the government.

(ii) Generally, the first hour of the Lok Sabha is devoted to questions and that hour is called the Question Hour. There are three types of questions which were asked by members in the Parliament.

These are

(a) **Starred Questions** These are the questions in which a member is required to give oral answers.

(b) **Unstarred Questions** These are the questions in which a member is required to give written answers.

(c) **Short Notice Questions** These are related to urgent public importance.

(iii) The motion to reduce the amounts demanded as grants is known as a Cut Motion.

There are following three types of cut motions

(a) **Policy Cut Motion** This represents the disapproval of the policy. It says that the amount of demand be reduced to ₹ 1.

A Member of Parliament has to give precise reasons for such a cut.

(b) **Economy Cut Motion** This motion means that a member would like to reduce expenditure by making a specific cut in the grant demanded. The form of this motion is that some specific amount of demand is to be reduced.

(c) **Token Cut Motion** This motion is widely used by members. Its object is to voice a particular grievance for which the Government of India is responsible. The motion says that the amount of the demand be reduced to ₹ 100.

4. (i) The President is the nominal head of India. He has legislative, executive, diplomatic, financial and even judicial powers. But Indian Constitution has made clear that the President shall act in accordance with the advice given by the Prime Minister and the Council of Ministers e.g. the President can declare emergency only if a written recommendation to do so is given to him by the Union Cabinet.

Further, a bill becomes a law only after it gets the assent of the President.

The President may give his assent or may send it back with some recommendations. If however, the houses pass the bill again or without amendments, the President have no power to withhold his assent from the bill.

(ii) There are mainly three limitations on the President's powers. These are

(a) There is the Prime Minister and the Council of Ministers to aid and advice the President in the exercise of his powers. In fact, in real sense the powers of the President are exercised by Prime Minister and Council of Ministers.

(b) All proclamation of emergencies made by the President under Articles 352, 356 and 360 have to be laid within one month before the Parliament for approval.

(c) The power of impeachment of the President is authorised by the Parliament for violating the Constitution in its letter and spirit.

(iii) The functions of Vice-President are as follows

- The Vice-President officiates as the President when the latter is unable to discharge his duties due to illness or absence from the country.
- If the office of the President falls vacant due to his resignation, death or impeachment, the Vice-President officiates as President for a maximum period of 6 months. The new President must be elected within the period of 6 months.
- The Vice-President acts as an ex-officio Chairman of the Rajya Sabha and regulates the proceedings of the house.
- He issues directions to the Chairman of various committees from time to time.

5. (i) The Chief Justice of a High Court is appointed by the President of India in consultation with the Chief Justice of the Supreme Court and the Governor of the State concerned. Other Judges of the High Court are appointed by the President in consultation with the Chief Justice of India, the Governor of the State and the Chief Justice of the High Court of the concerned state.

(ii) The acting Judges of a High Court are appointed by the following conditions

- When a Judge of a High Court is unable to perform his duties for any valid reason like illness, the President may appoint the acting Judge in his place. The acting Judge holds office till the regular judge is fit to resume his duties.
- The Chief Justice of a High Court may also request, with the prior consent of the President, the retired Judges of the High Courts to act as Judges of the High Court.
- Further, when the Chief Justice is unable to perform his duties or when the office of the Chief Justice of a High Court falls vacant, the President may appoint one of the Judges of the High Court as acting Chief Justice of the High Court.

(iii) To be qualified for appointment as a Judge of a High Court, a person must have the following qualifications

- He/she should be a citizen of India.
- He/she should have worked as a judge in any court in India for not less than 10 years.

Or He/she should have worked as an advocate in India for atleast 10 years.

In order to ensure the independence of the Judiciary at the state level, our Constitution has made some special provisions to safeguard the interests of Judges of the High Court.

These are as follows

- The Chief Justice and other Judges of the High Courts once appointed, hold office till they retire at the age of 62 years as they themselves resign from their office.
- A judge may be removed from his office by the President only through the procedure established in the Constitution.

6. (i) On 16th October, 1905, Partition of Bengal became effective. This day was observed by the people as a day of mourning. The Early Nationalists opposed this through press campaigns and petitions. The streets of Calcutta were full of the cries of 'Vande Mataram' which became the theme song of the National Movement.

The newspapers like 'The Bengalee', 'The Amrit Bazar Patrika', 'Sanjivani' criticised the government's policy. People of Bengal tied Rakhis on each other's hands as a symbol of brotherhood and the 'Arandhan' (not cooking anything in home) was put into effect.

(ii) The British Government used all kinds of repression. Thousands of people were arrested and put behind the bars. Lathicharge was common on peaceful and non-violent protesters. During 1905 to 1909, thousands of people were arrested and sent to jail. Schools and colleges were warned and grants to private institutions suspected of participating in this movement were discontinued. Lala Lajpat Rai, Sardar Ajit Singh, Bal Gangadhar Tilak were arrested. Even chanting of 'Vande Mataram' was forbidden.

By 1909, the movement had lost its momentum and the British had reasserted their authority.

(iii) Lord Curzon's two real motives behind the Partition of Bengal were as follows

(a) The province of Bengal was a huge territory and it was the main centre of Indian Nationalism at that time. To crush the nationalist spirit of Bengal, Curzon wanted to divide it into two parts.

(b) His other reason to divide Bengal was to set the Muslims and Hindus against each other. The new province of Eastern Bengal and Assam with Dhaka as capital was specially set up to create Muslims majority in that area.

7. (i) The basic ideas and methods given by Gandhiji to achieve freedom were as follows

- **Satyagraha** It is the novel method of mass agitation, which includes fasting, Non-cooperation and Civil Disobedience. Satyagraha was evolved by Gandhiji from the study of the works of Tolstoy and Hindu scriptures.
- **Non-Violence** Gandhiji's whole philosophy was based on non-violence. It is the weapon of strong, mighty and powerful individuals. Gandhiji had the opinion that neither an individual nor a country could gain anything by using violent methods.
- **Large scale Mass Involvement** The first valuable direction which Gandhiji provided to the freedom movement was a mass base. He took the freedom movement to every home.

(ii) Reasons leading to the Non-Cooperation Movement were as follows

Jallianwala Bagh Massacre (1919) The brutal killing of hundreds of unarmed Indians by British troops in Amritsar deeply shocked the nation and fueled widespread anger against British rule.

Rowlatt Act (1919) This act allowed the British government to imprison any Indian suspected of sedition without trial. It was seen as a direct attack on civil liberties and led to widespread protests.

Khilafat Movement The movement aimed to protect the Ottoman Caliphate, which was being dismantled after World War I. Gandhi saw an opportunity to unite Hindus and Muslims in a common cause against British rule.

Economic Exploitation The British economic policies had led to widespread poverty and unemployment in India. The exploitation of Indian resources and labour for British benefit was a major grievance.

(iii) The methods of Non-Cooperation adopted by the people were as follows

- Lawyers like CR Das, Motilal Nehru and Rajendra Prasad suspended their practices.
- Many students stopped going to the educational institutions which were run by British Government
- All Congress candidates withdrew from the elections and nearly two-thirds of the voters boycotted the elections.
- Mahatma Gandhi surrendered his title of Kaisar-e-Hind Rabindranath Tagore renounced his knighthood and many other people followed them.

8. (i) The Treaty of Versailles significantly contributed to the geopolitical tensions that eventually led to the Second World War. Imposed upon Germany at the end of World War I, the treaty was viewed by many, particularly within Germany, as excessively punitive. It required Germany to cede substantial territories, pay enormous reparations that strained its economy, and abide by strict military limitations. These conditions not only weakened Germany economically but also engendered deep-seated resentment and a sense of national humiliation among the German people.

This atmosphere of despair and indignation was exploited by extremist factions, most notably the Nazi Party led by Adolf Hitler. Hitler's rhetoric blamed the Weimar Republic's leaders for the treaty and promised to overturn its conditions, restore Germany's lost territories, and rebuild its military strength. These promises resonated with the humiliated populace, facilitating Hitler's rise to power. Once in control, Hitler's aggressive foreign policy aimed at undoing the Treaty's terms directly contributed to the outbreak of the Second World War as he sought to expand German territory and influence, defying the treaty's stipulations and challenging the global order established post-World War I.

(ii) The two causes that led to the Cold War were as follows

(a) There was an ideological conflict between the United States and the Soviet Union, with the US promoting capitalism and democracy, while the Soviet Union supported communism.

(b) The emergence of nuclear weapons created a sense of mutual fear and distrust, especially in the U.S., where there was a strong fear of communism spreading. These differences and tensions led to a long period of geopolitical rivalry and military buildup.

(iii) Four consequences of the Second World War were

(a) **Defeat of Axis Powers** The defeat of the Axis Powers led to the total surrender and subsequent military occupation of Germany, Italy, and Japan. This restructuring of major participations under Allied supervision aimed to ensure future peace by disarming these nations and establishing democratic governments.

(b) **Formation of the United Nations** In response to the failure of the League of Nations and the devastation of the war, the United Nations was formed in 1945. Its primary aim was to enhance international cooperation and prevent future conflicts. The establishment of various specialised agencies and programmes under its umbrella facilitated global collaboration in economic, social, and security issues.

(c) **Emergence of Cold War** The power vacuum post-World War II and ideological differences between the Soviet Union and Western allies escalated into the Cold War. This period was marked by political tension, nuclear arms race, and various proxy wars, shaping much of the late 20th century global politics.

(d) **Acceleration of Decolonisation** The war significantly weakened European colonial powers economically and politically, promoting independence movements in colonised countries across Asia and Africa. This shift led to the rapid end of colonial empires and the birth of multiple new nations within the two decades following the war.

9. (i) Person in picture 'A' is Gopal Krishna Gokhale. He belonged to the moderate section of the Congress. He was influenced by the ideals of Justice MG Ranade. The Moderates wanted to achieve self-governance within the British Empire and not for absolute independence.

Person in picture 'B' is Lala Lajpat Rai, one of the Assertive leaders of the Congress. The main objective of the Assertive Nationalists or extremists was the immediate attainment of 'Swaraj'. This meant complete independence and not just self-government, as was in the colonies of Australia and New Zealand, etc.

(ii) There were two types of ideology within Congress. Some of them were Moderates' ideology and some were Assertives philosophy. They used different types of method for struggle. These were as follow

(a) Moderates did not follow the policy of confrontation but highlighted their problems through meetings, use of press, memorandums and petitions, etc. They followed the method of three P's-Petitions, Prayers and Protests.

(b) Whereas Assertives believed in adopting the policy of non-violent resistance and vigorous political action to achieve their aims. They actually relied on the strength of the masses. The Assertives based the National Movement on people's religious and cultural beliefs. They followed the method of swadeshi, boycott, national education and passive resistance.

(iii) The contributions of Lala Lajpat Rai in the freedom struggle were

- He started a monthly magazine, 'The Young India' to spread the message of the Right of Indian to attain Swaraj. Through this magazine, he propagated his ideas of Radical Nationalism among the people of India.
- He opened orphanages, hospitals and schools. He set up 'Servants of the People Society' for the welfare of the downtrodden and outcastes.
- He was a great visionary. He was an active member of Arya Samaj and laid the foundation of DAV college, Lahore and various other educational institutions.
- He joined Madan Mohan Malviya in organising the Nationalist party and the Hindu Sangathan Movement for the protection of the interests of the majority community.

10. (i) The Security Council is the executive body of the UN. It comprises of 15 members, 5 permanent and 10 non-permanent.

The permanent members are USA, Britain, France, Russia and China. The election of non-permanent members are done by the General Assembly for a period of 2 years.

They are elected from a regional group which are as follows

(a) Afro-Asian Countries-5

(b) Latin-American Countries-2

(c) Western European and other Countries-2

(d) Eastern Europe-1

(ii) Three functions of the International Court of Justice are as follows

(a) The court plays a significant role in the codification of International Law.

(b) The court's jurisdiction extends to disputes pertaining to the interpretation of international law and to give judgement regarding the general principles of law recognised by nations.

(c) To give advisory opinion on specific legal questions to other organs of the UN like the General Assembly and the Security Council on any legal question.

(iii) The Security Council implements its decisions through several mechanisms

- **Imposition of Sanctions** The Security Council can impose sanctions on aggressor states, which are enforced by UN Member States.
- **The 'Unanimity Rule' (Veto Power)** Known as the Veto, this rule allows any of the five permanent members to block a resolution, even if all other members support it. This veto power can be seen as a strength of the Security Council, as it prevents any one-sided or unfair decisions and maintains a balance among the major powers.
- **Armed Intervention** The Security Council can authorise military action in cases of international conflict or aggression, as demonstrated by the intervention in Iraq when there was a majority decision.
- **Facilitating Negotiations** The Security Council can use various methods to bring conflicting parties to the negotiation table.

These tools help the Security Council enforce its resolutions and address international disputes.

SQP Code : **PB-7/15** Series ***i*-Succeed 7-25/15** Roll No.

Sample Question Paper 07

History & Civics 10th (Code 050)

General Instructions

1. Attempt all questions from Part I (Compulsory).
2. A total of 5 questions are to be attempted from Part II, 2 out of 3 questions from Section A and 3 out of 5 questions from Section B.
3. The intended marks for questions or parts of questions are given in brackets ( ).

Time : 2 Hrs.
Max. Marks : 80

Part-I Attempt all questions from this part

Que 1.

Choose the correct option. (16)

(i) Justice delayed is justice denied access to justice for the poor is a constitutional mandate to ensure fair treatment under our legal system hence Lok adalat's literally people's court was established to make justice accessible and affordable to all.
Source: The Hindu
Lok Adalat are the alternative dispute resolution system. Where was the first Lok Adalat held in India? [Application] (1)

(a) Madhya Pradesh (b) Rajasthan
(c) Gujarat (d) Andhra Pradesh

(ii) Given below are the few details.

Terms and Roles	Government Bodies and Positions
Money Bill	Lok Sabha
Ex-officio Chairman of Rajya Sabha	?
Emergency	President

Complete the above blank with the help of following options. [Understanding] (1)

(a) Speaker (b) Prime Minister
(c) Vice-President (d) Governor

(iii) Based on the image given below, which reflects the pardoning power given to the President of India under Article 72.
In which of the following situation can this power be exercised? [Understanding] (1)

(a) Either before or after the trial but never during the trial of the case
(b) At any time, before, during or after the trial
(c) Only after the trial and on the sentence of conviction
(d) During or after trial but never before trial

(iv) 'During a community dispute in Kanpur, two neighbouring shop owners, A and B, were involved in a prolonged conflict over a shared parking space. This dispute disrupted their business operations and caused tension in the community. To resolve the situation, the matter was referred to a Lok Adalat held in the district of Kanpur, where a peaceful settlement was facilitated through mediation. Both parties agreed to a rotating parking schedule thus avoiding a lengthy court process.

Case Study, Lok Adalat, District-Kanpur

Which advantage of the Lok Adalat is best illustrated by this case? [Application] (1)

(a) Ensures privacy and confidentiality
(b) Provides amicable solutions
(c) Reduces legal fees
(d) Decreases dependency on formal court settings

(v) Which among the following are the discretionary powers of President?

P. Dismissal of Council of Ministers
Q. Dismissal of Lok Sabha during No-Confidence Motion
R. Declaration of Emergency
S. Presenting Budget [Recall] (1)

(a) Pand Q (b) R and S
(c) P and S (d) Q and R

(vi) Prime Minister: Leader of Government : : President: .... [Recall] (1)

(a) Leader of State
(b) Leader of Parliament
(c) Leader of the Opposition
(d) Leader of Judiciary

(vii) Read the two statements given below regarding INA and select the option that show the correct relationship between A and R. [Analyse] (1)

Assertion (A) The practice of sati was banned in 1829 and the Widow Remarriage Act was passed in 1856.

Reason (R) The Indians disapproved the British interference in their social system.

Codes

(a) R contradicts A
(b) R is the reason for A
(c) A is true, but R is false
(d) A and R are independent of each other

(viii) Read the two statements given below and select the option that shows the correct relationship between A and R. [Analyse] (1)

Assertion (A) The dissatisfaction with the Treaty of Versailles was a significant factor that contributed to the outbreak of the Second World War.

Reason (R) The harsh terms imposed by the Treaty of Versailles led to severe economic and political instability in Germany, which created fertile ground for extremist ideologies like Nazism to take root.

Codes

(a) R contradicts A
(b) R is the reason for A
(c) A is true, but R is false
(d) A and R are independent of each other

(ix) Which of these is not correct about Subhash Chandra Bose? [Analyse] (1)

(a) He inaugurated the Indian National Planning Committee.
(b) He became an active worker of the Freedom Movement during Non-Cooperation.
(c) He was unanimously selected as the President of the Congress in 1938.
(d) He supported Gandhiji when Non-Cooperation Movement was withdrawn.

(x) The image given below shown the group which came to discuss the transfer of power to India. Who among the following was not a part of this group? [Recall] (1)

(a) Pethic Lawrence
(b) Stafford Cripps
(c) Mr AV Alexander
(d) Lord Mountbatten

(xi) The International Court of Justice consists of .... judges. [Recall] (1)

(a) 9 (b) 10
(c) 15 (d) 16

SP-07

(xii) Sonia is studying about a personality who became the first Governor General of Pakistan. Whom is she referring to? [Application] (1)

(a) Muhammad Ali Jinnah
(b) Maulana Abdul Kalam Azad
(c) Sir Syed Ahmed Khan
(d) Mohsin ul Mulk

(xiii) During the Quit India Movement, a local leader in Meerut proposed several methods to strengthen the movement against British rule. Given the ideologies and strategies adopted during this phase of the National Movement, which of the following methods is the leader not likely to approve? [Application] (1)

(a) Organising a large non-violent rally in the city centre
(b) Encouraging villagers to refuse to pay taxes
(c) Collaborating with a local British officer to obtain concessions
(d) Creating underground publications to spread the movement's message.

(xiv) The given image depicts the First World War. Which of the following causes responsible for the First World War? [Understanding] (1)

(a) Aggressive Nationalism and Imperialism
(b) Division of Europe
(c) Both (a) and (b)
(d) Treaty of Versailles

(xv) The Non-Aligned Movement came into existence mainly through the initiative of [Recall] (1)

(a) President Josip Tito
(b) Jawaharlal Nehru
(c) Gamal Abdel Nasser
(d) All of the above

(xvi) Identify the place from where the Second World War began with the German invasion. [Recall] (1)

(a) Poland (b) Rome
(c) Paris (d) Serbia

Que 2.

Read the extract given below and answer the question which follows.

Headline : SC okays judicial review of Armed Forces Tribunal decisions by High Courts

The Court's order became necessary due to a 2015 decision by the top court placing restriction on the High Court's power under Article 226 to entertain matters arising out of AFT.

This decision hampered the litigants before AFT to seek redress of their grievances as an appeal to the Supreme Court could only lie in matters raising 'a point of law of general public importance.'

Since pension and service disputes were purely personal matters, litigants before AFT were denied of a valuable right of judicial redress before High Courts.

Source: Hindustan Times 22nd March, 2023

(i) Based on the above passage discuss the provisions of Article 226. [Understanding] (2)

(ii) What is the term of the members of the Lok Sabha, and how is the Speaker of the Lok Sabha elected? [Analyse & Recall] (2)

(iii) Mention any two factors that helped in the growth of nationalism. [Recall] (2)

(iv) Who introduced 'Ilbert bill'? What was its purpose and why was it opposed? [Recall] (2)

(v) Suggest two achievements of the Assertive Nationalists. [Recall] (2)

(vi) Mention any two proposals of the Wavell Plan. [Recall] (2)

(vii) What were the two proposals related to the Princely States in the Mountbatten Plan? [Recall] (2)

SP-07

Part-II Section A (Civics) Attempt any two questions from this section

Que 3.

On the basis of the relations between the Centre and the States, Governments are of two types-Unitary and Federal. In this context, answer the following questions

(i) What do you mean by the Unitary Government? Mention its two characteristics. [Understanding & Recall] (1+2)

(ii) What is Federal Government? Mention its two important features. [Recall] (1+2)

(iii) Why does the framers of Constitution of India adopted for federal system of government? What is meant by the phrase 'Union of States'? [Analyse] (2+2)

Que 4.

The Indian Union Executive consists of the President, the Vice-President and the Council of Ministers headed by the Prime Minister. In this context, answer the following questions

(i) 'The President holds a position of authority and dignity'. In this context, how does he exercise his own individual judgement? [Understanding] (3)

(ii) Before holding the office, what does the Vice-President swear in his oath? [Recall] (3)

(iii) Mention any four points regarding the relationship between the Prime Minister and the President. [Recall] (4)

Que 5.

At apex of the judicial system is the Supreme Court of India, which supervises and controls the functioning of other courts. In this context, answer the following questions

(i) How are the salaries and allowances of the judges paid? [Recall] (3)

(ii) In the criminal cases, how does an appeal lie to the Supreme Court? [Recall] (3)

(iii) What do you mean by Judicial Review? Which Acts of Parliament were pronounced as null and void by Supreme Court under Judicial Review? [Understanding & Recall] (1+3)

Section B (History) Attempt any three questions from this section

Que 6.

The Revolt of 1857 had far reaching effects on the administration, economy and military structure in India. In this context, discuss

(i) Constitutional changes [Recall] (3)

(ii) Economic impact [Recall] (3)

(iii) Changes in Army organisation [Recall] (4)

Que 7.

The Lucknow Pact symbolised the unity in the Congress. In this context, answer the following questions

(i) What was the Lucknow Pact? Which two organisations joined hands in this Pact? [Analyse] (1+2)

(ii) Why was the pact criticised by some historians? [Recall] (3)

(iii) How did this pact foster unity between the Hindus and Muslims? [Recall] (4)

Que 8.

Read the excerpt given below and answer the questions that follow.

When European nations squared off against each other in the summer of 1914, it's doubtful that anyone envisioned it would mushroom into a four-year-long conflict that would be vastly more lethal than any previous war on that continent, both for military personnel and civilians.

Major powers such as Britain, France, the US and Germany kept detailed records of the war's human cost. But the carnage of World War I was so extreme and pervasive, and involved soldiers and civilians from so many different nations, that historians have had a difficult time agreeing on exactly how many people lost their lives.

(i) When did the above war take place? Who were the fighting sides of the war? [Recall] (1+2)

SP-07

(ii) What were the causes of the war? [Recall] (3)

(iii) What was the treaty that was signed after this war? Name any three provisions of this treaty. [Application & Recall] (1+3)

Que 9.

Study the picture and answer the following questions

(i) Identify the organisation with the help of picture given above and state its purpose of establishment. How the General Assembly ensure equal representation of all the nations? [Recall] (2+1)

(ii) General Assembly also elects the members of other principle organs of UN. Discuss. [Recall] (3)

(iii) State the recommendatory functions of the General Assembly. [Recall] (4)

Que 10.

With respect to Mountbatten Plan, answer the following questions

(i) State any three developments that paved the way for Mountbatten Plan. [Recall] (3)

(ii) State any three long-term impacts of Mountbatten Plan on the Indian politics. [Recall] (3)

(iii) Mention any four clauses related to the Mountbatten Plan. [Recall] (4)

Answers *in Topper's Style*

My Commitment *I affirm that I am reviewing these answers only after I have solved the Sample Question Paper 7 on my own. My purpose of looking the answers is solely to verify whether my answers were correct or not and to identify my mistakes in case my answers were wrong or I could not answer that.*

1. (i) (c) Gujarat (ii) (c) Vice-President

(iii) (c) only after the trial and on the sentence of conviction

(iv) (b) Provides amicable solutions

(v) (a) P and Q (vi) (a) Leader of State

(vii) (d) A and R are independent of each other

(viii) (a) R contradicts A

(ix) (d) He supported Gandhiji when Non-Cooperation Movement was withdrawn.

(x) (d) Lord Mountbatten (xi) (c) 15

(xii) (a) Muhammad Ali Jinnah

(xiii) (c) Collaborating with a local British officer to obtain concessions

(xiv) (c) Both (a) and (b)

(xv) (d) All of the above

(xvi) (a) Poland

2. (i) Provisions of Article 226 are as follows

- Article 226 gives High Courts the ability to issue instructions, orders and writs to any person or authority, including the government.
- Article 226 cannot be suspended, even in an emergency. It authorises a High Court to issue writs such as Mandamus, Habeas Corpus, Prohibition, Certiorari, and Quo Warranto.
- It empowers High Courts to enforce citizens' Fundamental Rights and for some other purposes.

(ii) The Lok Sabha, also known as the lower house of India's Parliament, has a term of five years from the date of its first session, unless dissolved sooner.

In the Lok Sabha, the speaker is elected from among its members by a simple majority of members present and voting in the house.

(iii) Two factors that helped in the growth of nationalism were as follows

(a) **Economic Exploitation** Britishers followed the policy of economic exploitation in India.

They collected land revenue, but were reluctant to do any welfare for the peasants.

(b) **Repressive Colonial Policies** All the policies made by British colonial

(iv) Sir Percy Ilbert introduced a bill named after him i.e. Ilbert Bill. The purpose of this bill was to remove judicial inequalities in the powers of the Indian and the British Magistrates.

It was hailed as a liberal and reasonable measure. But the British opposed this measure, so the bill could not be passed and was substantially modified to accommodate British interests.

(v) The Assertive Nationalists played an important role in the freedom movement of India.

Two achievements of the Assertive Nationalists were

(a) They specified the goal of the national struggle and organised mass movement for the attainment of total independence.

(b) They tried to cripple the administration by using methods of Non-Cooperation and Boycott.

(vi) Two proposals mentioned in the Wavell Plan were

(a) India would be given Dominion Status in the long run.

(b) The Constitution of India would be drafted by Indians themselves.

(vii) Two proposals related to the Princely States in the Mountbatten Plan were as follows

(a) The treaties with the Princely States would come to an end.

(b) They would be free to associate themselves with either of the dominions or to remain independent.

3. (i) Unitary Government is that government in which all the power is in the hands of one Central Government. Countries like England, Japan, France, etc. have Unitary Governments.

The two characteristics of the Unitary Government are as follows

(a) There is no division of subjects between the centre and the states as all the subjects are in the hands of the Central Government.

(b) The principle of single citizenship is adopted. There is no provision of seperate citizenship of provinces.

(ii) Federal Government is a government in which there is dual administration and there is distribution of powers between the centre and the states in accordance with the Constitution. Countries like USA, Canada, India, etc. have Federal Governments.

The two important features of the federal government are as follows

(a) The Constitutional Law is given the supreme position over ordinary law and special majority is needed to amend the Constitution

(b) The Constitution is given supremacy over an ordinary law. The Centre State Governments cannot pass any law which violates any provision of the Constitution.

(iii) The framers adopted the federal system of government due to

- the large size of the country.
- its socio-cultural diversity.
- The framers realised that the federal system not only ensures the efficient governance of the country but also reconciles nation unity with regional autonomy.
- The phrase 'Union of States', according to the father of the Constitution Dr. BR Ambedkar referred to two things
- The Indian federation is not the result of an agreement among the states.
- The states have no right to secede from the federation.

Thus, the federation is union because it is indestructible.

4. (i) The President exercises his discretion in the following ways

- He can return the advice of the Council of Ministers for its reconsideration at least for the first time in case of important Bills.
- He has power to get information about all matters of the Government.
- He has a duty to call the session of the Parliament at regular intervals or to consult the Election Commission on the elections in the country.

(ii) Before holding the office, the Vice-President takes an oath before the President (or some person appointed on his behalf by him). He swears in his oath

- to discharge the functions of the Vice-President
- to preserve, protect and defend the Constitution and the law.
- to devote himself to the service and well-being of the people of India.

(iii) From the following points, we can understand the relationship between Prime Minister and the President

(a) The Prime Minister is the only line of Communication between the Cabinet and the President. He conveys the Cabinet's decision to the President.

(b) The Prime Minister advises the President to summon and prorogue the Parliament and to dissolve the Lok Sabha.

(c) The Prime Minister advises the President on the appointment of Judges of Supreme Court, the Governors and Ambassadors and also in appointing or removing other high officials.

(d) The President cannot dismiss the Prime Minister as long as he enjoys the support of the majority in the Parliament.

5. (i) The salaries and allowances of the Chief Justice and other Judges of the Supreme Court are paid as may be determined by the Parliament, and charged on the Consolidated Fund of India.
As such, these are not required to be debated and voted upon by the Parliament. The salaries and allowances of the judges cannot be varied to their disadvantage except during the operation of financial emergency in the country.

(ii) In criminal cases, appeal lies to the Supreme Court as a matter of right (means without a certificate of the High Court) in two types of cases of death sentence. They are as follows
- Where a lower court aquits an accused and the High Court reverses this order and sentences the accused to death.
- Where the High Court withdraws a case under trial in a subordinate court, and sentences the accused to death.

Thus, it is clear that in case the accused is sentenced to death, the convicted person has a right to go in appeal to the Supreme Court.

(iii) The Judicial review means the power of the court to interpret the Constitution and determine the validity of a law passed by Legislature or an act of the Executive.
In 1970, the Supreme Court had declared the following Acts of Parliament as null and void, under its power of Judicial Review
- Presidential order concerning derecognition of the former princes.
- Banking Companies Act, 1969, for the nationalisation of 14 banks. Similarly, in August 1999, the Supreme Court held that 'merit' should be the sole criterion for admissions to post-graduate and other higher courses in medicine and engineering.

6. (i) The constitutional changes were that the Board of Control was abolished and the Board of Directors had no powers left. Now the power was to be exercised by the secretary of state for India, aided by a council. The secretary of state was a member of the British cabinet and his salary and allowances were to be paid out of the revenues of India.
Actual governance was to be carried on as before by the governor general who was also given the title of viceroy or crown's personal representative.

(ii) Economic impacts were as follows
- India was made a dumping ground of British manufactured goods.
- Many civil servants and military officers were sent to India from Britain. These officers drew heavy salaries thus put a heavy burden on India's economy.
- Thousands of Indian artisans and craftsmen lost their earnings as they could not compete with English goods.

(iii) Changes in the Army organisation included
- The Indian soldiers were to be excluded from any higher rank in the army.
- A distinction was made between martial and non-martial races.
- Supply of newspapers and magazines to the armies were stopped.

The ratio of Europeans and Indians in the Army was rearranged to 1:2 respectively.

7. (i) The Lucknow Pact was the outcome of the efforts made by the Congress and the Muslim League to come to an agreement regarding political reforms in India.
In December, 1916, the Congress and the League held their session at Lucknow.
The leaders of both the parties adopted a joint scheme which came to be known as the Lucknow Pact. In this pact, both agreed to join hands in order to fight against the British.

(ii) The Lucknow Pact was criticised by some historians on the ground that
- the Congress failed to retain its secular character by agreeing to a scheme of communal electorate.
- the compromise demanded more sacrifice on the part of the Hindus. This marked the beginning of the appeasement of Muslims by the Congress.
- the pact failed to involve the common masses either of Hindu or of Muslim community. It was merely an agreement at the level of leadership.

(iii) There were some special features of this pact, which played a crucial role to foster unity between the Hindus and Muslims. These were
- According to the pact, it was accepted that the minorities should be given adequate separate representation in elected bodies.
- None of the bill could be introduced by a non-official member if it affected the interest of any community and such a bill would not be passed if it was opposed by three-fourths of that community.
- The Congress compromised its secular character by accepting the scheme of a Muslim electorate. On the other hand, the League accepted the principles of election and majority rule.
- The leaders of the Congress and the League did not want to give the government any

excuse for delaying political reforms.
The adoption of the pact brought Hindu and Muslim communities closer. They slowly started believing in collective ideology and in fighting unitedly against foreign dominion.

8. (i) The above war took place between 28th July, 1914 to 11th November, 1918.
The war was fought between Allies, including Serbia, Russia, France, Britain, Italy and the United States. They were fought by Central powers consisted of Germany, Austria- Hungary, Bulgaria and the Ottoman Empire.

(ii) The causes of the above war were as follows

- Militant nationalism was the consequence of the aggressive nationalism which included the building of a huge army and appointing of a powerful class of military and naval officers.
- Sarajevo crisis is the immediate cause of this war. It took place on 28th June, 1914, when the crown prince of Austria, Archduke Francis Ferdinand and his wife were assassinated at Sarajevo.
- Imperialism is the other cause of this war. It occurs when a strong nation takes over a weaker nation or region and dominates its economic, political and cultural life.

(iii) Treaty of Versailles was signed after World War I. Three provisions of this treaty were

(a) Germany was held guilty of aggression in the war.

(b) He was also required to pay huge war reparations of 33 billion dollars for the losses incurred by the victorious nations.

(c) The Rhine Valley in Germany was to be demilitarised and German territory to the West of Rhine was to be occupied by the Allied troops for 15 years.

9. (i) The given organisation as depicted in the form of its symbol is United Nations Organisation. One of the objective of establishing United Nations is to take effective collective measures for the prevention and removal of threats to the peace suppression of acts of aggression or other breaches of peace.
The General Assembly ensures equitable geographical representation as the Presidency of the Assembly rotates each year among five groups of states i.e. Africa, Asia, Eastern Europe, Latin America and Western Europe.

(ii) The General Assembly elects the members of other principal organs of the United Nations, namely; the non-permanent members of the Security Council, members of the Economic and Security Council and judges of the International Court of Justice.
The assembly also elects members to its subsidiary organs and to the executive boards and governing councils of the United Nations agencies, funds and programmes.

(iii) The recommendatory functions of the General Assembly are

- It makes recommendations on general principles of co-operation for maintaining international peace and security, including disarmament.
- It discusses any question relating to international peace and security except where a dispute or situation is currently being discussed by the Security Council and make recommendations on it.
- It makes recommendations on any questions within the scope of the charter or affecting the powers and functions of any organ of the United Nations.

10. (i) Three developments which paved the way for Mountbatten Plan were

(a) On 26th October, 1946 representatives of the Muslim League were inducted into the interim government. The government seemed to be paralysed by non-cooperation of the members of the Muslim League.

(b) After consultation with Indian leaders, Mountbatten concluded that he would not unite the major parties.

(c) Lord Mountbatten personally went to England to inform the British Government about the situation of India and got his plan approved by them.

(ii) Three long-term impacts of Mountbatten plan on Indian politics were

(a) It gave birth to un-ended communal dispute between Hindus and Muslims.

(b) The demarcations of boundaries were not clearly defined.

(c) It left the Kashmir issue unsettled.

(iii) The four clauses of the Mountbatten Plan were as follows

(a) The country would be divided into two dominions India and Pakistan.

(b) The plan provided for the creation of Boundary Commission to settle the boundaries of the two dominions in case partition was decided upon.

(c) Treaties with Princely States would end, and they were free to join either of their two dominions or remain independent.

(d) The plan ended with a declaration that the transfer of power would take place not in June 1948, but much earlier than that.
The British Parliament would pass an act for the transfer of power before 15th August, 1947.

SQP Code : **PB-8/15** Series *i*-**Succeed 8-25/15** Roll No.

Sample Question Paper 08

History & Civics 10th (Code 50)

General Instructions

1. Attempt all questions from Part I (Compulsory).
2. A total of 5 questions are to be attempted from Part II, 2 out of 3 questions from Section A and 3 out of 5 questions from Section B.
3. The intended marks for questions or parts of questions are given in brackets ( ).

Time : 2 Hrs.

Max. Marks : 80

Part-I Attempt all questions from this part

Que 1.

Choose the correct option. (16)

(i) During a session of the Lok Sabha, the Speaker exercised his power to adjourn the house following a heated debate over budget allocations. This occurred after the required quorum was met, but the session was proving unproductive due to continuous disruptions.

From the passage above, what can we infer about the Speaker's powers? [Application] (1)

(a) The Speaker can adjourn the house without a quorum.

(b) The Speaker's decision to adjourn can be vetoed by the members.

(c) The Speaker has the authority to adjourn the house to ensure order and productivity.

(d) The Speaker must consult the President before adjourning the house.

(ii) Refer to the given details. [Understanding] (1)

	Powers	Meaning
1.	Reprieve	Cancellation of Punishment
2.	Respite	Temporary Relief
3.	Commute	?

Fill the above blank with the help of following options.

(a) Reduce

(b) Postpone

(c) Increase

(d) Change in nature of punishment

(iii) The image below depicts a scene from the Upper House of Parliament. The person presiding over the session, ensuring order and smooth functioning of the discussions, is most likely referred to as the [Understanding] (1)

(a) Vice-President

(b) Speaker

(c) Leader of Majority Party of Rajaya Sabha

(d) Prime Minister

(iv) 'In January 2024, during a political stalemate in the Indian Parliament where no party could secure a majority, the role of the President of India became crucial. The President, guided by constitutional provisions, invited the leader of the largest coalition in the Lok Sabha to form the government. This decision was based on the discretionary powers that the President holds in situations where clear majority is not evident after general elections.'

Based on the case study provided, what does this scenario illustrate about the President of India's role? [Understanding] (1)

(a) The President acts on the advice of the Council of Ministers in all situations.
(b) The President has the discretion to invite a party leader to form the government in the absence of a clear majority.
(c) The President only plays a ceremonial role and cannot influence government formation.
(d) The President must always invite the leader of the single largest party to form the government.

(v) Which among the following are the unitary features of Constitution of India? [Recall] (1)

P. Weak Centre
Q. Dual Citizenship
R. Single Constitution
S. Integrated Judiciary

(a) P and Q (b) R and S
(c) P and S (d) Q and R

(vi) .... : de facto : : President : de jure [Recall] (1)

(a) Prime Minister (b) Speaker
(c) Chief Justice of India (d) Chief Minister

(vii) Read the two statements given below regarding United Nation and select the option that shows the correct relationship between A and R. [Analyse] (1)

Assertion (A) Failure of League of Nations led to establishment of UN.

Reason (R) The main aim of UN is to maintain International peace and security.

(a) R contradicts A
(b) R is the reason for A
(c) A is true, but R is false
(d) A and R are independent of each other

(viii) Read the two statements given below and select the option that shows the correct relationship between A and R. [Analyse] (1)

Assertion (A) The formation of the League of Nations was intended to prevent further global conflicts after World War I.

Reason (R) The League of Nations was established as part of the Treaty of Versailles, which aimed to create a platform for international cooperation and conflict resolution.

(a) R contradicts A
(b) R is the reason for A
(c) A is true, but R is false
(d) A and R are independent of each other

(ix) 'A new policy introduced by the government of Country Z aims to foster unity among diverse religious communities within the nation, reflecting the spirit of the Lucknow Pact of 1916.' Who is most likely to be impacted by this policy? [Application] (1)

(a) Religious leaders (b) Educators
(c) Business owners (d) Political activists

(x) The given below personality was the political mentor of Mahatma Gandhi. Identify the personality. [Recall] (1)

(a) RC Dutt
(b) Gopal Krishna Gokhale
(c) Justice Ranade
(d) Gopal Hari Deshmukh

(xi) The International Court of Justice was established in .... by the Charter of UN. [Recall] (1)

(a) June 1945 (b) June 1946
(c) July 1945 (d) July 1946

(xii) Neha is studying about a personality who played an important role in launching Non-Aligned Movement. Whom is she referring to? [Application] (1)

(a) Tito (b) Jawaharlal Nehru
(c) Sukarno (d) Woodrow Wilson

(xiii) During a university seminar on 20th-century history, students examine the pivotal factors that influenced global events leading up to the Second World War. They discuss the role of ideological shifts and external political pressures. Considering the ideological fervour that characterised the period, which of the following actions is a student not likely to consider a major contributing factor to the rise of dictatorships in Europe? [Application] (1)

(a) The economic hardships and societal unrest following the Great Depression.
(b) The signing of non-aggression pacts between dictatorial regimes and democratic countries.
(c) Active collaboration and mutual support among democratic nations to stem the rise of totalitarian ideologies.
(d) The widespread discontent with democratic governments' inability to deal with economic and social issues effectively.

(xiv) The below image depicts the Non-Permanent members of the UNSC. How many Non-Permanent members are there in the United Nation Security Council? [Understanding] (1)

(a) Five (b) Ten (c) Six (d) Seven

(xv) The President and Vice-President of the International Court of Justice are elected for a term of .... [Recall] (1)

(a) two years
(b) three years
(c) four years
(d) five years

(xvi) Identify the countries which were part of the Axis Power in the Second World War. [Recall] (1)

(a) Poland, Germany and Japan
(b) France, Japan and Britain
(c) Germany, Italy and Japan
(d) Italy, Japan and Britain

Que 2.

Read the extract given below and answer the questions which follows.

Headline : Chief Justice visits District Court Complex Srinagar

Chief Justice, High Court of Jammu and Kashmir, and Ladakh, Justice N. Koteshwar Singh, today visited the District Court Complex, Srinagar. Chief Justice was accorded ceremonial guard of honour from the contingent of Jammu and Kashmir Police.

Source: Times of India 21st June

(i) On the basis of above news, discuss the composition and functions of District Judge [Understanding] (2)

(ii) Mention the qualifications required for membership in the Rajya Sabha. [Recall] (2)

(iii) Mention two declarations made by the British which upset the Mughal royalty. [Recall] (2)

(iv) What is Vernacular Press Act? [Recall] (2)

(v) Who was Jyotiba Phule? [Recall] (2)

(vi) Mention any two provisions from each side of the Gandhi-Irwin Pact signed in 1931. [Recall] (2)

(vii) Mention two aims of the League of Nations. [Recall] (2)

Part-II Section A (Civics) Attempt any two questions from this section

Que 3.

With reference to the Union Parliament, answer the following questions.

(i) Which House of the Parliament is considered as the powerful house and why? [Analyse] (3)

(ii) How is the Speaker of the Lok Sabha elected? Mention two functions of the Speaker during the session of Parliament. [Recall] (1+2)

(iii) Mention any four ways in which Lok Sabha exercises control over the Council of Ministers. [Recall] (4)

Que 4.

The Cabinet holds a pivotal position in the working of the Indian Parliamentary Government. In this context, answer the following questions :

(i) What do you mean by Cabinet? [Recall] (3)

(ii) Mention any three administrative powers of the Cabinet. [Recall] (3)

(iii) Distinguish between the Cabinet and Council of Ministers. [Application] (4)

Que 5.

The Supreme Court is the highest judicial form and final court of appeal under the Constitution of India.

In this context, answer the following questions:

(i) What is meant by the Appellate Jurisdiction? [Understanding] (3)

(ii) How does Supreme Court acts as the Guardian of Fundamental Rights? [Recall] (3)

(iii) Explain the impeachment procedure for the removal of judges of Supreme Court. [Recall] (4)

Section B (History) Attempt any three questions from this section

Que 6.

Describe the results of the First War of Independence with reference to the following :

(i) Policy towards the Indian Princes. [Recall] (3)

(ii) Rise of Nationalism in India. [Recall] (3)

(iii) Changes in the administrative set up of the British Territories in India. [Recall] (4)

Que 7.

The formation of the Muslim League and the Home Rule Movement had a wholesome effect on the affairs of the country. In this context, answer the following questions :

(i) What were the three main objectives of the Muslim League? [Recall] (3)

(ii) State the circumstances that led to the Lucknow Pact. [Recall] (3)

(iii) Mention any two features and two significance of the Lucknow Pact. [Recall] (2+2)

Que 8.

Read the excerpt given below and answer the questions which follow.

"The Treaty of Versailles was signed at the end of the First World War. It imposed heavy reparations and territorial losses on Germany, as well as restrictions on its military capabilities. This treaty was meant to ensure peace but instead it sowed the seeds of resentment and led directly to the rise of extremism in Germany."
The New York Times [Edited]

(i) What treaty is being discussed in the excerpt above? Which global conflict did it conclude, and in what year was this treaty signed? [Application & Recall] (1.5+1.5)

(ii) The treaty discussed above had profound impacts on the geopolitical landscape of Europe. Analyse this statement by mentioning any three impacts. [Analyse] (3)

(iii) How did the Treaty of Versailles impact Germany's territorial boundaries after World War I ? [Recall] (4)

Que 9.

In the given below historic Photograph, Pandit Jawaharlal Nehru, is seen giving his famous speech in the Constituent Assembly on 14th August, 1947. In this context, answer the following questions.

(i) What were the provisions of the Indian Independence Act, 1947? [Recall] (3)

(ii) State the clauses mentioned in the Mountbatten Plan. [Recall] (3)

(iii) Why did All India Congress Committee accept the Mountbatten Plan. [Recall] (4)

Que 10.

Nazism is the ideology and practice associated with Germany in the 20th century. In this context, answer the following questions.

(i) What is Nazism? [Recall] (3)

(ii) Why did Nazism become popular in Germany during 1930s? [Recall] (3)

(iii) What were the peculiar features of Nazi thinking? [Recall] (4)

Answers in Topper's Style

My Commitment *I affirm that I am reviewing these answers only after I have solved the Sample Question Paper 8 on my own. My purpose of looking the answers is solely to verify whether my answers were correct or not and to identify my mistakes in case my answers were wrong or I could not answer that.*

1. (i) (c) The Speaker has the authority to adjourn the house to ensure order and productivity.

(ii) (a) Reduce

(iii) (b) Speaker

(iv) (b) The President has the discretion to invite a party leader to form the government in the absence of a clear majority.

(v) (b) R and S

(vi) (a) Prime Minister

(vii) (d) A and R are independent of each other

(viii) (a) R contradicts A

(ix) (a) Religious leaders

(x) (b) Gopal Krishna Gokhale

(xi) (a) June 1945

(xii) (b) Jawaharlal Nehru

(xiii) (c) Active collaboration and mutual support among democratic nations to stem the rise of totalitarian ideologies.

(xiv) (b) Ten

(xv) (b) three years

(xvi) (c) Germany, Italy and Japan

2. (i) The District Court is the highest court of the district, and it decides both civil and criminal cases. A judge who decides civil cases is known as a district judge. Appeals against the decisions made by the district judges can be made in the High Court if the amount involved in the case is more than ₹ 5000.

A person desiring to become a district judge should have been an advocate for at least seven years in Union Judicial Service or the State Public Service Commission.

(ii) The qualifications required for membership in the Rajya Sabha are

- a person should be a citizen of India.
- a person should be of 30 years or older.
- a person should have such alternative qualifications as mandated in this behalf underneath any Law enacted by Parliament.

(iii) The two declarations made by the British that upset the Mughal royalty are

(a) Firstly, the British declared that after the death of Bahadur Shah, his successors would have to leave the Red Fort.

(b) Secondly, they also declared that Bahadur Shah's successors would not be allowed to use the royal titles and dignities to their names.

(iv) The Vernacular Press criticised the irrational policies of the British. To prevent this, Lord Lytton passed the Vernacular Press Act in 1878. According to this Act, the Vernacular papers could not publish any material that might incite feelings of dissatisfaction against the Government.

(v) Jyotiba Phule was the famous social reformer who founded the Satya Shodhak Samaj in 1873 to fought against the caste system. He pioneered the Widow Remarriage Movement in Maharashtra and worked for the education of women. He waged a life long struggle against Caste discrimination and Brahmanical supremacy.

(vi) The two provisions from each side of the Gandhi Irwin Pact signed in 1931 were

(a) Gandhiji called off the Civil Disobedience Movement and agreed to attend the Second Round Table Conference in London.

(b) From the Government's side, the Viceroy agreed to withdraw ordinances promulgated against the Civil Disobedience Movement. He also agreed to release people who had been jailed in connection with that movement and return seized property.

(vii) Two aims of the League of Nations were as follows

(a) All the states of the world were prohibited from entering into secret treaties and alliances.

(b) The member states were not supposed to maintain huge armies, warships and destructive armaments.

3. (i) There are two Houses in the Parliament, i.e. Rajya Sabha and Lok Sabha but Lok Sabha is considered to be more powerful in the Union Parliament because

- Members of the Lok Sabha are directly elected by the people.
- The Money Bill can only be introduced in the Lok Sabha. When the Money Bill is passed by the Lok Sabha, it is sent to the Rajya Sabha for its recommendations. But, the Lok Sabha may or may not accept the recommendations of Rajya Sabha.
- The final power to decide whether a particular Bill is a Money Bill or not, is vested on the Speaker of the Lok Sabha.

(ii) The Speaker of the Lok Sabha is elected from amongst its own members soon after the newly elected house meets for the first time.

The two functions of the Speaker are as follows

(a) The Speaker presides over all the meetings of the house. All speeches made in the Parliament are addressed to the Speaker.

(b) The Speaker has the final power to maintain order within the Lok Sabha and to interpret its rules of procedure.

(iii) Four ways in which Lok Sabha exercises control over the Council of Ministers are as follows

(a) **Right to Interpellation** It means that the members of Lok Sabha can ask questions from any minister, during the allotted time (question hour), regarding Government policies and implementation.

(b) **No-confidence Motion** The Council of Ministers are collectively responsible to the Lok Sabha. The ministers remain in the office as long as they enjoy the confidence of the majority of members in the Lok Sabha. It has power to pass no-confidence motion against the Council of Ministers.

(c) **Adjournment Motion** This is tabled by the members of Lok Sabha on to discuss and debate a serious matter.

(d) **Monetary Controls** A cut motion may be moved during the budget session. It is ensured that the money is spent in accordance with the decision of the Parliament. It studies the reports of the Comptroller and Auditor General (CAG).

4. (i) The Cabinet is collective decision making body of the Government of India. It heads almost all the important ministries of the Central Government like home, defence, finance, external affairs and so on. The Cabinet Ministers consist of Prime Minister and other Ministers of Cabinet rank which is of 15 to 20 members. The Cabinet meets as a body, frequently and usually once in a week to deliberate and take decisions regarding the transaction of the Government business. Cabinet directs the Council of Ministers by taking policy decisions which are binding on all ministers.

(ii) The three administrative powers of the Cabinet are as follows

(a) It is a policy-making body which formulates the external and domestic policies of the Government.

(b) It coordinates the activities of all the ministries and departments. Each ministry is put under the care of one or more ministers, i.e. Ministers of State and Deputy Ministers. Also, ultimate policy is decided by the cabinet which has to be followed by the incharge of the ministers.

(c) It is the supreme executive authority of the Central Government.

(iii) The differences between the Cabinet and Council of Ministers are

Cabinet	Council of Ministers
It includes only Cabinet Ministers.	It includes all three categories of ministers i.e. Cabinet Ministers, Ministers of State and Deputy Ministers.
It directs the Council of Ministers by taking policy decisions which are binding on all ministers.	Its functions are determined by the Cabinet.
It enforces the collective responsibility of the Council of Ministers to the Lok Sabha.	It is collectively responsible to the Lower House (Lok Sabha) of the Parliament
It supervises the implementation of its decisions by the Council of Ministers.	It implements the decisions taken by the Cabinet.

5. (i) Appellate jurisdiction means that the Supreme Court is the final court of appeal. It has the power to grant special leave of appeal against the judgement delivered by any subordinate court in our country. It may consist of appeals by leave of the appellate court or by right.

Depending on the type of case and decision, appellate review primarily consist of

- an entirely new hearing.
- a hearing where the appellate court gives deference to factual findings of the lower court.
- a review of particular legal rulings made by the lower court.

(ii) The Supreme Court plays the role of the guardian of Fundamental Rights of the citizens as it has the power to issue order or writs. It includes Habeas corpus, Mandamus, Prohibition, etc for the enforcement of Fundamental Rights. Indian Constitution under Article 32 guarantees to the citizens, the rights to move to the Supreme Court for the enforcement of the Fundamental Rights.

Article 13 of the Constitution prohibits the Parliament from enacting an ordinary legislation which abridges or takes away the Fundamental Rights. Any law made against this provision of the Constitution shall be declared void by the Supreme Court.

(iii) According to Article 124 (4) of the Constitution and the judges Enquiry Act (1986), a judge of the Supreme Court can be impeached on the grounds of proved misbehaviour or incapacity. The initiation of the process of impeachment can be taken by 100 members of Lok Sabha or 50 members of Rajya Sabha. It has to be admitted to a three-member committee i.e. the Chief Justice or a judge of Supreme Court, a Chief Justice of a High Court and distinguished jurist for investigation.

If found guilty, then the motion is send to the house. Such address must be supported by a special majority of each house of parliament (i.e. a majority of the total membership of that house and majority of not less than 2/3rd of the members of that house present and voting). After the motion is passed, an address presented to the President for the removal of the judge. Finally, the President passes an order for the removal of the judge.

6. (i) In 1858, the British Parliament passed the Government of India Act, by which the responsibility to govern India was transferred to the British Queen and the British Parliament. There was a change in the policy of the new Government towards Indian Princes in order to turn their loyalty towards British. These changes were

- It assured them that all treaties entered into with the company would be honoured.
- Their territories would not be annexed to the British crown.
- Doctrine of Lapse was abolished and the right to adoption was recognised.

(ii) Reasons responsible for the rise of Nationalism in India after First War of Independence were as follows

- The First War of Independence aroused national feelings and paved the way for the rise of the National Movement.
- The sacrifice of the Great Indian leaders like Rani Laxmibai, Nana Saheb, Tantia Tope, Mangal Pandey, etc and general people served as the source of inspiration for the struggle for freedom.
- This war became a symbol of challenge to the mighty British as man's inborn desire for freedom and patriotism could not be subdued.

(iii) After the First War of Independence, some changes in the administrative set up of the British Territories introduced were

- In 1858, the British Parliament passed the Government of India Act in which, the responsibility to govern India was transferred from East India Company to the British Queen and the British Parliament.
- The Board of Directors of the East India Company were abolished and the responsibility of India's administration was passed on to a separate minister, known as the 'Secretary of State' for India. He would be advised by a council consisting of fifteen members.
- The British Government had lost faith in Indian soldiers. All important posts in army were given to British officers.
- The Governor-General was made the Viceroy who was the representative of the British sovereign in India.

7. (i) Three main objectives of the Muslim League were as follows

(a) To keep the Muslim intelligentsia away from the mainstream of Indian National Movement.

(b) To promote feelings of loyalty among Indian Muslims towards the British Government.

(c) To protect the political and other rights of the Muslims and present them before the Government in mild language.

(ii) Circumstances that led to the Lucknow Pact were

- Muslims were unhappy with the unsympathetic treatment of Caliph or the ruler of Turkey by British in the First World War.
- Prominent Muslim leaders like Abdul Kalam Azad and Ali brothers spread nationalist ideas among Muslims.
- The changes in the objectives of Muslim League also led to the Lucknow Pact, as initially they were supporting the British government but later they switched towards the goal of self government.

(iii) Two main features of Lucknow Pact were

(a) Half the members of the viceroy executive council were to be Indian, elected by the members of the imperial Legislative Council.

(b) There shall be self-government in India. Muslims should be given 1/3rd representation in Central Government.

Two significance of the Lucknow Pact were

(a) The Lucknow Pact symbolised Hindu-Muslim unity as the Congress and Muslim League prepared a joint programme for demanding self governance.

(b) The Lucknow Pact became the symbol of unity between the two sections of the Congress i.e. extremists and moderates.

8. (i) The treaty discussed is the Treaty of Versailles. This treaty famously concluded the First World War and was signed on 28th June, 1919.

The Treaty of Versailles was intended to establish a peace settlement with Germany and to prevent further conflicts by holding Germany accountable for the war and imposing strict punitive measures.

The signing of this treaty marked the formal end of World War I, an event that had brought unprecedented destruction and changed the geopolitical landscape of Europe.

The treaty, however, is often criticised for its harsh treatment towards Germany, which many believe laid the groundwork for future upheavals, including World War II.

(ii) The Treaty of Versailles had significant impacts on the geopolitical environment of Europe. These were

- **Economic Impact** The treaty imposed enormous reparations on Germany, amounting to about 33 billion dollars. This financial burden devastated the German economy, leading to severe hyperinflation and contributing to the economic instability that plagued the Weimar Republic. The economic hardships faced by the German population created fertile ground for dissatisfaction and unrest, which extremist groups exploited.
- **Political Impact** By forcing Germany to cede territory and accept full responsibility for the war (the War Guilt Clause), the treaty stirred nationalistic and unforgiving sentiments among Germans. The loss of territories such as Alsace-Lorraine to France, and parts of Prussia to the new Polish corridor, not only altered the map of Europe but also left millions of Germans living outside the newly defined borders of Germany, creating reclaiming pressures.
- **Military Impact** The treaty drastically limited Germany's military capabilities, restricting its army to 100,000 troops, forbidding drafts, and banning submarines and aircraft. These limitations were intended to prevent Germany from becoming a military threat again. However, these restrictions were viewed as humiliating by many Germans, contributing further to the collective sense of injustice and betrayal, which militaristic leaders later used to justify rearmament and expansionist policies.

(iii) The Treaty of Versailles significantly altered Germany's territorial boundaries after World War I. It mandated the cession of territories to neighbouring countries, including Alsace-Lorraine to France, Eupen-Malmedy to Belgium and parts of Upper Silesia to Poland.

The city of Danzig (now Gdansk) was declared a free city under League of Nations administration. These territorial losses reduced Germany's size and population, affecting its economic resources and industrial capabilities.

The treaty also imposed demilitarisation and allied occupation in the Rhineland region to prevent future aggression. These territorial and military restrictions aimed to weaken Germany's power and prevent it from reinitiating conflict, but also fueled resentment and laid the groundwork for future geopolitical tensions and conflicts.

9. (i) The provisions of the Indian Independence Act 1947 regarding the Constituent Assembly were as follows

- The constituent assemblies of both the dominions were to act as the central legislatures.
- The assemblies were to act as sovereign bodies for the purpose of making the Constitution and other laws.
- They were to be governed in accordance with the act of 1935 till the new Constitution was framed.

(ii) Following were the clauses mentioned in the Mountbatten Plan

- Partition of India into two different and sovereign states-India and Pakistan.
- The plan provided Partition of Punjab and Bengal.
- Princely states were given the choice of joining either of the two countries or to remain independent.
- Existing Constitution would continue to work and draft the Constitution for free India.
- Creation of a Boundary Commission to decide the boundary of two dominions.
- India's independence to be pre-poned to 15th August, 1947.

(iii) The All India Congress Committee accepted the Mountbatten Plan due to the following reasons

- Large-scale communal riots' engulfed the whole country convinced all the political leaders that the only solution to communal problem lay in the partition of India.
- The Muslim league had joined the Interim Government to obstruct and not to cooperate. Experience of working with the league convinced the Congress that a joint administration with the league was not possible.
- The leaders felt that partition would rid the Constitution of separate electorates and other undemocratic procedures. India could evolve a truly secular and democratic nation.

10. (i) Nazism was a system, a structure of ideas about the world and politics. This political system was introduced by Hitler in Germany which established dictatorship and propagated extreme hatred towards the Jews.

Nazism subscribed the theory of racial hierarchy and social Darwinism.

It aimed to overcome social divisions and create a homogeneous society based on national unity.

(ii) Some of the main causes of the rise and popularity of Nazism in Germany are as follows

- The humiliating Treaty of Versailles was harsh and devastating for the economy and national honour of the Germans. It's clauses became the causes of the rise of Nazism.
- Germany witnessed grave economic crisis and Hitler promised the people prosperity and peace. Therefore, Hitler's ideas of Nazism were accepted by the people.
- Hitler had a strong personality and had a mass appeal which contributed a lot to the popularity of Nazism in Germany.

(iii) The peculiar features of Nazi thinking were

- They believed that the strong should rule the world and the rest should accept their leadership.
- They believed in racial hierarchy, where the Nordic German Aryans were at the top and the Jews were at the lowest category.
- The Nazis believed that the Jews were their greatest enemies. So, the Jews were tortured and killed.
- From a very young age, children were indoctrinated both inside and outside school with the Nazi ideology of nationalism and war.
- The Nazis believed in the geo-political concept of Lebensraum or living space, i.e. new territories had to be acquired for the German nation.
- Women had to play the role of a good mother and wife and were excluded from all responsible position in political and academic spheres.

SQP Code : **PB-9/15** Series ***i*-Succeed 9-25/15** Roll No.

Sample Question Paper 09

History & Civics 10th (Code 50)

General Instructions

1. Attempt all questions from Part I (Compulsory).
2. A total of 5 questions are to be attempted from Part II, 2 out of 3 questions from Section A and 3 out of 5 questions from Section B.
3. The intended marks for questions or parts of questions are given in brackets ( ).

Time : 2 Hrs.

Max. Marks : 80

Part-I Attempt all questions from this part

Que 1.

Choose the correct option. (16)

(i) 'In a recent session of the Lok Sabha, a new bill regarding digital privacy was introduced. During the session, the Speaker played a crucial role in moderating the debate, ensuring that all parliamentary procedures were followed, including the maintenance of the quorum, managing the question hour, and overseeing the voting process.' [Application] (1)

Which of the following statements is not true according to the functions of the Parliament?

(a) The Speaker of the Lok Sabha oversees the introduction and debate of new bills.

(b) The Rajya Sabha has the exclusive power to introduce money bills.

(c) The Lok Sabha requires a quorum of 10% of its members to conduct business.

(d) The Speaker is responsible for ensuring that parliamentary procedures are adhered to during sessions.

(ii) Consider the following details.

	Emergency Types	Articles
1.	National Emergency	352
2.	State Emergency	?
3.	Financial Emergency	360

Fill in the blank with the help of below options. [Understanding] (1)

(a) 355 (b) 356 (c) 358 (d) 361

(iii) The given below image depicts the chairman of Rajya Sabha, who among the following also acts as the ex-officio chairman of Rajya Sabha? [Understanding] (1)

(a) Vice-President (b) President

(c) Comptroller and Auditor General of India

(d) Attorney General of India

(iv) 'A complex civil litigation case was originally filed in the District Court but was escalated to the Sessions Court due to the serious nature of the allegations and the amount of money involved. The Sessions Court handled the trial, applying its jurisdiction over civil matters involving higher claim values.' [Application] (1)

Case Study, Sessions Court

Which distinction between the Court of the District Judge and the Sessions Court is highlighted in this case?

(a) Jurisdiction over criminal cases

(b) Jurisdiction over civil cases

(c) Speedy trial mechanisms

(d) Lok Adalat referral systems

(v) Which among the following can be introduced only in Lok Sabha? [Recall] (1)

P. Money Bill

Q. Budget

R. Formation of New States

S. Creation of All India Services

Codes

(a) P and Q (b) R and S

(c) P and S (d) Q and P

(vi) The Person X was arrested without any warrant hence which of the following writ can be issued? [Understanding] (1)

(a) Habeas Corpus (b) Mandamus

(c) Certiorari (d) Prohibition

(vii) Read the two statements given below regarding Lucknow Pact and select the option that shows the correct relationship between A and R. [Analyse] (1)

Assertion (A) The unity between the Muslim League and the Congress due to Lucknow Pact strengthened the Indian National Movement.

Reason (R) Acceptance of the principle of separate electorate for Muslims by the Congress undermined the political unity of the country.

(a) R contradicts A

(b) R is the reason for A

(c) A is true, but R is false

(d) A and R are independent of each other

(viii) Read the two statements given below and select the option that shows the correct relationship between A and R. [Analyse] (1)

Assertion (A) The Treaty of Versailles led directly to the rise of Nazism in Germany.

Reasoning (R) The Treaty imposed heavy reparations on Germany, severely weakened its economy, and humiliated the German people, creating conditions ripe for extremist ideologies.

(a) R contradicts A

(b) R is the reason for A

(c) A is true, but R is false

(d) A and R are independent of each other

(ix) Which of the following fact is not correct about Fascism? [Analyse] (1)

(a) Fascism favored equal control in all the sections of the society.

(b) Fascists promoted the concept of democracy.

(c) It supported the notion of one party and one leader.

(d) Fascists focused on nationalism and on individual institutions.

(x) Gandhi Irwin Pact: March 1931 :: Second Round Table Conference: .... [Recall] (1)

(a) September to December 1931

(b) September to January 1932

(c) September to October 1931

(d) September to November 1931

(xi) The headquarter of UNESCO is situated in .... [Recall] (1)

(a) Geneva (b) Rome (c) Washington (d) Paris

(xii) Sakshi is reading about a person who discussed plan for Partition of India with Big 7 leaders. Who is she referring to? [Application] (1)

(a) Lord Wavell (b) Lord Mountbatten

(c) Lord Curzon (d) Lord Linlithgow

(xiii) During a Civil Disobedience Movement a group in a small town decided to protest against the unjust tax imposed on water. Being strong followers of Mahatma Gandhi's methods, they convened to discuss various non-violent ways to express their dissent. However, one of the suggested methods conflicted with Gandhi's principles. [Application] (1)

Which of the following protest methods would followers of Gandhian principles, not likely to approve?

(a) Organising a violent individual actions of Violence

(b) Holding a silent sit-in protest outside the tax office

(c) Carrying out a violent strike against tax collectors

(d) Sending a petition to the colonial authorities outlining their grievances

(xiv) The image given below depicts the Lucknow Pact of 1916. Which of the following is a drawback of the Lucknow Pact? [Recall] (1)

(a) The Congress lost its secular character by accepting separate electorates for Muslims and hence paved the way for communal tensions.
(b) It emphasised separate political existence for the Hindus and Muslims.
(c) Communal Veto in legislation was provided by this pact.
(d) All of the above

(xv) The First Non-Aligned Movement Summit was attended by ………… Afro-Asian nations and one European Union. [Recall] (1)

(a) 25 (b) 20
(c) 21 (d) 24

(xvi) Identify the country which waged a genocidal war during the Second World War. [Recall] (1)

(a) Italy (b) Germany
(c) USA (d) France

Que 2.

Read the extract given below and answer the questions which follows.

Headline : Supreme Court asks President to appoint ECs and CEC's on the advice of Committee.

On 2nd March, the Supreme Court made a ruling regarding the appointment of the Chief Election Commissioner (CEC) and Elections Commissioners (ECs) in India.

Source: Mint

(i) On the basis of the above news, discuss any two executive powers of President. [Understanding] (2)
(ii) What is the term of office for members of the Lok Sabha, and what is the primary function of the Speaker within its proceedings? [Analyse] (2)
(iii) Who was Mangal Pandey? Why did he disobey orders of his senior officers? [Recall] (1+1)
(iv) Who introduced the Arms Act of 1878? What did it declare? [Recall] (2)
(v) Name some precursors of Indian National Congress. [Recall] (2)
(vi) When did NAM officially came into existence? Who were the architects of the Non-Aligned Movement? [Recall] (1+1)
(vii) Who used the term Cold War first? What does it mean? [Recall] (1+1)

Part-II Section A (Civics) Attempt any two questions from this section

SP-09

Que 3.

Discuss the relationship between the two Houses of the Parliament with reference to the following.

(i) Introduction of Non-Money Bills in the House. [Recall] (3)
(ii) Introduction of Money Bill in the House. [Recall] (3)
(iii) What is meant by the estimates on expenditure in the General Budget? Explain in detail. [Recall] (4)

Que 4.

In the parliamentary form of Government, the Council of Ministers is the real executive of the government. In this context, answer the following questions.

(i) What do you understand by the term Council of Ministers? What are its composition? [Understanding & Recall] (1+2)
(ii) As we know the Council of Minister is headed by the Prime Minister. Mention his relation towards the Council of Ministers. [Application & Recall] (3)

(iii) Mention any four distinction between Council of Ministers and Cabinet. [Recall] (2+2)

Que 5.

At the district level in the State Judiciary, there are Subordinate Courts which hear the cases. In this context, answer the following questions.

(i) What is meant by Lok Adalat? Why it is set up? [Understanding] (2+1)

(ii) What is the scope of Lok Adalats in India? [Analyse] (3)

(iii) What do you understand by Family Court? Which kinds of matters are dealt by the Court? [Understanding & Recall] (2+2)

Section B (History) Attempt any three questions from this section

Que 6.

In the context of the Rise of Nationalism, explain the following

(i) Role of Press [Recall] (3)

(ii) The Economic Exploitation of India [Recall] (3)

(iii) Literary Movements [Recall] (4)

Que 7.

With reference to the First World War, answer the following questions.

(i) Discuss the significance of the armament race and the division of Europe which resulted in the First World War. [Recall] (3)

(ii) Analyse the role of the League of Nations following World War I and its failure to prevent the Second World War. [Analyse] (3)

(iii) What was the significance of First world war and how was it monumental in reshaping the global landscape? [Analyse & Recall](4)

SP-09

Que 8.

Read the excerpt given below and answer the question which follows.

Around the same time, in 1913, Jinnah had finally joined the Muslim League. Remarkably, he continued to be a member, simultaneously, of the Congress, which he had joined in 1906. He was held in high esteem in both Congress and Muslim League circles, and was popularly known as an 'ambassador of Hindu-Muslim unity'. Tilak and Jinnah had already worked together in the previous decade. Hence, a confluence of India's two main political streams led to the historic Lucknow Pact in 1916.

(i) Mention some national events that led to signing of Lucknow Pact. [Recall] (3)

(ii) Discuss any three features of Lucknow Pact. [Recall] (3)

(iii) Describe any two achievements and limitations of Lucknow Pact. [Recall] (4)

Que 9.

In the historic photograph given below Pandit Jawaharlal Nehru is seen giving his famous speech in the Constituent Assembly on 14th August, 1947.

In this context, answer the following questions.

(i) Mention three important reasons due to which the All-Indian Congress Committee was reluctant to accept Mountbatten Plan. [Recall] (3)

(ii) Mention the provisions of the Indian Independence Act of 1947 regarding the dominion status for the two countries. [Recall] (3)

(iii) Mention any four factors which led to the British to Quit India. [Recall] (4)

Que 10.

The Great War of 1914 was not due to any single cause, but due to the accumulation of explosive material for many years. With reference to this, answer the following questions.

(i) Explain briefly the Balkan Tension. [Recall] (3)

(ii) Explain briefly about the militant or intense nationalism. [Recall] (3)

(iii) (a) State any two terms of the Treaty of Versailles that helped to weaken the military power of Germany. [Recall] (2)

(b) Discuss briefly the division of Europe into two hostile groups. [Recall] (2)

Answers *in Topper's Style*

My Commitment *I affirm that I am reviewing these answers only after I have solved the Sample Question Paper 9 on my own. My purpose of looking the answers is solely to verify whether my answers were correct or not and to identify my mistakes in case my answers were wrong or I could not answer that.*

1. (i) (b) The Rajya Sabha has the exclusive power to introduce money bills.
   (ii) (b) 356
   (iii) (a) Vice-President
   (iv) (b) Jurisdiction over civil cases
   (v) (a) P and Q
   (vi) (a) Habeas Corpus
   (vii) (d) A and R are independent of each other
   (viii) (b) R is the reason for A
   (ix) (b) Fascists promoted the concept of democracy.
   (x) (a) September to December 1931
   (xi) (d) Paris
   (xii) (b) Lord Mountbatten
   (xiii) (c) Carrying out a violent strike against tax collectors
   (xiv) (a) The Congress lost its secular character by accepting separate electorates for Muslims and hence paved the way for communal tensions.
   (xv) (a) 25
   (xvi) (b) Germany

2. (i) Some of the executive powers of the President are

   (a) The President is the head of the Indian Union. All executive orders are issued by the Prime Minister and his cabinet on the name of the President.

   (b) All key appointments are made on the name of the President on the advice of the Prime Minister and his cabinet.

   (ii) The term of office for members of the Lok Sabha, which is the lower house of India's Parliament, is five years from the date of its first sitting unless dissolved sooner.

   The primary function of the Speaker within its proceeding is maintaining order during debates, deciding on all procedural issues and ensuring that the house operates smoothly.

   (iii) Mangal Pandey was a sepoy (soldier) in British Army and posted in Barrackpore during 1857.

   He refused to obey orders because the cartridges which his officers wanted to use were rumoured to be greased with the fat of cows and pigs. He thought that use of such cartridge would mean loss of his religious beliefs.

   (iv) Lord Lytton introduced the Arms Act of 1878. It declared that it was criminal offence for Indians to keep arms and to trade in them without license, but the Europeans were exempted from this law. Surendranath Banerjee said that, 'The Arms Act imposed on us a badge of racial inferiority'.

   (v) The Indian Association (1876) and the Poona Sarvajanik Sabha are the two main associations that were the precursors of the Indian National Congress.

   - The Indian Association established in 1876. It was founded by Surendranath Banerjee and Ananda Mohan Bose. The association aimed at the promotion of the political, intellectual advancements of the people.
   - Poona Sarvajanik Sabha, started under the leadership of Justice Ranade.

   (vi) NAM officially came into existence in 1961, in Belgrade. The main architects of the Non-Aligned Movement were

   - Jawaharlal Nehru of India
   - Josip Broz Tito of Yugoslavia
   - Sukarno of Indonesia
   - Gamal Abdel Nasser of Egypt
   - Kwame Nkrumah of Ghana

(vii) The term 'Cold War' was first used by Bernard Baruch. The Cold War reflects a period of mutual mistrust and extreme political unfriendliness which divided the world into two blocs.

USA and its allies formed the Western Bloc and USSR and its allies formed the Eastern Bloc, which lasted from 1945 till 1992, when the erstwhile USSR collapsed and the Paris Treaty announced the end of the Cold War.

3. (i) In case of ordinary or Non-Money Bills, the Rajya Sabha has almost equal powers as that of the Lok Sabha. An ordinary bill may originate in either House of the Parliament. When the bill is passed by both the houses, it becomes an act upon receiving the President's assent. In case of difference of opinion between the two houses in regard to any ordinary bill, the final decision is taken in a joint session of the two houses in order to resolve the deadlock.

In joint session, the Lok Sabha enjoys more power as the membership of Lok Sabha is more than the membership of Rajya Sabha.

(ii) In case of Money Bills, the Rajya Sabha has practically no powers. All money bills relating to taxation or expenditure must be initiated in the Lok Sabha and then it is referred to the Rajya Sabha for its approval.

Rajya Sabha must return the Money Bill with or without its recommendations within 14 days from the date of its receipt.

If Rajya Sabha does not return the bill within this period, the bill shall be deemed to have been passed by both the houses in its original form.

If the Rajya Sabha returns the bill with some recommendations, the Lok Sabha has total liberty to accept or reject any of these recommendations. So referring of Money bills to the Rajya Sabha is a mere constitutional formality.

(iii) The annual budget of the Union Government contains the General Budget for the financial year. The estimates on expenditure in the General Budget are of two types. They are

(a) Expenditure charged on the Consolidated Fund of India which includes the salaries and allowances of the President, Vice-President, Speaker, Deputy Speaker, Deputy Chairman of Rajya Sabha, Judges of the Supreme Court, Comptroller and Auditor General of India and pension of judges of High Court.
This expenditure does not require the annual vote of the Parliament, but it can discuss the estimates.

(b) Estimates required to meet the other expenditure of the Government of India are put up before the Lok Sabha in the form of Demands for Grants. These are thoroughly debated and voted upon by the members.
In this respect, the Lok Sabha has the power to impose, abolish or alter any tax or duties, etc.

4. (i) The term Council of Ministers is the name given to the supreme executive organ of the government. The term is usually equivalent to the word cabinet.

The Council of Ministers consists of three categories of ministers, namely, Cabinet Ministers, Ministers of State and Deputy Ministers.

- **Cabinet Ministers** Major ministries are headed by the Cabinet Ministers. They attend cabinet meetings and play an important role in deciding policies. Their responsibility extends over the entire gamut of the government.
- **The Ministers of State** They can either be given independent charge of ministries or departments or can be attached to Cabinet Ministers.
- **Deputy Ministers** Do not hold independent portfolio but are attached with cabinet ministers and ministers of state.

(ii) The Prime Minister plays a crucial role in relation to the Council of Ministers. These are explained as follows

- The Prime Minister recommends persons to be appointed as Ministers by the President.
- The Prime Minister allocates and reshuffles various portfolios among the Ministers.
- The Prime Minister can ask a Minister to resign or advice the President to dismiss him in case of difference of opinion.

(iii) The differences between Council of Ministers and Cabinet are given below

Council of Ministers	Cabinet
It is a wider body consisting of 60 to 70 ministers.	It is a smaller body consisting of 15 to 20 ministers.
It does not meet as a body to transact government duties. It has no collective functions.	It meets as a body frequently and usually to transact government duties. It has collective functions.
Its functions are determined by the Cabinet.	It directs the Council of Ministers by taking policy decisions which are binding on all Ministers.
It is collectively responsible to the Lok Sabha.	It enforces the collective responsibility of the Council of Ministers to the Lok Sabha.

5. (i) Lok Adalat means 'People's Court'. These Courts were set up by the recommendation of 'Justice Bhagwati' to encourage the settlement of disputes speedily and through compromise between parties. Lok Adalats are presided over by Judicial officers

and other persons who possess such qualifications as may be prescribed by the State. In 1982 for the first time Lok Adalats were held in Gujarat.

The Lok Adalats are set up to provide legal and quick justice to those who are not in a position to engage lawyers and to bear the expenses of the legal proceedings.

(ii) The scope of Lok Adalat can be understood through the following points

- The system of Lok Adalats have now become so popular that various government departments like the Telephone Department and the Electricity Boards have begun to hold Lok Adalats solving hundreds of cases in a single day.
- These courts can play an important role in the settlement of family rivalry, dispute between the neighbours and minor cases of assault and injury.
- In Delhi, all pending disputes concerning Delhi Development Authority, MTNL and National Insurance Co. Ltd are to be settled in the Lok Adalats.

(iii) The Family Courts Act was enacted in 1984 which provides to set up family courts in cities having population more than 10 lakh and at such other places the state government may deem necessary.

Family Courts are subordinate to the High Court, which has power to transfer the cases from one Family Court to the other. These courts are to secure speedy settlement of disputes relating to marriage, family affairs and related matters.

The matter which are dealt in the Family Court are as follows

- Matrimonial relief which include nullify of marriage, judicial separation, divorce, restoration of conjugal rights.
- Declaration as to the validity of marriage and matrimonial status of the person, property of spouses or any of them.
- Declaration as to the legitimacy of any person, guardianship of a person or custody of any minor maintenance including the proceeding under the Criminal Penal Code (CrPC).

6. (i) The introduction of Printing Press was a significant event for promoting nationalistic sentiments amongst Indians. The press and newspapers enabled people to be informed and educated. During the later half of the 19th century, a large number of newspapers like The Amrit Bazar Patrika, The Hindu, The Patriot, The Maharatta, The Kesari, The Azad, The Indian Mirror, etc. were started.

These papers fostered patriotism and ideas of liberty and justice in our country. They criticised the unjust policies of the government and helped in forming a general opinion which was in favour of overthrowing the British rule.

(ii) The Economic Exploitation of India is to be understood through the following points

- Agricultural India was made an economic colony to serve the interests of Industrial England.
- India was made to accept ready made British goods either duty free or at nominal duty rates, while Indian products were subjected to high import duties in England.
- The British capital invested in Indian markets especially in railways, shipping, oil exploration, tea and coffee plantations in order to get huge profits and was sent to England. All this led to extreme economic exploitation.

(iii) The literary movement in India greatly helped in the rise of nationalism. It began in 18th and 19th centuries when lot of literature was written. Literature became an important instrument for promoting social reforms, awareness of social problems, patriotism and nationalism. During this period, prose writing became important and new forms of literary writings such as novel, short story, drama and essay began to develop.

- Writers like Bankim Chandra Chattopadhyay, Rabindranath Tagore, Bharatendu Harishchandra, etc. played an important role in promoting consciousness among people.
- Bankim Chandra's famous novel 'Anandamath' (1882) was considered as the 'Bible of Modern Patriotism'. 'Vande Mataram' and other patriotic songs written by Bankim Chandra Chatterjee and patriotic songs written by Rabindranath Tagore, Dwijendralal Roy, Muhammad Iqbal inspired Indians and prepared them for the national struggle.

7. (i) The armament race and the division of Europe were key factors leading to the First World War. The arms race involved countries like Germany, Britain and France rapidly increasing their military strength, causing mutual fear and suspicion. Simultaneously, Europe was divided into two major alliances: the Triple Entente (France, Russia and the UK) and the Triple Alliance (Germany, Austria-Hungary, and Italy). These alliances meant that any conflict could quickly escalate, as happened after the assassination of Archduke Franz Ferdinand, leading to a widespread war.

(ii) The League of Nations was formed after World War I to maintain peace and prevent future conflicts. However, it failed to prevent World War II due to several reasons such as,

- Key countries like the USA never joined and others like Germany and the Soviet Union had limited membership.
- The League required unanimous decisions, which often led to inaction.
- It had no armed forces to enforce its resolutions.

- The rise of aggressive nationalism in countries like Germany, Italy and Japan further undermined its efforts, leading to its failure and replacement by the United Nations.

(iii) The First World War was a monumental conflict that reshaped the global landscape, altering the course of history and setting the stage for profound changes in the international order. Here are the key points regarding its significance and how it paved the way for a new world order

- **End of Empires** The war led to the collapse of four major empires: the German, Austro-Hungarian, Ottoman and Russian empires. This dissolution significantly altered the geopolitical map of Europe and the Middle East, leading to the creation of new nation-states and altering political boundaries.
- **Rise of the United States** The First World War marked the emergence of the United States as a world power. The U.S. economy strengthened significantly during the war and post-war, the U.S. played a crucial role in shaping the post-war economic and political order, advocating for principles like self-determination and open markets.
- **Social Changes** The war had profound social impacts, including the acceleration of social change movements such as women's suffrage.
- **Technological and Military Innovations** The war drove rapid advancements in military technology, including the development of tanks, aircraft and chemical weapons.

8. (i) National events that led to signing of Lucknow Pact were

- Firstly, the partition of Bengal was cancelled.
- Subsequently, nationalist Muslims such as Abul Kalam Azad and the Ali Brothers seized upon this opportunity to promote nationalist sentiments among Muslims, advocating for self-government.
- Thirdly, Tilak was released from imprisonment in 1914.
- Lastly, several Muslim leaders were detained under the Seditious Meetings Act by the British government. These developments led to a closer alignment between the Congress and the Muslim League.
- Initially, the League had 'support of the British Government' as one of its official goals. However, in 1913, the League's constitution was amended to include a system of self-government under the British Crown as its ideal.

(ii) The three features of Lucknow Pact were

(a) The Imperial Legislation of India should not control India's defence (including making war and signing treaties) and foreign affairs.

(b) Four-fifths of the members of the Provincial Legislature were to be directly elected and one-fifth should be nominated.

(c) Muslims were to be elected through a separate electorate. Minorities should be given adequate representation in elected bodies.

(iii) Two achievements of Lucknow Pact were

(a) It led to Hindu–Muslim unity. While Congress accepted the scheme of separate electorates for the Muslims, the Muslim League accepted the principle of election and majority rule.

(b) The signing of the Lucknow Pact also reunited the Early and Assertive Nationalists (both wings of the Congress were split in the 1907 Session at Surat).

Two limitations of Lucknow Pact were

(a) The Lucknow Pact did not involve the masses and was confined to only rich and educated Hindus and Muslims.

(b) Acceptance of the principle of separate electorate for Muslims by the Congress undermined the political unity of the country.

9. (i) The three important reasons due to which the All Indian Congress Committee was reluctant to accept Mountbatten Plan were

(a) Extension of the British rule was harmful for India. The British instigated the native rulers of Indian states to remain independent. So, the Congress thought that it was better to accept partition of the country than have confusion created by the 'Divide and Rule' policy of the British.

(b) The Congress believed that it could not have a joint administration with the League against the prior bitter experience.

(c) Large-scale communal riots that engulfed the whole country proved beyond doubt that it was better to accept the Partition of the country than to have bloodshed.

(ii) The provisions which were related to the dominion status for two countries are as follows

- **Separate Governor-General** There would be a Governor-General for each of the Dominions who shall function as a Constitutional Head. The right to the king or queen to veto laws was given up and was given to the Governor-General.
- **Power to Constituent Assemblies to make Laws** The Constituent Assemblies of the two Dominions were to serve as their Central Legislatures. They were to act as sovereign bodies for the purpose of making the Constitution as well as other laws for the Dominions.
- **Safeguarding the Interests of the Existing Officers** They were appointed by the Secretary of State, who would not make any such appointments in future.

(iii) The main factors which led to the British to quit India were as follows

(a) The Second World War had changed the world power balance. Britain was no longer powerful enough to withstand the upcoming march of nationalist movements.

(b) The resentment against British rule ran at a high pitch. At the end of the war, all this pent-up resentment broke out in dealing a final blow to foreign rule.

(c) The Royal Indian Navy Mutiny gave a final blow to the British rule in India.
The Mutiny was supported by the Indian Air Force and the Local police.

(d) The International pressure on England for India's freedom by countries like China, Russia and America.

10. (i) The Balkan Tension emerged in the 19th century, when a large part of the Balkans started disintegrating from the Ottoman Empire. One by one, nation broke away from its control and declared their independence. All European powers, via Russia, Germany, England and Austria were interested to extend ties and their hold on the Balkans.

Within the Austrian Empire, the most restive nationality was the Southern Slavs. They wanted to join the independent Kingdom of Serbia and the provinces of Bosnia-Herzegovina. This tension among the countries led to a series of war and ultimately the First World War.

(ii) The 19th century became an era of narrow and militant nationalism which means love for one's own nation and hatred towards other nations. Each nation thought about its own national interests which resulted into aggressive nationalism.

Fierce competition in economic and defense areas were the causes of growing nationalistic feelings.

Germany, Italy and Japan worked to increase their influence in their colonies in the least developed countries. All military strong nations competed against each other in wining over other colonial power. Aggressive and fierce economic competition gave rise to fear, confusion, insecurity and mutual hatred in the whole Europe. This was followed by expansionist policies in the name of nationalism which led to rise of imperialism.

(iii) (a) The two terms of the Treaty of Versailles that helped to weaken the military power of Germany were as follows

(a) Germany was restricted to keep its military. It was allowed to keep only a small army of one lakh soldiers, 15,000 navel men and 36 ships.

(b) Germany was forced to give up its colonies and other acquired areas in Africa and Europe.

(b) Europe was divided into two hostile camps at the early 20th century and they were

- **Triple Alliance** In 1882, Germany and Austria-Hungary strengthened their bond by forming the Triple Alliance with Italy. All three nations pledged to support if any of them would be attacked by France. If any member found itself at war with two or more nations at once, the alliance would come to their aid.
- **Triple Entente** It was formed in 1907 among Russia, France and Britain, to counter the effects of the formation of the Triple Alliance.

SQP Code : **PB-10/15** Series ***i*-Succeed 10-25/15** Roll No. | | | | | | | | |

Sample Question Paper 10

History & Civics 10th (Code 50)

General Instructions

1. Attempt all questions from Part I (Compulsory).
2. A total of 5 questions are to be attempted from Part II, 2 out of 3 questions from Section A and 3 out of 5 questions from Section B.
3. The intended marks for questions or parts of questions are given in brackets ( ).

Time : 2 Hrs.

Max. Marks : 80

Part-I Attempt all questions from this part

Que 1.

Choose the correct option. (16)

(i) 'The power of judicial review of the Supreme Court of India was highlighted in the landmark case of Kesavananda Bharati v. State of Kerala in 1973, where the court outlined the basic structure doctrine, protecting the core principles of the Constitution from amendments that may alter its essential character.' [Application] (1)

In the context of the excerpt provided, what is the primary role of the Supreme Court's power of judicial review?

(a) To amend the Constitution to keep it up to date with modern laws.

(b) To evaluate the constitutionality of legislative and executive actions.

(c) To provide advisory opinions to the government on legal matters.

(d) To oversee the functioning of lower courts in the country.

(ii) Given below are the few details. [Understanding] (1)

Articles	Provision
?	Impeachment of Judge
126	Judge of SC as acting Chief Justice of SC
141	Law making power of SC
125	Salaries, emoluments of judges of SC

Fill in the blank with correct option.

(a) 125 (b) 124 (c) 130 (d) 147

(iii) The below image depicts the upper house of the parliament, Rajya Sabha. How Many members are nominated in Rajya Sabha by the President of India? [Understanding] (1)

(a) 15 (b) 12 (c) 16 (d) 10

(iv) During a severe national crisis triggered by a natural disaster across multiple states, the President of India was confronted with a decision to invoke emergency powers. This action was necessary to streamline and centralise the disaster response efforts, ensuring that aid and relief operations could be conducted efficiently and without jurisdictional conflicts between the affected states. Acting upon the advice of the Union Cabinet, and after careful consideration of the ongoing situation, the President declared a state of emergency under Article 352 of the Constitution. [Application] (1)

What Constitutional authority did the President of India exercise in declaring a state of emergency during the national crisis?

(a) The President acted under the advice of the Supreme Court.
(b) The President used discretionary powers without consulting anyone.
(c) The President declared emergency powers based on the advice of the Union Cabinet.
(d) The President took direct control of the state governments.

(v) Which among the following are the Legislative Powers of President of India? [Recall] (1)

P. Address to Parliament
Q. Sending Messages to House
R. Appointment of PM
S. Introducing Budget in Parliament

(a) P and Q (b) Q and R
(c) R and S (d) P and S

(vi) Lok Sabha : .... : : Rajya Sabha: Upper House [Recall] (1)

(a) Greater House (b) Lower House
(c) Central House (d) House of Authority

(vii) Read the two statements given below and select the option that shows the correct relationship between A and R. [Analyse] (1)

Assertion (A) The Mountbatten Plan led to the partition of India into two separate nations, India and Pakistan, in 1947.

Reason (R) The plan was proposed by Lord Mountbatten to provide a solution to the religious and political conflicts between Hindus and Muslims in the subcontinent.

(a) R contradicts A
(b) R is the reason for A
(c) A is true, but R is false
(d) A and R are independent of each other

(viii) .... emphasised upon the neutrality of Asian and African states in the Cold War Era. [Recall] (1)

(a) President Sukarno of Indonesia
(b) President Kwame Nkrumah of Ghana
(c) Jawaharlal Nehru of India
(d) President Colonel Gamel Abdel Nasser of Egypt

(ix) 'The government of Country Y has announced a new policy similar to the objectives pursued by the Extremist faction within the Indian National Congress during the early 20th century. Who will be primarily targeted by this policy?' [Application] (1)

(a) The educational institutions
(b) The agricultural sector
(c) The colonial administrative officials
(d) The nationalistic movements

(x) Personality in the given below image played a pioneering role in the abolition of Sati. Identify the personality. [Recall] (1)

(a) Raja Rammohan Roy
(b) Lokmanya Tilak
(c) Bipin Chandra Pal
(d) Justice Ranade

(xi) He was known as 'Punjab Kesari', 'Sher-e-Punjab', he is .... [Recall] (1)

(a) Surendranath Banerjee
(b) Bal Gangadhar Tilak
(c) Bipin Chandra Pal
(d) Lala Lajpat Rai

(xii) Poorva is studying about a personality who founded London India Society and was the first Indian to be elected to British House of Commons. Name the personality. [Application] (1)

(a) Gopal Krishna Gokhale
(b) Dadabhai Naoroji
(c) Surendranath Banerjee
(d) Justice Ranade

(xiii) Which of the following is not correct about the Cold War? [Analyse] (1)

(a) Increased harmony between US and USSR.

(b) A state of extreme political tension between US and USSR.

(c) USA believed in democracy and capitalism.

(d) USSR believed in Communism based on Marxist Theory.

(xiv) Which of the following territories in France wanted to retrieve from Germany during the First World War? [Recall] (1)

(a) Saint Pierre and Miquelon

(b) Alsace and Lorraine

(c) Wallis and Futuna

(d) Reunion and Lorraine

(xv) In the late 19th century, as socio-religious reform movements gained momentum in India, leaders like Raja Rammohan Roy and Jyotiba Phule were at the forefront of advocating for social changes. These changes included efforts against caste discrimination and the push for education for all, including women. At a hypothetical meeting discussing further strategies to promote their reformist agenda, various methods were proposed. [Application] (1)

Considering their historical context and approaches to social reform, which of the following methods would Raja Rammohan Roy be least likely to approve?

(a) Organising a public debate to discuss the importance of education reform.

(b) Leading a protest demanding the abolition of caste restrictions.

(c) Creating a secretive society to promote their causes undercover.

(d) Publishing articles in newspapers advocating for social justice and reform.

(xvi) Identify the personality who founded the Satya Shodhak Samaj in 1873. [Recall] (1)

(a) Jyotiba Phule

(b) Raja Rammohan Roy

(c) Surendranath Banerjee

(d) Dadabhai Naoroji

Que 2.

Read the extract given below and answer the question which follows.

Headline : Honour to be back in India at such historic time, says US Ambassador Garcetti.

Shortly after presenting his credentials to President Droupadi Murmu, US Ambassador Eric Garcetti on Thursday said he would focus on raising the bilateral partnership to 'new heights' with both sides working together on 'defining issues' of the time.

Sources: Deccan Chronicle; 11th May

(i) Based on the above news, discuss any two diplomatic powers of the President. [Understanding] (2)

(ii) Explain the role and importance of the Speaker of the Lok Sabha in the parliamentary proceedings of India. [Recall] (1+1)

(iii) What was the General Service Enlistment Act? [Recall] (2)

(iv) Mention any two social evils that existed in India during the 19th century. What measures did the British Government take to stop them? [Recall] (2)

(v) Name two leaders who took the Anti-Partition Movement of Bengal outside Bengal. Who supported the movement led by these leaders? [Recall] (1+1)

(vi) Why did Subhash Chandra Bose resign from the post of the President of the Congress in 1939? [Recall] (2)

(vii) State any two similarities between Nazism and Fascism. [Recall] (2)

Part-II Section A (Civics) Attempt any two questions from this section

Que 3.

Keeping in view the powers of the Union Parliament, answer the following questions.

(i) Mention three of its Legislative Powers. [Recall] (3)

(ii) What are the three levels of government in federal setup in India? [Recall] (3)

(iii) Mention the devices through which the Parliament exercises control over the executive. [Recall] (4)

Que 4.

The President of India is the head of the state. In this context, answer the following questions.

(i) Mention briefly about the term of the office of the President. [Recall] (3)

(ii) Before holding the office, the President has to make to an oath or affirmation. In his oath what does he swear? [Recall] (3)

(iii) Mention the discretionary powers exercised by the President of India. [Understanding] (4)

Que 5.

The subordinate courts are the courts below the rank of the High Court in a state. With reference of this, answer the following questions.

(i) What are the Subordinate Courts? [Recall] (3)

(ii) Who appoints the Judges of the Subordinate Court? [Recall] (3)

(iii) Clearly describe the graded Civil Courts in a district. [Recall] (4)

Section B (History) Attempt any three questions from this section

Que 6.

With reference to the factors or causes that led to the Second World War, answer the following questions

(i) Discuss the Japanese invasion of China. [Recall] (3)

(ii) How did failure of League of Nations lead to the rise of dictatorship? [Recall] (3)

(iii) Give a brief idea about the Second World War. How rise of Fascism becomes another cause of the Second World War? [Recall] (2+2)

Que 7.

With reference to the Surat Split and the objectives and methods of struggle of the Radicals, answer the following questions.

(i) What was the Surat Split of 1907 and why was it significant in the history of the Indian National Congress? [Recall] (2+1)

(ii) What were the main objectives of the Radicals within the Indian National Congress by the early 20th century? [Recall] (3)

(iii) Describe the methods of struggle adopted by the Radicals in the Indian National Congress around the time of the Surat Split. [Recall] (4)

Que 8.

Read the excerpt given below and answer the questions that follows.

The Mountbatten Plan, unveiled in June 1947, outlined a detailed procedure for transferring power from British rule to Indian hands and proposed the partition of British India into two independent dominions, India and Pakistan. The plan was accepted by most major political parties, including the Congress and the Muslim League, leading to the rapid decolonisation of South Asia.

The Indian Independence Act, implemented the provisions of the Mountbatten Plan. It granted independence to the new dominions of India and Pakistan, allowing them to adopt or enact new Constitutions and make their own laws.

(i) When was the Indian Independence Act passed, and what were two primary clauses of this Act? [Recall] (1+2)

(ii) How did the Mountbatten Plan address the issue of partition? [Recall] (3)

(iii) What were the key clauses of the Mountbatten Plan? [Recall] (4)

Que 9.

Study the picture below and answer the questions that follow.

(i) (a) Name the organisation associated with the above emblem. [Recall]

(b) Mention any two functions of this organisation. [Recall] (1+2)

(ii) Mention three achievements of WHO in the field of health. [Recall] (3)

(iii) What are the main activities of the WHO? [Recall] (4)

Ques 10.

(i) What were the primary causes of the First War of Independence in 1857? [Recall] (3)

(ii) Describe three major consequences of the First War of Independence; 1857. [Recall] (3)

(iii) Outline the role of socio-religious factors in instigating the First War of Independence, 1857. [Understanding] (4)

Answers in Topper's Style

My Commitment *I affirm that I am reviewing these answers only after I have solved the Sample Question Paper 10 on my own. My purpose of looking the answers is solely to verify whether my answers were correct or not and to identify my mistakes in case my answers were wrong or I could not answer that.*

1. (i) (b) To evaluate the constitutionality of legislative and executive actions.

(ii) (b) 124 (iii) (b) 12

(iv) (c) The President declared emergency powers based on the advice of the Union Cabinet.

(v) (a) P and Q

(vi) (b) Lower House

(vii) (a) R contradicts A

SP-10

(viii) (c) Jawaharlal Nehru of India

(ix) (d) The nationalistic movements

(x) (a) Raja Rammohan Roy

(xi) (d) Lala Lajpat Rai

(xii) (b) Dadabhai Naoroji

(xiii) (a) Increased harmony between US and USSR.

(xiv) (b) Alsace and Lorraine

(xv) (c) Creating a secretive society to promote their causes undercover.

(xvi) (a) Jyotiba Phule

2. (i) Two diplomatic powers of the President are

(a) The President appoints the Indian Ambassadors to the other countries.

(b) All treaties and international agreements are concluded on the name of the President.

(ii) The Speaker holds a crucial role in the functioning of the lower house of India's Parliament. The Speaker's primary responsibility are as follows

- To maintain order during house debates, make sure that debates are conducted in a fair and impartial manner.
- The Speaker has the authority to adjourn the house or suspend sessions.
- During a tie on any decision in the house, the Speaker exercises a casting vote.

(iii) The General Service Enlistment Act of 1856 provided that all the sepoys of the Bengal army should be ready for service anywhere within or outside India.

Under the provision of the act, they could be sent overseas also, but as sea voyage was against the accepted belief of Brahmins, the Indian troops considered the act as a disregard to their feelings.

(iv) Social evils that existed in India during the 19th century include, 'Sati' where the widow was burnt on the funeral pyre of her husband and the pathetic condition of widows in the society.

Raja Rammohan Roy condemned these social evils and the British Government supported him and passed legislation for the suppression of Sati and the remarriage of widows.

(v) Bal Gangadhar Tilak and Lala Lajpat Rai took the Anti-Partition Movement of Bengal outside the Bengal. Boycott and Swadeshi were two novel methods to protest against Partition of Bengal.

The movement led by Tilak and Lajpat Rai, received the support of the youth who were ready to make sacrifices for the freedom of their country.

(vi) Subhash Chandra Bose resigned from the post of the President of the Congress in 1939 because it was getting increasingly difficult for him to work as Congress President. His pro-people, progressive and radical attitude made him popular. Despite the disapproval of Mahatma Gandhi, Subhash Chandra Bose won the President Post of the Congress by defeating Gandhiji's candidate Pattabhi Sitaramayya, in Tripuri Congress session. The followers of Gandhiji did not allow Subhash Chandra Bose to function effectively.

(vii) Two similarities between Nazism and Fascism were as follows

(a) Both Hitler and Mussolini were against democracy and wanted to crush opposition. They both believed in one party and one man rule.

(b) They both believed in aggressive nationalism and imperialistic policies.

3. (i) Three Legislative Powers of the Union Parliament are as follows

(a) The Parliament has exclusive powers to make laws on all the 100 subjects mentioned in the Union List including important subjects like defence, communication, finance, foreign policy, etc.

(b) The Parliament can make laws on the state subjects when specific conditions exist. e.g. when the state is under President's rule.

(c) The Parliament possesses residuary powers. It means that it can make laws with respect to all those matters which are not mentioned in Union List, State List and even in the Concurrent List.

(ii) The three levels of government in a federal set up in India are

- **Central Government** It is responsible for matters that affect the entire country or are of national importance.
- **State Government** Each state in India has its own government that governs the state as per the subjects listed in the State List of the Constitution such as law and order, agriculture, health, etc.
- **Local Authorities** (Municipal corporations and Panchayats) It consist of Panchayats in rural areas and Municipalities in urban areas.

These three levels of government are distributed to easily control the country's administration.

(iii) The devices, through which the Parliament exercises control over the executive are known as executive powers.

They are as follows

- **Interpellation or Inquiry** A valuable device against the slackness of the government, comprising of the question hour, discussion, etc. through which the government is answerable about its policies and performance to the opposition.
- **Adjournment Motion** It aims at censuring the acts of omission and commission of the ministers to bring matters of public importance.
- **Monetary Controls** A cut motion may be moved during the budget session. It ensures that the money is spent in accordance with the decision of the Parliament. It studies the reports of the Comptroller and Auditor-General of India (CAG).
- **Vote of No-Confidence** If a government does not follow the provisions of the Constitution, the Parliament can show No-Confidence to the government.

4. (i) The President holds office for a term of five years and is eligible for re-election. Besides, the President may vacate his office by the following ways

- By resigning from the office before the expiry of the term.
- In case of death or removal by impeachment.

The vacancy must be filled up as soon as possible and in no case later than six months from the date of the occurrence of such vacancy.

(ii) Before holding upon the office, the President has to make and subscribe to an oath or affirmation. In his oath, the President swears

- to faithfully execute the office.
- to preserve, protect and defend the Constitution and Law.
- to devote himself to the service and well-being of the people of India.

(iii) The President has no constitutional discretion; he/she has some situational discretion. These are as follows

- Appointing the Prime Minister when no party has a clear majority in the Lok Sabha or when the Prime Minister in the office dies suddenly and there is no obvious successor.
- Dismissal of the Council of Minister when it cannot prove the confidence of the Lok Sabha.
- Dissolution of the Lok Sabha if the Council of Ministers has lost its majority. Appointment of the Prime Minister.
- In case of sudden death, where the ruling party is unable to immediately elect a leader.

5. (i) All the courts at the district level and below are known as Subordinate Courts. Every state is divided into districts for judicial administration. The High Court is the Apex Court in the state. Just below the High Court there are District Courts.

Administration of justice at the district level is entrusted on three types of courts *viz*, Civil Courts, Criminal Courts and Revenue Courts. These three courts are part of the district court. The Civil Courts are those which deal with cases related to land, property, money transaction, etc.

- The Criminal Courts exercises jurisdiction in cases related to murder, robbery, theft, assault, etc. District Court is referred to as Session Court when it exercises its jurisdiction on criminal matters. Revenue Courts deal with cases relating to the maintenance of land records and the assessment and collection of land revenue.

(ii) The Judges of the Subordinate Court are appointed by the Governor in consultation with the Chief Justice of High Court. Most of them are appointed through competitive examinations held by the State Public Service Commission. The District Judge should have been in the Judicial service of the State for 7 years. Other judges of the Subordinate Court who are appointed through competitive examination must have atleast 3 years' experience as an advocate or as a pleader.

(iii) In a district, the graded Civil Courts are as follows

- **The Civil Courts** The highest Civil Court of the district is the Court of the District Judge. The District Judge, sometime along with the Additional District Judge supervises all the Civil Courts in the district. In his judicial capacity, he takes up cases involving a sum of more than ₹ 5000. Appeal against its decision can be brought to the High Court.
- **Sub-Judges's Court** The Sub-Judges's Court comes next to the District Court. It deals with cases involving not more than ₹ 5000. Appeals against its decision can be brought to the District Judges's Court.
- **Munsif's Court** These courts are lower than the Courts of the Sub-Judges. A Munsif's Court deals with civil cases involving not more than ₹ 2000. Appeals against its decision lie with the Sub-Judges's Court.
- **Small Courts** These courts deal with cases of nominal money value. The Junior Judges head these courts. There is no appeal against their decisions.

6. (i) The Japanese invasion of China becomes one of the causes of the Second World War. Japan and China fought the First World War on the side of Allies. After the war, Japan became ambitious and started developing its army.

- Japan was hit badly by the economic depression in 1931. Japanese people lost their faith in the government.
- They turned towards their army to find a solution to their economic problems. In order to produce more goods, Japan needed natural resources for its factories.
- The Japanese army invaded China, an area which is rich in minerals and resources.
- In 1931, Japan attacked over China and seized Manchuria and renamed it as Manchukuo, an independent state.
- China asked for help from the League of Nations but Japan ignored that and continued to occupy China and Korea.

(ii) After World War I, the League of Nations was established with the aim of preventing future conflicts and maintaining global peace and security. However, the major powers that held influence within the League often disregarded its mandates and regulations, thereby undermining its effectiveness. Consequently, the League of Nations proved to be ineffective and failed in achieving its primary objectives.

Simultaneously, many newly formed governments in European countries struggled to establish stable political and economic conditions. This instability created fertile ground for the rise of dictators such as Hitler and Mussolini, who exploited these conditions to seize power and impose authoritarian rule.

(iii) The Second World War was a direct result of the turmoil left behind by First World War. A lot of events throughout the world led to the beginning of Second World War. The main causes were the failure of the League of Nations to establish peace in the world and the Treaty of Versailles was set aside and expansionist policies were prevailed. The Second World War was more fatal than the First World War. Basically, the Second World War was a war for democracy.

Fascism becomes another cause of the Second World War as it led to totalitarian form of government.

- Dictatorship due to the adoption of Fascism got established in Italy under the leadership of Benito Mussolini. He focused on recovering the lost glory of the Old Roman Empire.
- He came out with changes in administration and followed an aggressive policy.
- Italy captured Abyssinia and Albania.
- The League of Nations declared that Italy was in the wrong direction and international restrictions should be imposed on Italy as the aggressor.

7. (i) The Surat Split occurred during the Indian National Congress's annual session in Surat in 1907, marking a major division within the party.

The split was primarily between the Moderates, who sought gradual reforms and methods of peaceful agitation, and the Radicals (or Extremists), who demanded swifter and more extensive political reforms through more assertive methods.

The Surat Split was significant in the history of the Indian National Congress due to the following reasons.

- The split led to a weakening of the Congress as a unified political organisation at a crucial time in the freedom struggle.

- It demonstrated the growing influence and dissatisfaction of younger members against the older leadership's cautious approach.
- The event paved the way for the emergence of more radical forms of resistance against British rule, as embodied by leaders like Bal Gangadhar Tilak, Lala Lajpat Rai, and Bipin Chandra Pal.

(ii) The main objectives of the Radicals within the Indian National Congress by the early 20th century were

- **Swaraj** The Radicals aimed for Swaraj or self-rule, which was a more immediate and complete form of political freedom than what the Moderates advocated.
- **Wider Participation** They sought to mobilise a broader segment of the Indian population into the freedom struggle, beyond the elite and educated classes who primarily constituted the Congress's base at the time.
- **Aggressive Methods** Unlike the Moderates, who preferred petitions and peaceful protests, the Radicals supported more direct forms of protest, including boycotts, public demonstrations, and the Swadeshi Movement (the use of indigenous goods and the boycott of foreign products).
- **Cultural Revival** The Radicals also emphasised the revival of Indian culture and education systems as a means to strengthen national identity and resist cultural imperialism.

(iii) The methods of struggle adopted by the radicals in the Indian National Congress around the time of the Surat Split were

- **Boycott** The Radicals advocated for the boycott of British goods and institutions as a means to hit at the economic foundations of the British in India.
- **Public Mobilisation** They organised mass protests, demonstrations, and public meetings to galvanise support and create a wider awareness and participation among the common people.
- **Educational Reforms** Emphasis was placed on establishing national schools and colleges to educate young Indians in a spirit of nationalism and to counteract the influence of British-led education.
- **Press and Publications** The Radicals made extensive use of the press to propagate nationalist ideas, criticise British policies, and mobilise public opinion against colonial rule.

8. (i) The Indian Independence Act was passed on 18th July, 1947, by the British Parliament. This legislation led to the end of British rule in India and the creation of two independent dominions, India and Pakistan.

The primary causes of the act were

- **Partition Clause** This clause authorised the division of British India into the two new dominions of India and Pakistan.
  The division was based primarily on religious demographics, aiming to create separate nations for the majority Hindu and Muslim populations. This decision was influenced by years of communal tension and demands from various political groups, most notably the Muslim League, which sought a separate nation for Muslims.
- **Legislative Powers Clause** Under this clause, the dominions of India and Pakistan were given complete autonomy over their internal and external affairs. This provision abolished the use of British royal instruments in government and discontinued the British monarch's role in governing these territories. Both countries were allowed to draft their Constitutions and develop independent legislative bodies. This shift was critical in allowing each new nation to forge its path in legislative and constitutional matters, laying the groundwork for their future as sovereign states.

(ii) The Mountbatten Plan, addressed the issue of partition by proposing the division of British India into two independent nations, India and Pakistan.

- It outlined clear principles for partition, granting autonomy and sovereignty to both nations to draft their own Constitutions.
- The plan allowed for the transfer of power to be expedited, with provisions for the Princely States to accede to either nation based on geographical and demographic considerations.
- This partition framework aimed to manage the transition from colonial rule to independent states, despite the ensuing challenges and conflicts.

(iii) The key clauses of the Mountbatten Plan were

- **Partition of India** The plan proposed the partition of British India into two dominions, India and Pakistan, based on religious majorities. This was aimed at resolving the ongoing conflict between Hindus and Muslims in the region.
- **Immediate Transfer of Power** The plan proposed the transfer of power to the new dominions by 15th August, 1947, significantly accelerating the timetable for British withdrawal from India.
- **Princely States' Status** The princely states were given the option to decide whether to join India or Pakistan. This autonomy was crucial as there were over 560 princely states, each with its own governance.
- **Constituent Assemblies** Each new dominion would have its own Constituent Assembly, which would have the power to draft and enact a new Constitution.
- **Bengal and Punjab Partition** Special provisions were made for the partition of the provinces of Bengal and Punjab, with the respective provincial assemblies voting in separate sections to decide whether to join India or Pakistan.

9. (i) (a) The above emblem belongs to the World Health Organisation (WHO).

(b) Functions of this organisation are as follows
- To help countries to build up infrastructure in health sectors. It helps them by giving important drugs and other supplies needed for medical care.
- To promote research to cure and prevent diseases. The WHO has arranged for the investigation of cancer and heart diseases in many countries in order to identify disease causing micro organisms, improve vaccines and to train research workers.

(ii) Achievements of WHO in the field of health are as follows
- Complete eradication of small pox and nearly elimination of guinea worm.
- There is significant reduction in diarrhoeal deaths.
- Rare occurrence of cholera and plague epidemics.

(iii) The main activities of the WHO are
- The WHO aims to eradicate polio within the next few years from the whole world. For this, it runs worldwide programmes.
- The WHO carries campaigns to discourage tobacco use.
- The WHO has drafted, a global plan of action on worker's health to protect and promote health at the workplace.

10. (i) The First War of Independence in 1857, commonly referred to as the Sepoy Mutiny, was triggered by a confluence of political, economic, military, and socio-religious factors. Some of the causes were as follows
- **Politically** the aggressive expansion and annexation policies of the British, such as the Doctrine of Lapse and the annexation of princely states like Awadh on grounds of misgovernance, alienated the ruling elite weakened traditional power structures.
- **Economically** the peasantry was distressed due to heavy land taxes and the disruption of traditional agricultural practices,
- Artisans faced ruin due to the invasion of British manufactured goods which outcompeted local products.
- Indian soldiers or sepoys in the British East India Company's army faced racial discrimination, were paid less than their British counterparts, and were often sent on missions overseas, which violated their religious and social values.
- The final spark was provided by the introduction of the Enfield rifle; the cartridges for this rifle were rumoured to be greased with cow and pig fat, which were considered impure in Hinduism and Islam, respectively.
- This is not only caused outrage due to the insensitivity to local religious customs but also encapsulated the broader perception that British rule was inherently disrespectful and exploitative towards Indian traditions and sentiments.

(ii) The three major consequences of the First War of Independence, 1857 were

(a) The revolt led to the dissolution of the British East India Company, and the administration of India was transferred directly under the British Crown through the enactment of the Government of India Act, 1858. This shift signalled a new phase of rule, with Queen Victoria promising to respect the religious beliefs, social customs, and inheritance laws of Indians in her Proclamation of 1858, attempting to rectify the distrust caused by previous policies.

(b) The composition of the British forces in India was significantly changed to prevent such occurrences in the future. The ratio of British to Indian soldiers was increased, and recruitment strategies were altered to favour groups deemed more loyal to the British regime, like the Sikhs and Gurkhas. Additionally, there was a major overhaul in military leadership and strategy to maintain stricter control and oversight.

(c) The British also expanded public works and infrastructure projects, like railways and telegraphs, aiming to modernise India while improving administrative efficiency and famine response.

These changes, although initially imposed to secure British interests, gradually laid the groundwork for modern state institutions in India.

(iii) The socio-religious factors that contributed to the 1857 rebellion stem from deep-rooted resentments against the policies implemented by the British, which were seen as direct threats to the cultural and religious foundation of Indian society. These were
- The British enacted several social reforms, including the abolition of practices such as Sati and the introduction of the Widow Remarriage Act, which, while progressive, were perceived by many as an overreach into religious matters.
- Christian missionary work that included the building of churches and conversions, instilled fears of religious conversion and cultural erosion.
- Introduction of the new Enfield rifle cartridges, which were rumoured to be greased with cow and pig fat. This not only offended Hindu and Muslim soldiers but also symbolised that the Britishers did not respect the religious sentiments of Indians.
- This incident confirmed the suspicions of many Indians about the ultimate intentions of the British. It acted as a collective grievance among Indians and sparked widespread rebellion.

Thus, the socio-religious dimension of the grievances played a crucial role in mobilising a wide range of Indian society against British rule, making the rebellion a landmark event in Indian history.

SQP Code : **PB-11/15** Series ***i*-Succeed 11-25/15** Roll No.

Sample Question Paper 11

History & Civics 10th (Code 50)

General Instructions

1. Attempt all questions from Part I (Compulsory).
2. A total of 5 questions are to be attempted from Part II, 2 out of 3 questions from Section A and 3 out of 5 questions from Section B.
3. The intended marks for questions or parts of questions are given in brackets ( ).

Time : 2 Hrs.
Max. Marks : 80

Part-I Attempt all questions from this part

Que 1.

Choose the correct option (16)

(i) 'The Supreme Court's original jurisdiction extends to cases involving disputes between the Union and one or more states, or between different states. This jurisdiction is a critical aspect of India's federal structure as it helps maintain a balance by resolving issues that could affect the national integrity.'
Which type of cases fall under the original jurisdiction of the Supreme Court? [Application] (1)

(a) Disputes between private citizens
(b) Disputes involving commercial contracts
(c) Disputes between different states or between states and the union
(d) Appeals against decisions of high courts

(ii) Given below are details of few cases. [Understanding] (1)

Courts	Cases
Court of District Judge	Land and money cases
Sessions Court	?
Lok Adalats	Matrimonial cases

Fill the above blank with the help of options given below.

(a) Arbitration (b) Guardianship
(c) Murders and theft (d) Writs

(iii) Which statements accurately describes the procedure for a no-confidence motion in the Indian Parliament? [Analyse] (1)

(a) A no-confidence motion, once passed in the Rajya Sabha, leads to the dissolution of the government.
(b) A no-confidence motion needs the support of 50 members to be admitted for discussion in the Lok Sabha.
(c) A no-confidence motion can be introduced and passed in either house of Parliament to challenge the government's majority.
(d) A no-confidence motion, if passed in the Lok Sabha, requires the Prime Minister and the Council of Ministers to resign.

(iv) Which among the following are the functions of Prime Minister? [Recall] (1)

P. Allocation and reshuffling of Port folios.
Q. Presiding the meeting of Council of Ministers.
R. Introducing the budget
S. Declaring war

(a) P and Q (b) P and R
(c) R and S (d) Q and S

(v) 'In 1991, during a political crisis where no single party could secure a majority in the Lok Sabha after general elections, the President of India played a pivotal role.

The President invited the leader of the largest coalition formed post-election to form the government, despite the leader not being from the single largest party.'

Based on the case study, what does this scenario illustrate about the President's powers in India? [Application] (1)

(a) The President always nominates the leader of the single largest party to form the government.
(b) The President has no discretion and must follow the directive of the outgoing Prime Minister.
(c) The President's discretionary power allows him to decide whom to invite to form the government in the absence of a clear majority.
(d) The President can dissolve Lok Sabha without inviting anyone to form a government.

(vi) .... has the power to enlarge the jurisdiction and powers of the Supreme Court in respect to the Union List and other matters. [Recall] (1)

(a) Executive (b) Prime Minister
(c) Parliament (d) Cabinet

(vii) Read the two statements given below regarding Nazism and select the option that shows the correct relationship between A and R. [Analyse] (1)

Assertion (A) The communists had organised themselves in Germany, and they had succeeded in capturing many seats in the Reichstag.

Reason (R) Hitler criticised the growing influence of communism and asked the Germans to vote for him as Nazis could alone check the rising tide of communism.

(a) R contradicts A
(b) R is the reason for A
(c) A is true, but R is false
(d) A and R are independent of each other

(viii) Read the two statements given below and select the option that shows the correct relationship between A and R. [Analyse] (1)

Assertion (A) The Lucknow Pact of 1916 marked a significant turning point in the history of the Muslim League.

Reason (R) The Pact represented an agreement between the Muslim League and the Indian National Congress to work together for the formation of a self-governing system in India.

(a) R contradicts A
(b) R is the reason for A
(c) A is true, but R is false
(d) A and R are independent of each other

(ix) The personality shown below wrote the autobiography: The Story of My Deportation. Identify the personality. [Recall] (1)

(a) Bipin Chandra Pal (b) Lala Lajpat Rai
(c) Lokmanya Tilak (d) RC Dutt

(x) Lala Lajpat Rai : Punjab Kesari :: Bipin Chandra Pal : .... [Recall] (1)

(a) Father of Revolutionary Thought in India
(b) Grand Old Man of India
(c) Father of the Indian Renaissance
(d) Desh Ratna

(xi) Mahatma Gandhi withdrew the Non-Cooperation Movement on .... [Recall] (1)

(a) 10th February, 1921
(b) 12th February, 1922
(c) 14th February, 1922
(d) 15th February, 1922

(xii) 'In 1931, during the Second Round Table Conference in London, an Indian delegate was noted for his adherence to the principles of non-violence and cooperation. The discussions revolved around increasing Indian participation in governance. Despite differing opinions, this delegate advocated for dialogue and legislative reforms as a way to progress.'

Based on his beliefs, which of the following strategies is the delegate not likely to endorse during the negotiations? [Application] (1)

(a) Supporting Civil Disobedience in India to pressure British negotiators
(b) Proposing constitutional reforms for greater Indian autonomy
(c) Engaging in diplomatic discussions to find a common ground
(d) Drafting a detailed proposal for responsible governance shared between the British and Indians

(xiii) The image shows 'Subhash Chandra Bose', founder of Forward Bloc. In the light of the given image, which of the following statements best describes the primary objective of the Forward Bloc? [Recall] (1)

(a) To negotiate with the British for incremental reforms and greater Indian participation in government.
(b) To promote the use of violent means to end British rule in India.
(c) To consolidate all the leftist elements within the Indian National Congress.
(d) To establish a broad anti-imperialist front comprising various social groups against British rule in India.

(xiv) When was the Provisional Government of Free India formed? [Recall] (1)

(a) 21st October, 1943
(b) 21st November, 1943
(c) 21st December, 1943
(d) 21st January, 1944

(xv) During the First World War, on the Western front Germany and .... were engaged in a fierce conflict. [Recall] (1)

(a) Britain
(b) Austria
(c) Russia
(d) France

(xvi) Identify the charismatic personality who was regarded as 'Duce'. [Recall] (1)

(a) Benito Mussolini
(b) Adolf Hitler
(c) Woodrow Wilson
(d) Winston Churchill

Que 2.

Read the extract given below and answer the questions which follows.

Headline : Assault on on-duty police officials: Sessions court upholds order to frame charges.

A sessions court here upheld on Monday the order of a Magisterial Court to frame charges against a man accused of assaulting on-duty police officials in 2014.

(i) On the basis of above news, write a note on Criminal Court. [Understanding] (2)

(ii) What special powers does the Lok Sabha have that the Rajya Sabha does not? [Recall] (2)

(iii) Why the First War of Independence was a failure? State two points. [Recall] (2)

(iv) Mention two important contributions of Lala Lajpat Rai. [Recall] (2)

(v) Write about an incident which convinced Indians that independence from British rule was necessary. [Recall] (2)

(vi) What was the moral code laid down by Gandhiji for Satyagrahis? [Recall] (2)

(vii) Mention the countries associated with the two blocs during Cold War. [Recall] (2)

Part-II Section A (Civics) Attempt any two questions from this section

Que 3.

Indian Constitution has provided for Parliamentary form of government. Considering the Constitutional Provision, answer the following questions.

(i) What is the difference between unicameral and bicameral legislature? [Analyse] (3)

(ii) How can Indian Constitution be amended? [Recall] (3)

(iii) Write any three privileges enjoyed by a Member of Parliament. [Recall] (4)

Que 4.

The Vice-President occupies the second highest office in the country and is next to the President. In this context, answer the following questions.

(i) How does a Vice-President gets elected? [Recall] (3)

(ii) What are the conditions of the office of the Vice-President? [Recall] (3)

(iii) What are the powers and functions of the Vice-President? [Recall] (4)

Que 5.

With reference to the Judiciary, answer the following

(i) What is the criminal appellate jurisdiction of the High Courts? [Recall] (3)

(ii) Explain when and how the judges can be removed from office? [Recall] (3)

(iii) Name the three types of courts at the district level. Explain the different categories of cases that fall under the jurisdiction of each. [Recall] (4)

Section B (History) Attempt any three questions from this section

Que 6.

Mass Movement in India due to Anti-Partition agitation was indirectly initiated by Lord Curzon. In this context, answer the following questions.

(i) How Lord Curzon favoured the 'Partition of Bengal'? [Recall] (3)

(ii) What were the double advantage that Curzon hoped to achieve by the partition? [Recall] (3)

(iii) In what way the nationalists interpreted Lord Curzon's Partition? How did they opposed it? [Recall] (2+2)

Que 7.

With reference to the Rise of Dictatorships in Europe, answer the following questions.

(i) Discuss and compare the similarities between Mussolini's Fascism in Italy and Hitler's Nazism in Germany. [Analyse] (3)

(ii) Enlist at least four causes for the rise of Fascism in Italy. [Application & Recall] (3)

(iii) Compare and contrast four ideological differences between Mussolini's Fascism and Hitler's Nazism. [Analyse] (4)

Que 8.

Read the excerpt given below and answer the question which follows.

1905 saw a change in the direction of India's nationalist struggle and deepened a communal divide that would haunt India for decades to come. The reason: Lord Curzon, the imperial Viceroy, decided it was time to divide British India's largest province, the Bengal Presidency, the Partition of Bengal also galvanised Indian nationalists, furious at the British divide and rule strategy. New forms of protest, from calls of boycott to advocacy of swadeshi, emerged.

(i) When did the above event take place? Who was the Viceroy of India during the above event? What was the main motive of Curzon behind the Partition of Bengal? [Recall] (1+1+1)

(ii) What was the people's reaction to the Partition of Bengal? [Recall] (3)

(iii) Explain the other events that took place in 1905. [Recall] (4)

SP-11

Que 9.

Look at the picture given below carefully and answer the following questions.

(i) Which event is seen in the above picture? Mention any two causes that led to this event. [Recall] (1+2)

(ii) What was the programme of the movement? [Recall] (3)

(iii) What were the consequences of the movement? [Understanding] (4)

Que 10.

The United Nations and its agencies are concerned with maintaining world peace, promoting social progress, better standards of life, remove diseases and so on.

In this regard answer the following questions.

(i) State the objective of the UN. [Recall] (3)

(ii) Write about the activities undertaken by UNESCO. [Recall] (3)

(iii) Which is the main organ of UN? Mention its functions. [Recall] (1+3)

Answers *in Topper's Style*

My Commitment *I affirm that I am reviewing these answers only after I have solved the Sample Question Paper 11 on my own. My purpose of looking the answers is solely to verify whether my answers were correct or not and to identify my mistakes in case my answers were wrong or I could not answer that.*

1. (i) (c) Disputes between different states or between states and the union

(ii) (c) Murders and theft

(iii) (d) A no-confidence motion, if passed in the Lok Sabha, requires the Prime Minister and the council of ministers to resign.

(iv) (a) P and Q

(v) (c) The President's discretionary power allows him to decide whom to invite to form the government in the absence of a clear majority.

(vi) (c) Parliament

(vii) (d) A and R are independent of each other

(viii) (a) R contradicts A

(ix) (b) Lala Lajpat Rai

(x) (a) Father of Revolutionary thought in India

(xi) (b) 12th February, 1922

(xii) (a) Supporting civil disobedience in India to pressure British negotiators

(xiii) (d) To establish a broad anti-imperialist front comprising various social groups against British rule in India.

(xiv) (a) 21st October, 1943

(xv) (d) France

(xvi) (a) Benito Mussolini

2. (i) Criminal Courts a court that has jurisdiction to try and punish offenders against criminal laws. It deal with cases related to murder, robbery, theft, assault, etc. The Criminal Courts can be classified into the five categories namely Sessions Court, Court of Chief Judicial Magistrate, Court of First Class Magistrate, Court of Second Class Magistrate and Court of Third Class Magistrate.

(ii) The Lok Sabha has the exclusive power to initiate and pass a no-confidence motion against the Council of Ministers. If the motion passes, the Prime Minister and their cabinet must resign. The Rajya Sabha does not have this power, emphasising the Lok Sabha's primary role in determining the government's stability.

(iii) The First War of Independence failed to end the British rule in India due to the following reasons

(a) There was no centralised leadership or any well defined military plans.

(b) It was not a mass struggle as parts of East, West and South India remained unaffected by the uprising.

(iv) Two important contributions of Lala Lajpat Rai were

(a) He protested against the Rowlatt Act and the Jallianwala Bagh Massacre. He founded the Home Rule League of America in 1917 in New York.

(b) He supported the Non-Cooperation Movement of Gandhi at the Nagpur session of the Congress in 1920.

(v) Many incidents convinced the Indians that independence from British rule was necessary. Among them, an important incident was the threat of Japanese attack from the Myanmar side during the Second World War. Japan was an Axis power and Britain was an Allied power.

India being a colony of British was threatened of an attack from Japan. This convinced the Indian leaders that for India's safety, the British should withdraw from India.

(vi) Gandhiji believed in truth and non-violence. The moral code laid down by Gandhi for Indians was Satyagraha which means the quest for truth.

He showed the path of non-violence to achieve goals. Followers of Gandhiji were called Satyagrahis.

- Gandhi initiated mass movements and people got associated with the moral path shown by him in large numbers.

(vii) During Cold War, one bloc was Democratic/ Capitalist bloc and another was Communist/ Socialist bloc.

Democratic Capitalist Block headed by US and comprised of Britain, France, Belgium, Italy, Canada, Australia, Netherlands, Greece, Pakistan and Turkey.

Communist/Socialist Bloc, headed by USSR and comprised of countries of Eastern Europe like Romania, Hungary, Bulgaria, Poland, Czechoslovakia, Yugoslavia and Albania.

3. (i) Unicameral and bicameral legislature are the two types of legislature. Differences between them are

Unicameral Legislature	Bicameral Legislature
It consists of one house of legislature.	It comprises of two houses of legislature, the upper house and the lower house.
It consists only of lower house and is represented on the basis of population.	It consists almost equal number of representatives from each state or province.
Unicameral legislature system is implemented in China.	Bicameral legislature system is in USA, UK and India.

(ii) The Parliament can amend the Indian Constitution in following ways

- Some provision of Constitution can be amended by simple majority. e.g. Amendment for admission or establishment of new states.
- By special majority of Parliament. e.g. Amendment of Fundamental Rights.
- By special majority of Parliament and by ratification of states. e.g. Amendment to election of the President and its manner.

(iii) The three privileges enjoyed by individual Member of Parliament are as follows

(a) **Freedom from Arrest** During the session of Parliament and 40 days before the beginning and 40 days after the end of a session.

(b) **Freedom of Speech** No member is liable to any proceedings in any court for anything said or any vote given by him in Parliament or its committees.

(c) **Freedom from Jury Service** Member of Parliament can refuse to give evidence and appear as a witness in a case pending in a court when the Parliament is in session.

4. (i) Like the President, the Vice-President of India is elected indirectly by an Electoral college, through the system of Proportional Representation by means of Single Transferable Vote.

This Electoral college consists of

- Both the elected as well as the nominated Members of the Parliament.
- It does not include the members of the State Legislative Assemblies.

Election is carried by secret ballot and an absolute majority of the votes is also required for the election of the Vice-President.

(ii) The conditions of the office of the Vice-President are

- The Constitution of India lays down the condition for a person to be eligible for the post of Vice- President. He/She should be qualified for the election as a member of Rajya Sabha.
- The person should not hold any office of profit under the Union Government or any State Government or any other public authority.
- The person should not be a member of either house of the Parliament or State Legislature.

(iii) The powers and functions of Vice-President are as follows

- The Vice-President acts as an ex-officio Chairman of the Rajya Sabha.
- The Vice-President acts as the President when a vacancy occurs in the office of the President due to his/ her removal or his/her death or otherwise.
- When the sitting President is unable to discharge his/her functions, the Vice-President acts as the President until the President resumes his/her office.
- Vice-President regulates the Rajya Sabha proceedings, decides the order of speeches and decides the admissibility of a resolution. He may suspend or adjourn the Rajya Sabha in case of grave disorder.

5. (i) Criminal Appellate Jurisdiction of High Court is given below
   - Appeals from the judgements of Session Courts and Additional Session Courts lie to the High Court, if the sentence is one of imprisonment for more than 7 years.
   - Appeals against the death sentence awarded by a Session Court or an Additional Session Court should be confirmed by the High Court before it can be executed, whether there is an appeal by the committed person or not.
   - Appeals from the judgements of the Assistant Session Judge, Metropolitian Magistrate or other Magistrates lie to the High Court.

   (ii) A judge of High Court remains in office till the age of 62 years and can be removed only by the order of the President. Following procedure is adopted for removal
   - The President issues a removal order only after an address by the Parliament has been presented for removal.
   - The address must be supported by a special majority of each house of the Parliament by two-third majority.
   - Only then the President passes an order for the removal of the judges. This procedure is called the impeachment of the judge.

   (iii) The three types of courts at the District level are the Civil Courts, Criminal Courts and Court of Revenue. Cases that fall under the jurisdiction of each are as follows
   (a) **The Civil Courts** The Civil Courts hear cases of land, property, money transactions, marriage, divorce, will and guardianship.
   (b) **The Criminal Courts** The highest Criminal Court of the district is the Court of the Sessions Courts. Usually, it is presided over by the District Judge. In the Sessions Court, serious cases of murder, robbery and dacoities are tried.
   (c) **Court of Revenue** These courts deal with cases relating to the maintenance of land records and assessment and collection of land revenue.

6. (i) Lord Curzon's Scheme of Partition of Bengal was implemented on 16th October, 1905. Curzon favoured the partition in the following ways
   - Curzon justified the Partition of Bengal Presidency, saying that the area of Bengal was very large and it was also the most thickly populated province in British India.
   - It was difficult for the British to administer the same efficiently. Hence, according to Lord Curzon, Partition of Bengal was administrative neccessity.
   - Two provinces were necessary for the smooth administration. Therefore, Bengal was divided into West Bengal that included Western parts of Bengal, Bihar and Odisha and East Bengal that included Eastern districts of Bengal.

   (ii) Double advantage that Curzon hoped to achieve through the partition were
   - Bengal was the nerve centre of Indian politics at that time so to destroy the political influence of educated middle class, it was partitioned. In this way, the ideas of nationalism would be prevented from spreading thereby weakening the national movement.
   - By setting up the new province of East Bengal, a Mohammedan province was created where Muslims would be in majority. Dacca was made a parallel centre to Calcutta thus, counterbalancing Hindus with Muslims.

   (iii) The Indian nationalists clearly saw the intentions behind the partition and condemned it. They thought that this was done in order to divide or break the Hindu-Muslim unity; they felt that administrative efficiency could have been better secured to stop the tide of nationalism, to curb Bengali influence by not only placing Bengalis under the administration, but by reducing them to a minority in Bengal.
   Nationalists oppose and condemned the partition in the following ways
   - They called protest meetings and campaigns.
   - The day of partition was declared as the day of 'National Mourning' people observed fast on that day.
   - Congress leaders initiated mass movement to show their disapproval.

7. (i) Following were the similarities between the Mussolini's Fascism in Italy and Hitler's Nazism in Germany
   - **Authoritarianism** Both ideologies enforced total state control, suppressing opposition via secret police and state-controlled media.
   - **Nationalism** Mussolini and Hitler promoted national revival, appealing to citizens disillusioned by instability.
   - **Anti-Communism** Both leaders opposed communism, gaining support from industrialists and conservatives.
   - **Militarism** They pursued aggressive militarism and expansionism, with Mussolini aiming for an Italian empire and Hitler seeking Lebensraum.
   - **Propaganda and Cult of Personality** Both leaders used media to depict themselves as saviors essential for their nations' resurgence.

   (ii) Four causes for the rise of Fascism in Italy were as follows
   (a) **Economic Hardship** Post-World War-I challenges included high unemployment, inflation, and stagnant growth, along with unmet expectations from war spoils and territorial gains.

(b) **Political Instability** Frequent government changes and ineffective leadership led to widespread disillusionment with the parliamentary system and democratic governance.

(c) **Anti-Communist Sentiment** The middle and upper classes feared a potential socialist or communist uprising.

(d) **Treaty of Versailles Disappointment** National discontent over the Treaty of Versailles outcomes fueled a desire to reclaim pride and assert Italy's power.

These factors created a fertile environment for Mussolini's Fascist movement, which promised economic revival, political stability and nationalistic resurgence.

(iii) The differences between ideologies of Mussolini's Fascism and Hitler's Nazism were

- **Race** Hitler's Nazism was distinctly characterised by a racial ideology, promoting the idea of the Aryan race's superiority and anti-semitism, leading to the Holocaust. On the other hand, Mussolini's Fascism was initially less focused on race and more on nationalism, although it later adopted similar racial laws under Nazi influence.
- **Expansionism** Both ideologies were expansionist but differed in scope and justification. Hitler aimed for Lebensraum (living space) to the east, based on racial grounds to secure territory for the Aryan race. On the other hand, Mussolini sought to recreate a Roman Empire, motivated by historical and national prestige.
- **The Role of the State** Nazism viewed the state as a means to an end to achieve racial purity and national greatness. Fascism promoted the state as supreme, with Mussolini famously stating, "Everything within the state, nothing outside the state, nothing against the state."
- **Economic Policies** While both regimes implemented policies to control the economy and suppress labour movements, Fascism was more openly corporatist, seeking collaboration between employers and workers mediated by the state. On the other hand, Nazism focused more on full employment and autarky, alongside extensive rearmament programmes.

8. (i) The Partition of Bengal took place in 1905.
Lord Curzon was the Viceroy of India during the above event.
The main motive of Curzon behind the Partition of Bengal was to apply Divide and rule policy among the Hindus and the Muslims.

(ii) People's reactions to the Partition of Bengal were

- On 16th October, 1905, the Partition of Bengal came into effect. The leaders of the protest movement declared it a 'Day of Mourning' throughout Bengal. It was also observed as a 'day of fasting'.
- The streets of Calcutta were full of the cries of Vande Mataram, which became the theme song of the National Movement.
- People showed their anger by boycotting foreign goods. They observed fasts and pledged support to the nationalists for forcing the government to cancel the partition.

(iii) In the year 1905, the Swadeshi and Boycott Movements started as a part of the agitation against the Partition of Bengal.

'Swadeshi' literally means 'one's own country'. The aim of the Swadeshi Movement was the promotion of indigenous industries for strengthening the nation. It was a weapon forged by the people to achieve industrial and economic regeneration.
'Boycott Movement' meant 'abstaining from the purchase of British goods'.

It includes the following conditions

- Boycott of English goods like clothes, salt and sugar, etc.
- Rejection of English speech.
- Rejection of government posts and seats in Legislative Council.
- Social boycott of people, who purchased foreign goods.

9. (i) The event seen in the given picture is Dandi March, also known as Salt March. This event started in 1930 and it led to the Mass Movement known as Civil Disobedience Movement. Two causes leading to this movement were

(a) Opposing the Simon Commission by the Indians as no Indian was included in the Commission that was coming to review the constitutional situation in India.

(b) Protesting the Salt Tax that was levied on salt by the British Government and to gain the right of making salt that was banned by British Government.

(ii) The event of Dandi March started when Gandhiji along with 78 followers, started his March from Sabarmati Ashram on 12th March, 1930 for Dandi, the coastal town of Gujarat. On 6th April, he reached Dandi and ceremonially violated the Salt Law, by manufacturing salt by boiling sea water. The March was over 240 miles. This marked the beginning of the Civil Disobedience Movement.

The Civil Disobedience Movement adopted following programmes

- Defiance or violation of Salt Laws.
- Non-payment of taxes and revenues.
- Boycott of foreign cloth and British goods of all kinds.
- Boycott of liquor.

(iii) The Civil Disobedience Movement had some significant consequences on India's freedom struggle. These were
- It created political consciousness and a deep sense of patriotism in the minds of the people.
- It brought women out of their homes and made them equal partners in the freedom struggle.
- It made the British Government to realise the need for constitutional reform. As a consequence the Government of India Act, 1935 was passed.

10. (i) The objectives of the United Nations are as follows
- To maintain international peace and security, to take collective measures for the prevention and removal of threats to peace, to suppress acts of aggression or other breaches of peace.
- To develop friendly relations among nations based on respect for the principle of equal rights and self-determination of people.
- To achieve international cooperation in solving international economic, social, cultural, or humanitarian problems and encouraging respect for human rights and for fundamental freedoms.

(ii) United Nations Educational, Scientific and Cultural Organisation (UNESCO) is an agency of the UN that is based in Paris. It undertakes various educational, scientific and cultural activities. They are
- It organises seminars and conferences of scientists of various countries and circulates information through journals, press and exhibition.
- It promotes research in the fields of Geology, Mathematics, Physics and Oceanography.
- It helps in correcting the imbalance in scientific and technological manpower that exists.
- It encourages the study of Social Science in order to focus attention on combating all forms or discrimination.

(iii) The main organ of the UN is General Assembly that is also known as Parliament of the United Nations. It respresents all nations of the world.
The functions of General Assembly are
- To discuss any question related to international peace and security.
- To receive reports from the Security Council and other organisations.
- To elect non-permanent members of the Security Council.
- To appoint Secretary General of the UN.

SQP Code : **PB-12/15** Series ***i*-Succeed 12-25/15** Roll No. | | | | | | | |

Sample Question Paper 12

History & Civics 10th (Code 50)

General Instructions

1. Attempt all questions from Part I (Compulsory).
2. A total of 5 questions are to be attempted from Part II, 2 out of 3 questions from Section A and 3 out of 5 questions from Section B.
3. The intended marks for questions or parts of questions are given in brackets ( ).

Time : 2 Hrs.

Max. Marks : 80

Part-I Attempt all questions from this part

Que 1.

Choose the correct option. (16)

(i) 'Under Article 226 of the Indian Constitution, High Courts have the power to issue certain writs. This article empowers High Courts to issue writs for the enforcement of Fundamental Rights as well as for any other purpose.'

Which amendment to the Indian Constitution introduced clause (1A) to Article 226, allowing High Courts to issue directions, orders, or writs to any Government. [Application] (1)

(a) 42nd Amendment (b) 44th Amendment

(c) 73rd Amendment (d) 15th Amendment

(ii) Given below are the few details.

Terms	Meanings
Habeas corpus	You shall have the body
Mandamus	We command
Prohibition	?
Certiorari	To be certified

Complete the above blank with the help of options given below. [Understanding] (1)

(a) Forbid (b) Allow

(c) Call upon (d) Advise

(iii) The given below image depicts the judiciary in India. Judiciary in India is independent and works on the principle of separation of power.

Which of the following provision ensures the independence of judiciary in India? [Application] (1)

(a) Appointment of judges by the members of judiciary itself
(b) Ban on practice after retirement
(c) Salaries and emoluments of judges cannot be altered to their disadvantages
(d) All of the above

(iv) The Parliament can legislate on .... subjects of State List. [Recall] (1)

(a) 31 (b) 41

(c) 51 (d) 61

(v) Which among the following is not a type of Revenue Court? [Recall] (1)

P. Board of Revenue
Q. Commissioner's Court
R. Court of Record
S. Appeals Court

(a) P and Q (b) P and R
(c) R and S (d) Q and S

(vi) Civil court : Civil cases : : Session court: .... cases [Recall] (1)

(a) Revenue (b) Divorce
(c) Corporate (d) Criminal

(vii) Read the two statements given below regarding NAM and select the option that shows the correct relationship between A and R. [Analyse] (1)

Assertion (A) India played an important role in NAM and world affairs during the Cold War.

Reason (R) It supported many countries in the efforts to attain Independence.

(a) R contradicts A
(b) R is the reason for A
(c) A is true, but R is false
(d) R and A are independent of each other

(viii) Read the two statements given below and select the option tht shows the correct relationship between A and R. [Analyse] (1)

Assertion (A) The Civil Disobedience Movement led by Mahatma Gandhi significantly weakened British colonial rule in India.

Reason (R) The movement mobilised a large section of the Indian population to defy British laws non-violently, causing widespread administrative disruptions and economic losses to the British regime.

(a) R contradicts A
(b) R is the reason for A
(c) A is true, but R is false
(d) R and A are independent of each other

(ix) Which of these statements are odd one out about the immediate objectives of the Indian National Congress? [Analyse] (1)

(a) To promote cordial relations between Congress and Muslim League.
(b) To get public opinions through discussions and debates.
(c) To consolidate a feeling of nationalism irrespective of caste, class or religious differences.
(d) To present popular demands before the government.

(x) The University shown in the image was established during which movement? [Recall] (1)

(a) Civil Disobedience Movement
(b) Non-Cooperation Movement
(c) Quit India Movement
(d) Swadeshi Movement

(xi) The Public Service Commission was appointed by the British in .... [Recall] (1)

(a) 1882 (b) 1883
(c) 1886 (d) 1889

(xii) Manish is doing a research on a reformer who established first girls school along with his wife. Whom is he referring to? [Application] (1)

(a) Jyotiba Phule
(b) Justice Ranade
(c) Raja Rammohan Roy
(d) Ishwar Chandra Vidyasagar

(xiii) Which of the following was not a reaction of the Government to the Quit India Movement? [Application] (1)

(a) Rebellious villages had to pay huge sums as fines.
(b) Prisoners were tortured, killed and arrested.
(c) Government supported the movement in some parts of India.
(d) Press was completely muzzled.

(xiv) Which of the following was a common ideology of the dictators? [Recall] (1)

(a) Faith in Totalitarian rule
(b) One Party One Leader
(c) Aggressive Nationalism and Imperialism
(d) All of the above

(xv) Identify the revolutionary from the given below image who played a vital role during the revolt of 1857. [Recall] (1)

(a) Nana Sahib (b) Mangal Pandey
(c) Tantya Tope (d) Kunwar Singh

(xvi) 'In the year 1942, the leader of a local community, inspired by the Quit India Movement, organised a gathering to decide on the best course of action to support the national call for an immediate end to British rule in India. The group discussed several methods to participate effectively in the movement while adhering to the principles set forth by Mahatma Gandhi'.
Based on the principles of the Quit India Movement, which of the following methods is the leader of the community not likely to approve? [Application] (1)
(a) Organising a peaceful demonstration in the town square.
(b) Sabotaging railway tracks used by the British to transport goods.
(c) Boycotting British-made products and promoting swadeshi goods.
(d) Sending a delegation to negotiate with local British administrators for more autonomy.

Que 2.

Read the extract given below and answer the questions which follows.

Headline : Acting Chief Justice inaugurates new buildings at Nagapattinam, Thanjavur Acting Chief Justice of Madras High Court, T Raja on Sunday inaugurated the District Munsif-cum-Judicial Magistrate Court at Thirukkuvalai and additional court buildings for additional Mahila Court, Fast Track Mahila Court, and Family Court in Nagapattinam.

(i) On the basis of above news discuss in brief about District Munsif Court. [Understanding] (2)
(ii) Mention any three relations of Prime Minister with the Parliament of India. [Recall] (2)
(iii) Why was the Rowlatt Act (1919) passed? [Recall] (2)
(iv) How did assertive nationalists expanded the base of the National Movement? [Recall] (2)
(v) Which agency of the UN looks after the interests of the children in the world? What was the original purpose of setting up this agency? [Recall & Understanding] (2)
(vi) Which UN principle emphasised the right of peoples to self-determination ? [Recall] (2)
(vii) State two reasons for US entry into the First World War. [Recall] (2)

SP-12

Part-II Section A (Civics) Attempt any two questions from this section

Que 3.

The Parliament of India is a House where Ministers discuss public matters and orders. In this regard answer the following questions.

(i) How does the Constitution of India deal with the allocation of seats in the Rajya Sabha? [Recall] (3)
(ii) Mention three powers which are common to both houses of the Parliament? [Recall] (3)
(iii) Under what conditions a person cannot be chosen as a Member of Parliament? [Analyse] (4)

Que 4.

With reference to the functions of the Union Council of Ministers headed by Prime Minister, answer the following questions.

(i) Mention three important functions of the Prime Minister as the head of the Union Council of Ministers. [Recall] (3)

(ii) How Prime Minister acts as a link between the Cabinet and the President? [Recall] (3)

(iii) How is the Prime Minister of India appointed? [Recall] (4)

Que 5.

The Supreme Court is the Apex Court in the entire judicial set-up in India. In this context, answer the following questions.

(i) India has adopted the single-integrated Judicial system. Why? [Analyse] (3)

(ii) How does the Supreme Court resolve dispute through Judicial Review? [Recall] (3)

(iii) In the extensive jurisdiction of the Supreme Court, state the difference between the Original Jurisdiction and the Appellate Jurisdiction. Mention two functions that come under Original Jurisdiction. [Recall] (2+2)

Section B (History) Attempt any three questions from this section

Que 6.

The First War of Independence of 1857 was a culmination of people's dissatisfaction with the British rule. In this context, enumerate the following.

(i) Annexation of Oudh [Recall] (3)

(ii) Activities of Missionaries [Recall] (3)

(iii) Indigo Cultivators [Recall] (4)

Que 7.

The aim of the United Nations Organisation is not only to save the succeeding generations from scourge of another war, but to promote social progress. With reference to this, answer the following questions.

(i) Working of ILO towards social welfare. [Recall] (3)

(ii) Important functions of the UNESCO. [Recall] (3)

(iii) Role of the Security Council in maintaining world peace. [Recall] (4)

Que 8.

'The first or early phase of Indian Nationalism is also termed as Moderate Phase (1885-1905). Moderate leaders were W.C Banerjee, Gopal Krishna Gokhale, R.C Dutt, Ferozeshah Mehta, George Yule, etc. Moderates have full faith in British Government and adopted the PPP path i.e. Protest, Prayer, and Petition'. With reference to the First Phase of the Indian National Movement, answer the following questions.

(i) What were the primary objectives of the Early Nationalists in the Indian National Movement? [Recall] (3)

(ii) Describe any three methods of struggle used by the Early Nationalists in their fight against British colonial rule. [Recall] (3)

(iii) Outline the contributions of Dadabhai Naoroji, Surendranath Banerjee and Gopal Krishna Gokhale in the early phase of the Indian National Movement. [Analyse] (4)

Que 9.

Look at the picture given below carefully and answer the following questions.

(i) (a) Identify the event in the above picture. Name the Indian leader whom you can recognise. [Recall]

(b) State any two provisions of the Gandhi-Irwin Pact signed before this event. [Recall] (1+2)

(ii) What was the reason behind the failure of the conference? [Recall] (3)

(iii) Explain the main features of the National Movement which started after the failure of this conference. [Recall] (4)

Que 10.

With reference to rise of Hitler and coming of Nazism in Germany, answer the following questions.

(i) Explain the Hitler's influence among the people. [Recall] (3)

(ii) How did Hitler establish a totalitarian state in Germany? [Analyse] (3)

(iii) (a) Mention the background of Germany before the establishment of Nazism. [Recall]

(b) What were the impacts of economic crises on Germany after the First World War? [Recall] (2+2)

Answers

1.

(i) (d)	(ii) (a)	(iii) (d)	(iv) (d)
(v) (a)	(vi) (d)	(vii) (b)	(viii) (b)
(ix) (a)	(x) (b)	(xi) (c)	(xii) (a)
(xiii) (c)	(xiv) (d)	(xv) (b)	(xvi) (b)

Scan this QR code from your mobile phone to get the explanations of this paper.

SQP Code : **PB-13/15**

Series ***i*-Succeed 13-25/15**

Roll No. | | | | | | | | |

Sample Question Paper 13

History & Civics 10th (Code 50)

General Instructions

1. Attempt all questions from Part I (Compulsory).
2. A total of 5 questions are to be attempted from Part II, 2 out of 3 questions from Section A and 3 out of 5 questions from Section B.
3. The intended marks for questions or parts of questions are given in brackets ( ).

Time : 2 Hrs.

Max. Marks : 80

Part-I Attempt all questions from this part

Que 1.

Choose the correct option. [Application] (16)

(i) 'In the 75th year of supreme court establishment, the Supreme Court of India is organising a Special Lok Adalat from 29th July, 2024 to 3rd August, 2024 to facilitate amicable settlements of suitable pending cases. The statement said organising the Lok Adalat was pursuant to the commitment to accessible and efficient justice delivery for all sections of the society.'

Source : The Hindu

What is not an advantages of Lok Adalats as a justice delivery system? (1)

(a) Quick Justice delivery
(b) Cost-effective
(c) Complicated
(d) Efficient

(ii) Consider the following details. [Understanding]

Judicial Jurisdiction	Supreme Court Jurisdiction
Original Jurisdiction	Centre-State Disputes
Appellate Jurisdiction	Constitutional Cases
Revisory Jurisdiction	Review Own Judgement
Writ Jurisdiction	?

Fill the above blank with the help of options given below. [Understanding] (1)

(a) Habeas Corpus (b) Advise to President
(c) Disputes Between States (d) Court of Record

(iii) President wants to impose President's rule in State X. What is the other name of President's rule? [Understanding] (1)

(a) National Emergency (b) State Emergency
(c) Financial Emergency (d) Armed Conflict

(iv) Which aspect of judiciary is being depicted in the image through the scale? [Understanding] (1)

(a) Fairness and impartiality
(b) Judicial activism
(c) Corruption in the judiciary
(d) Judicial accountability

(v) Identify the Articles that were not suspended during the National Emergency. [Recall] (1)

P. 20 Q. 21 R. 15 S. 25

(a) P and Q (b) P and R

(c) R and S (d) Q and S

(vi) President: Supreme Commander of the Armed Forces :: Vice-President: .... [Recall] (1)

(a) Commander of National Police

(b) Commander of State Militias

(c) Chairman of the Rajya Sabha

(d) Head of Disaster Management

(vii) Read the following statements given below regarding Revolt of 1857 and select the correct relationship between A and R. [Analyse] (1)

Assertion (A) The sepoys of Meerut were joined by the local soldiers of Delhi.

Reason (R) They killed many British officers and declared Bahadur Shah Zafar as the leader of the revolt.

(a) R contradicts A

(b) R is the reason for A

(c) A is true, but R is false

(d) A and R are independent of each other

(viii) There was a growth of nationalism in country A similar to that in India. Which of the following were the causes of growth of Nationalism in India? [Understanding] (1)

(a) No welfare of peasants

(b) Changes in land law

(c) Heavy duties on export

(d) All of the above

(ix) Read the statements given below and select the option that shows the correct relationship between A and R. [Analyse] (1)

Assertion (A) The socio-religious reform movements in the 19th and early 20th centuries significantly contributed to the awakening of national consciousness in India.

Reason (R) Reformers like Raja Rammohan Roy and Jyotiba Phule challenged traditional social structures and promoted ideas of equality and justice, which laid the groundwork for broader socio-political changes in Indian society.

(a) R contradicts A

(b) R is the reason for A

(c) A is true, but R is false

(d) A and R are independent of each other

(x) The personality shown below founded the Satyashodhak Samaj. Identify the personality. [Recall] (1)

(a) Raja Rammohan Roy

(b) Jyotiba Phule

(c) Dayananda Saraswati

(d) Lokmanya Tilak

(xi) .... was the last Viceroy of India. [Recall] (1)

(a) Lord Wavell

(b) Lord Patrick Lawrence

(c) Lord Curzon

(d) Lord Mountbatten

(xii) Isha is studying about a personality who established Arya Samaj. Who is she referring to? [Application] (1)

(a) Dayananda Saraswati

(b) Jyotiba Phule

(c) Justice Ranade

(d) Pandita Ramabai

(xiii) Which of the following is/are not an impact of Fascism? [Analyse] (1)

(a) Catholic religion was made the state religion.

(b) Italy followed an aggressive Foreign policy.

(c) It emphasises on Freedom of Press.

(d) All political parties lost their existence except Mussolini's Party.

(xiv) The given below famous image depicts the time when the Gandhi-Irwin pact was signed. With reference to the image, In which of the following year was the Gandhi-Irwin pact signed? [Recall] (1)

(a) 1930 (b) 1928
(c) 1942 (d) 1931

(xv) Regular session of the General Assembly begins each year on third Tuesday in .... and continues till third week of December. [Recall] (1)
(a) August
(b) September
(c) October
(d) November

(xvi) Identify the UN specialised agency that was also awarded the Noble Prize for Peace in 1965. [Recall] (1)
(a) WHO
(b) UNESCO
(c) UNICEF
(d) ILO

Que 2.

Read the extract given below and answer the questions which follows.

Headline : 4% of Supreme Court Judges of All Time are Women.

In 73 Years of the Indian Supreme Court, there have been 268 Judges. Of these, only 11 Judges have been women. So far, the SC has not had a woman Chief Justice. If the principle of appointing the senior most judge as the CJI is followed, Justice BV Nagarathna will be India's first woman Chief Justice. However, her tenure as CJI will be 36 days.

Source: Supreme Court Observer.

(i) On the basis of above news, write the qualifications required for the post of judge of Supreme Court. [Understanding](2)

(ii) Following are the terms related to parliamentary procedures. Explain the following terms in short [Recall] (1+1)
(a) Question Hour (b) Quorum

(iii) How did Dalhousie's policy become a political cause for the Revolt of 1857? [Recall] (2)

(iv) Mention two developments that paved the way for the approval of Mountbatten Plan. [Recall] (2)

(v) Enumerate role of press in fostering national unity. [Recall] (2)

(vi) Which countries remained neutral during Second World War? [Recall] (2)

(vii) How was Fascist regime established in Italy? [Recall] (2)

Part-II Section A (Civics) Attempt any two questions from this section

Que 3.

With reference to the powers and functions of the Speaker of the Lok Sabha, discuss the following points.

(i) Special power enjoyed by Speaker of the lower house. [Recall] (3)

(ii) Grounds on which Speaker decides his seat to be vacant. [Recall] (3)

(iii) Election and tenure of the Speaker. [Recall] (4)

Que 4.

In addition to normal powers, the President has extraordinary emergency powers. In this context, explain the following.

(i) Financial emergency (Article 360). [Recall] (3)

(ii) Presentation of national emergency. [Recall] (3)

(iii) President's rule and its two effects. [Recall] (2+2)

Que 5

The High Courts in the states are just below the Supreme Court and keeps subordinate power on the lower court to it. In this context, answer the following questions.

(i) When can the President appoint an acting Chief Justice of the High Court? [Recall] (3)

(ii) How does a High Court control over the Subordinate Courts? [Recall] (3)

(iii) Name two types of cases in which the High Court exercises Original Jurisdiction. [Recall] (4)

Section B (History) Attempt any three questions from this section

Que 6.

The early Congressmen were liberal in their views and programmes. This led to the Rise of Radical Nationalists who demanded more forceful action against the British. In this context, discuss the following questions.

(i) Reasons why the early Congressmen were called 'Moderates'. [Recall] (3)

(ii) How did the Moderates differ from the Assertive Nationalists in realising their objectives? [Analyse] (3)

(iii) How did Tilak bring a new wave in Indian politics that was distinct from the early Congressmen? [Recall] (4)

Que 7.

It the context of Non-Cooperation Movement, answer the following questions

(i) What techniques were used in Non-Cooperation Movement? [Recall] (3)

(ii) How was the movement different from the earlier movements? [Recall] (3)

(iii) Why Khilafat movement got associated with Non-Cooperation Movement? What were their demands? [Recall] (2+2)

Que 8.

Read the excerpt given below and answer the questions that follow.

These nationalists were Rajnarain Bose, Ashwini Kumar Dutta and Vishnu Shastri Chiplunkar. The other assertive nationalists were Bal Gangadhar Tilak, Aurobindo Ghosh, Bipin Chandra Pal and Lala Lajpat Rai. They wanted nothing less than complete independence and were ready to follow any means to achieve the same.

Source : Times of India

(i) What was the aim of Early Nationalists? What were the methods of Early Nationalists? What were the causes of rise of assertive nationalism? [Analyse & Recall] (1+1+1)

(ii) What was the criticism about the Early Nationalists? [Recall] (3)

(iii) What are the four basic beliefs of the Early Nationalists? [Recall] (4)

Que 9.

Look at the picture given below carefully and answer the following questions.

(i) Identify the leader and provide a brief idea about him. [Recall] (3)

(ii) State any three features of Nazism. [Recall] (3)

(iii) Give reason why did he invade Poland? [Recall] (4)

Que 10.

United Nations was set-up to give peace a chance in solving world's disputes. In context of this statement, answer the following questions.

(i) How the Security Council of UN maintain international peace and security? [Recall] (3)

(ii) Explain the role of World Health Organisation in combating diseases. [Recall] (3)

(iii) Discuss the role of International Court of Justice. How it plays an important role in codification of international laws? [Analyse & Recall] (2+2)

Answers

1. (i) (b)	(ii) (a)	(iii) (b)	(iv) (b)
(v) (b)	(vi) (c)	(vii) (b)	(viii) (d)
(ix) (b)	(x) (b)	(xi) (d)	(xii) (a)
(xiii) (c)	(xiv) (d)	(xv) (b)	(xvi) (c)

Scan this QR code from your mobile phone to get the explanations of this paper.

SQP Code : **PB-14/15** Series *i*-**Succeed 14-25/15** Roll No. | | | | | | | | |

Sample Question Paper 14

History & Civics 10th (Code 50)

General Instructions

1. Attempt all questions from Part I (Compulsory).
2. A total of 5 questions are to be attempted from Part II, 2 out of 3 questions from Section A and 3 out of 5 questions from Section B.
3. The intended marks for questions or parts of questions are given in brackets ( ).

Time : 2 Hrs.

Max. Marks : 80

Part-I Attempt all questions from this part

Que 1.

Choose the correct option. (16)

(i) The Supreme Court of India serves as the apex judicial body in the country and has the ultimate authority on interpreting the Constitution. It exercises a range of powers, including appellate, original and advisory jurisdictions.
What is a key feature of the judgements made by the Supreme Court? [Application] (1)

(a) They are preliminary and need ratification by the Parliament.
(b) They are binding on all lower courts across the country.
(c) They require confirmation by the President of India.
(d) They can be appealed to the International Court of Justice.

(ii) Consider the following details. [Understanding] (1)

Responsibility	Roles
Leader of Lok Sabha	Prime Minister
President	De Jure
Salaries and allowances of Ministers	?
Appointment of Prime Minister	President

Fill in the above blank with the help of correct options given below.

(a) Parliament
(b) Prime Minister
(c) President
(d) Lok Sabha

(iii) Which of the following statements best describes the jurisdiction of the Supreme Court of India? [Understanding] (1)

(a) The Supreme Court only has appellate jurisdiction, dealing with appeals from lower courts.
(b) The Supreme Court Cannot issue Writs.
(c) The Supreme Court's jurisdiction includes original, appellate and advisory roles.
(d) The Supreme Court can only hear cases that are referred to it by the President of India.

(iv) .... prior permission is required to introduce certain types of bills in the Parliament. [Recall] (1)

(a) Prime Minister
(b) President
(c) Speaker
(d) Council of Ministers

(v) Which of the following are the Judicial powers of the President? [Recall] (1)

P. Appointment of Chief Justice

Q. Issuing of writs

R. Pardon the punishment

S. Changing the seat of Supreme Court

(a) P and Q (b) P and R

(c) R and S (d) Q and S

(vi) Read the two statements given below and select the option that shows the correct relationship between A and R. [Analyse] (1)

Assertion (A) The Supreme Court of India has the power to strike down laws passed by the Parliament if they are found to be unconstitutional.

Reason (R) The Supreme Court's authority to conduct judicial review enables it to ensure that all laws adhere to the principles laid out in the Constitution of India.

(a) R contradicts A

(b) R is the reason for A

(c) A is true, but R is false

(d) A and R are independent of each other

(vii) Read the two statements given below regarding World War I and select the option that shows the correct relationship between A and R. [Analyse] (1)

Assertion (A) Damages caused by World War I and the total impact of the war was till now unprecedented in history.

Reason (R) War was fought by several nations and affected almost all countries and was extensively spread.

(a) R contradicts A

(b) R is the reason for A

(c) A is true, but R is false

(d) A and R are independent of each other

(viii) What was the primary reason Mahatma Gandhi suspended the Non-Cooperation Movement in 1922? [Recall] (1)

(a) The successful negotiation of the Gandhi-Irwin Pact.

(b) The British government's agreement to grant India full independence

(c) The violent incident at Chauri Chaur.a where protesters killed 22 policemen.

(d) The resolution of the Khilafat issue which was one of the driving causes of the movement.

(ix) Identify the given below personality who recorganised the Hindustan Public Association. [Recall] (1)

(a) Gopal Krishna Gokhale

(b) Feroz Shah Mehta

(c) Chandra Shekhar Azad

(d) Bhagat Singh

(x) Identify the event that does not directly involve Mahatma Gandhi's leadership. [Recall] (1)

(a) Dandi March

(b) Quit India Movement

(c) Simon Commission Protests

(d) Civil Disobedience Movement

(xi) Japan withdrew from League of Nations in the year .... [Recall] (1)

(a) 1931

(b) 1933

(c) 1934

(d) 1935

(xii) Santosh is studying about the policies of British. Their most famous policies of Divide and Rule was introduced during whose tenure? [Application] (1)

(a) Lord Mayo

(b) Lord Linlithgow

(c) Lord Curzon

(d) Lord Dalhousie

(xiii) Gandhi-Irwin Pact : March 1931 :: Second Round Table Conference : .... [Recall] (1)

(a) September to December, 1931

(b) September to January, 1932

(c) September to October, 1931

(d) September to November, 1931

(xiv) What was the main principle for which the Second World War was fought? [Understanding] (1)

(a) Protecting the national interests
(b) Maintaining military alliances
(c) To make the world safe for democracy
(d) Removal of aggressive policies

(xv) Which organisation is represented by the blue silhouette in the given below image? [Recall] (1)

(a) WHO (b) ILO
(c) UNIDO (d) UNICEF

(xvi) Identify the aspects promoted by NAM countries. [Recall] (1)

(a) Opposed colonialism, imperialism and racial discrimination.
(b) Support sovereign equality of all states.
(c) Followed an aggressive Foreign Policy.
(d) Both (a) and (b)

Que 2.

Read the extract given below and answer the questions which follows.

Headline : Union Finance Minister Nirmala Sitharaman presented the Union Budget 2023-24 in the Parliment Hon'ble Speaker, I present the budget for 2023-24. This is the first budget in Amrit Kaal.

This budget hopes to build on the foundation laid in the previous budget, and the blueprint drawn for India@100.

(i) With reference to above news, discuss the financial powers of Parliament. [Understanding] (2)
(ii) How is the authority of the Prime Minister kept under check? [Recall] (2)
(iii) What is meant by the British policy of expansion? [Recall] (2)
(iv) What changes the British government made in Indian Civil Services and why? [Recall] (2)
(v) Who founded Home Rule League in India? What was its objective? [Recall] (2)
(vi) What are the two important ideals of the Brahmo Samaj? [Recall] (2)
(vii) What is meant by Misery belt? Why its called so? [Recall] (2)

Part-II Section A (Civics) Attempt any two questions from this section

Que 3.

Each House of the Parliament has its own presiding officer. With regard to this, answer the following questions.

(i) Mention any three provisions that the Speaker can make to discipline the Lok Sabha proceedings? [Recall] (3)
(ii) What do you understand by Speaker Pro-tem? How does he avail his power and duty? [Understanding] (1+2)
(iii) Who is the Chairman of Rajya Sabha? Mention his powers and functions as the presiding officer of Rajya Sabha. [Application & Recall] (1+3)

Que 4.

The Council of Ministers headed by the Prime Minister is the real executive authority in our politico-administrative system.

In this regard answer the following questions.

(i) Under the Article 75 of the Constitution, mention the responsibilities of the Council of Ministers. [Recall] (3)
(ii) Under Article 78 of the Constitution what are the duties of the Prime Minister? [Recall] (3)
(iii) Before entering upon his office, a minister administers oath by whom? What are the oath of office he swear? [Recall] (1+3)

Que 5.

The country's judicial system has a Supreme Court at its apex. In this context, discuss the following points.

(i) Under what circumstances does the Supreme Court grant a special leave for appeal? [Recall] (3)

(ii) Where is the seat of Supreme Court? Under what condition the seat of the Supreme Court was established? [Recall] (1+2)

(iii) Explain the appellate jurisdiction of Supreme Court over civil and criminal matters. [Recall] (2+2)

Section B (History) Attempt any three questions from this section

Que 6.

From 1905-1916, the independence movement was lead by the assertive nationalists and several important pacts like Lucknow Pact were signed between the moderates and extremists. In this context, answer the following questions.

(i) What was the significance of Lucknow Pact? [Recall] (1+2)

(ii) Discuss the contributions of Bal Gangadhar Tilak and Lala Lajpat Rai to the Indian independence movement. [Recall] (1+2)

(iii) Analyse the factors leading to the formation of the Muslim League and its objectives. [Analyse] (4)

Que 7.

The Civil Disobedience Movement has a historical importance in India's National Movement. In this context, write briefly on the following points.

(i) The incidents leading to the Civil Disobedience Movement. [Recall] (3)

(ii) Conference attended by Gandhi in 1931. [Recall] (3)

(iii) The Gandhi-Irwin Pact. [Recall] (4)

Que 8.

Read the excerpt given below and answer the questions that follows.

Today is 20th May, a day to remember Bipin Chandra Pal. On this day, the greatest freedom fighters and visionary leaders of India left the world for his heavenly abode. Born on 7th November, 1858 in Sylhet (now in Bangladesh), Bipin Chandra Pal emerged a prominent leader during the early years of the Indian Independence Movement. Along with his contemporaries Bal Gangadhar Tilak and Lala Lajpat Rai, he formed the triumvirate of the extremist leaders known as the "Lal-Bal-Pal" trio. These three leaders played a pivotal role in shaping the radical phase of the freedom struggle.

(i) What is the other popular name of Bipin Chandra Pal. Which newspaper was started by him? Name any two newspapers in which his writings were published. [Recall] (1+1+1)

(ii) Give any three contributions of this personality. [Recall] (3)

(iii) State any four methods that he advocated for the achievement of their aims. [Recall] (4)

Que 9.

Study the picture given below and answer the questions that follow.

(i) Identify the leader in the picture. What was his policy against the jews? [Recall] (1+2)

(ii) Why did he invade Poland and how it became an immediate cause of Second World War? [Recall] (3)

(iii) State any two factors of each that led to the rise of dictatorship in Germany and Italy respectively. [Recall] (2+2)

Que 10.

The UNO was established to prevent war and maintain world peace and secure political, social and economic conditions of the world. In this regard, explain the following points.

(i) Milestones in the formation of the UNO. [Recall] (3)

(ii) Agency setup to deliver relief to children and mothers after Second World War and its two functions. [Recall] (3)

(iii) Difference between the ICJ's voluntary and compulsory jurisdiction. [Recall] (4)

Answers

1.

(i) (b)	(ii) (a)	(iii) (c)	(iv) (b)
(v) (b)	(vi) (a)	(vii) (d)	(viii) (c)
(ix) (c)	(x) (c)	(xi) (b)	(xii) (a)
(xiii) (a)	(xiv) (c)	(xv) (d)	(xvi) (d)

Scan this QR code from your mobile phone to get the explanations of this paper.

SQP Code : **PB-15/15**	Series *i*-**Succeed 15-25/15**	Roll No.

Sample Question Paper 15

History & Civics 10th (Code 50)

General Instructions

1. Attempt all questions from Part I (Compulsory).
2. A total of 5 questions are to be attempted from Part II, 2 out of 3 questions from Section A and 3 out of 5 questions from Section B.
3. The intended marks for questions or parts of questions are given in brackets ( ).

Time : 2 Hrs.

Max. Marks : 80

Part-I Attempt all questions from this part

Que 1.

Choose the correct option. [16]

(i) 'The appellate jurisdiction of the Supreme Court of India is one of its primary functions. This jurisdiction ensures that there is a uniform interpretation of law across the country.'

What is the role of the Supreme Court's appellate jurisdiction? [Application] (1)

(a) To initiate and try cases as the first court of record

(b) To hear appeals from decisions of lower courts

(c) To advise the President on legal matters

(d) To enforce laws directly in the states

(ii) Consider the following details. [Understanding] (1)

Financial power	Demand for grants
Legislative power	Making laws
Executive power	No-confidence Motion
Judicial power	?

Complete the above blank with the help of options given below.

(a) Impeachment of President

(b) Appointment of Judges

(c) Creation of new High Court

(d) Salaries of Judges

(iii) The below image depicts the Prime Minister with the Council of Ministers. The Prime Minister as the head of the Council of Ministers aids and advises the President. Which Article corresponds best to the above given fact? [Understanding] (1)

(a) 72 (b) 75

(c) 74 (d) 80

(iv) There are .... different categories of ministers in the Union Council of Ministers. [Recall] (1)

(a) four (b) three

(c) five (d) six

(v) Identify the military functions of the President of India. [Recall] (1)

P. Supreme Commander of Armed Forces

Q. Appointment of Chiefs of Army, Navy and Air force

R. Setting up new Army bases

S. Presenting Army budget

(a) P and Q (b) Q and R

(c) R and S (d) P and S

(vi) Read the two statements given below and select the option that shows the correct relationship between A and R.

Assertion (A) The Parliament of India is bicameral, consisting of two houses: the Rajya Sabha and the Lok Sabha.

Reason (R) This bicameral structure allows for more detailed scrutiny of legislation, with each house bringing different perspectives, particularly the Rajya Sabha representing the states. [Analyse] (1)

(a) R contradicts A

(b) R is the reason for A

(c) A is true, but R is false

(d) A and R are independent of each other

(vii) Read the two statements given below regarding Assertive Nationalism and select the option that shows the correct relationship between A and R.

Assertion (A) The partition of Bengal provided a congenial environment for the growth of Assertive Nationalism.

Reason (R) The main aim of the Assertive Nationalists was the attainment of Swarajya or complete independence and not just dominion status in India. [Analyse] (1)

(a) R contradicts A

(b) R is the reason for A

(c) A is true, but R is false

(d) A and R are independent of each other

(viii) Abolition of Sati: 1829 :: Legislation of Widow Remarriage: .... [Recall] (1)

(a) 1851 (b) 1852

(c) 1856 (d) 1857

(ix) Which of the following is not a similarity between the ideologies of Fascism and Nazism? [Analyse] (1)

(a) Both had faith in totalitarian rule.

(b) Both believed in aggressive nationalism and imperialism.

(c) Both believed in racial supremacy.

(d) Both were against democratic political systems.

(x) The personality shown below founded the servants of India Society. Identify the personality. [Recall] (1)

(a) Justice Ranade

(b) Gopal Krishna Gokhale

(c) Ishwarchandra Vidyasagar

(d) Lokmanya Tilak

(xi) The title of Hitler's book, Mein Kampf, in English means .... [Recall] (1)

(a) Well Being

(b) My Country

(c) My Struggle

(d) My Life

(xii) Meera is studying about a personality who founded Brahmo Samaj. Whom is she referring to? [Application] (1)

(a) Raja Rammohan Roy

(b) Dayanand Saraswati

(c) Atmaram Pandurang

(d) Jyotiba Phule

(xiii) Which of the following statement is odd one out about International Court of Justice? [Analyse] (1)

(a) The court plays a significant role in the codification of International law.

(b) The court elects its President and Vice-President for 5 years of time.

(c) The court consists of 15 judges.

(d) The Justice is the principal organ of the UN.

(xiv) Which feature characterises the movement represented by the logo shown below? [Understanding] (1)

(a) It remained against military alliances like NATO, SEATO and Warsaw Pact.
(b) It stands for passivism.
(c) It actively participates in the politics among nations.
(d) Both (a) and (c)

(xv) The Terms of Treaty of Versailles were mainly decided by the President of USA and Prime Ministers of France and .... [Recall] (1)

(a) Great Britain
(b) Austria
(c) Greece
(d) Switzerland

(xvi) Identify the National Movement Leader who formed the Natal Indian Congress (NIC) and suffered imprisonment. [Recall] (1)

(a) Subhash Chandra Bose
(b) Lala Lajpat Rai
(c) Mahatma Gandhi
(d) Abdul Kalam Azad

Que 2.

Read the extract given below and answer the question which follows.

Headline : Karnataka High Court's Twitter verdict sparks debate on free speech.

In July 2022, Twitter took the Indian Government to court over its orders to block certain accounts and tweets. Several free speech experts hailed it as a significant lawsuit.

It was the first instance of a social media company suing the government over its content takedown orders, often criticised for being arbitrary and opaque.

Source: Times of India, August 2022

(i) On the basis of the above news discuss the original jurisdiction of High Courts. [Understanding] (2)

(ii) Following are some terms related to parliamentary functions. Explain the following terms. [Recall] (2)
(a) Prorogation (b) Adjournment

(iii) Write any two social reforms advocated by the British which affected the religious traditions of Indian people. [Recall] (2)

(iv) The Mountbatten Plan had passed which two proposals for Princely States? [Recall] (2)

(v) Mention two proposals of the Wavell Plan. Why was it rejected? [Recall] (2)

(vi) Explain the capitalist and the communist bloc formed after the Second World War. [Recall] (2)

(vii) How the United Nations finances its welfare projects? [Recall] (2)

Part-II Section A (Civics) Attempt any two questions from this section

Que 3.

With reference to the Parliament of India i.e. the supreme organ to legislate, answer the following.

(i) Methods to exercise control over executives. [Recall] (4)

(ii) Electoral functions [Recall] (3)

(iii) Difference between Presidential and Parliamentary system. [Recall] (3)

Que 4.

The Executive of the government consists of President, Vice-President and Council of Ministers headed by Prime Minister. With reference to this answer the following questions.

(i) Why is the President of India referred to as rubber stamp in the Union Executive? [Recall] (3)

(ii) Write any three co-ordinating functions of the Cabinet. [Recall] (3)

(iii) Mention any four ways in which the Constitution ensure the pre-eminent position of the Prime Minister in relation to the Union Council of Ministers. [Recall] (4)

Que 5.

The High Court is the Apex of the Judiciary in the state. In this context, answer the following questions.

(i) State the composition of the High Court. State the qualifications required to become a High Court Judge. [Recall] (2+2)

(ii) How Legislative and Executive organs of the government are checked by High Court? [Recall] (3)

(iii) Mention the administrative control of High Court over the Subordinate Courts. [Recall] (3)

Section B (History) Attempt any three questions from this section

Que 6.

With reference to rise of Nationalism, explain each of the following points.

(i) Aims of the Indian Association of Calcutta. [Recall] (3)

(ii) Contributions of Sir Syed Ahmad Khan. [Recall] (3)

(iii) Gradual changes in the objective of Congress. [Recall] (4)

Que 7.

In the aftermath of World War II, the United Nations was established to foster international cooperation and prevent future conflicts. In this context, answer the following questions.

(i) What are the primary objectives of the United Nations? Why was it formed? [Recall] (1+2)

(ii) Which countries are permanent members of the Security Council and why do they hold this status? [Recall] (1+2)

(iii) Discuss the role and functions of the International Court of Justice briefly. [Application] (4)

Que 8.

Read the excerpt given below and answer the questions that follows.

The 158th birth anniversary of the freedom fighter Lala Lajpat Rai, was celebrated with full honour at his birthplace Dhudike village of Moga, Saturday. Rai was born at the house of his maternal grandparents in Dhudike on 28th January, 1865. Punjab Cabinet Minister Aman Arora accompanied by MLA Nihal Singh Wala Manjit Singh, Bilaspur and MLA Dharamkot Devinderjit Singh Laddi Dhose paid rich tributes to Rai at his memorial established at Dhudike village.

(i) What was the above personality was popularly known as? Which newspapers were started by above personality? Name any three works of the above personality. [Recall] (1+1+1)

(ii) Mention any three contributions of above personality. [Recall] (3)

(iii) Identify the methods of struggle adopted by the moderates and the radicals. [Recall] (4)

Que 9.

Look the picture carefully and answer the following questions.

(i) Identify the event in the above picture. Name the important people seen in the above picture. Mention the year when the event took place. [Recall & Understanding] (3)

(ii) List the main clauses of the Indian Independence Act. [Recall] (3)

(iii) Explain the consequence of the Mountbatten plan on India. [Recall] (4)

Que 10.

United Nations works for the world peace as well as for cultural and economic development. With reference to this statement, answer the following questions.

(i) State any three objectives of the United Nations. [Recall] (3)

(ii) When and where was the United Nations formed? State any three principles of United Nations. [Recall] (3)

(iii) (a) Define the Veto Power of the Security Council?

(b) Discuss briefly about the powers and functions of the United Nations General Assembly.

[Recall & Application] (4)

Answers

1. (i) (b)	(ii) (a)	(iii) (c)	(iv) (b)
(v) (a)	(vi) (a)	(vii) (d)	(viii) (c)
(ix) (c)	(x) (a)	(xi) (c)	(xii) (a)
(xiii) (b)	(xiv) (d)	(xv) (a)	(xvi) (c)

Scan this QR code from your mobile phone to get the explanations of this paper.

Knowledge Booster Zone

Welcome to the Knowledge Booster Zone !

This section is dedicated to enhancing your understanding of key concepts. Here, you will find chapter-wise revision notes designed to solidify your **foundational knowledge**. Use these notes to review and reinforce what you've learned, ensuring you're well-prepared for each topic.

Progress Tracker Tick the chapters as you revise them.

- ☐ The Union Legislature
- ☐ The Union Executive : The President and Vice-President
- ☐ The Prime Minister and Council of Ministers
- ☐ The Supreme Court
- ☐ The High Courts and Subordinate Courts
- ☐ The First War of Independence-1857
- ☐ The Rise of Nationalism and the Indian National Congress
- ☐ First Phase of the Indian National Movement
- ☐ Second Phase of the Indian National Movement
- ☐ The Muslim League and Lucknow Pact
- ☐ National Movement and Mahatma Gandhi
- ☐ Forward Bloc and Indian National Army
- ☐ Independence and Partition of India
- ☐ The First World War
- ☐ Rise of Dictatorship : Fascism and Nazism
- ☐ The Second World War
- ☐ The United Nations and its Major Agencies
- ☐ The Non-Aligned Movement

CIVICS

Chapter 1 The Union Legislature

- The legislature is the law-making body of a political unit.
- In Indian democratic political system, the union legislature is called Parliament which consists of three bodies i.e. the President, the Council of States which is also called **Rajya Sabha** (Upper House) and the House of the people that is also called **Lok Sabha** (Lower house).
- The former represents the States and Union Territories of India while the later represents the people of India as a whole.

Federal Set-up in India

- In a federal system of Government, there is an association of states, in which all the administrative powers are divided between the Central and the State Governments by the Constitution.
- India has opted for a federal system of government.

Federal Features of the Constitution of India

The federal features of the Constitution of India are as follows

- **Dual Government** The Constitution establishes a Federal System, i.e. Union at the Centre and the States at the periphery.
- **Division of Powers** The Constitution divided the powers between the Centre and States in terms of lists, i.e. Union List, State List and Concurrent List in the 7th Schedule.
- **Independent Judiciary** There should be an independent judiciary headed by Supreme Court, for the purpose of protecting the supremacy of the Constitution and to settle down the disputes between the Centre and the States.
- **Bicameralism** The Constitution of India provides for a bicameral legislature, to protect the interest of the states against the undue interference of the Centre.

Lok Sabha

- The Lok Sabha is called the House of the People.
- It is the lower house of the Parliament.
- Its members are directly elected by the people of India.

Term

- The normal duration of the Lok Sabha is 5 years, but it may be dissolved earlier by the President.
- The normal duration may be extended for 1 year at a time by an act passed by the Parliament during a period of Emergency.
- The new Lok Sabha must be elected within 6 months once the emergency has ceased to operate.

Composition

- The total strength of Lok Sabha is 552. Out of this, 530 members are elected by the people from different states, while 20 members are from the Union territories and 2 members are nominated by the President for the seats reserved for Anglo-Indians from Anglo-Indian community. In January 2020, the Anglo-Indian reserved seats in the Parliament and State Legislatures of India were abolished by the 104th Constitutional Amendment Act, 2019.
- At present, the Lok Sabha consists of 545 members, 530 are from States, 13 are from Union Territories and two are nominated by the President of India.

Qualifications for Membership

- The candidate must be a citizen of India.
- The candidate must have attained the age of 25 years.
- The candidate must have his/her name in the electoral rolls in any part of the country.

Parliamentary Procedures

There are some parliamentary proceedings, which are as follows

Sessions of the Parliament

There are usually three sessions in a year which are as follows

- The Budget Session (February to May)

- The Autumn or Monsoon Session (July to September).
- The Winter Session (November to December).

Summoning of the Session

- The President of India summons each House of the Parliament time-to-time for meetings.
- The Constitution states that, there should not be a gap of more than 6 months between two consecutive sittings of the Parliament.

Quorum for the Session

- Quorum is the minimum number of members required to be present in the house before it can transact (organise) any business.
- It is one-tenth (1/10th) of the total number of members in each house including the presiding officers.

Question Hour

- It is the first hour of every parliamentary sittings in which members ask questions from the government.
- There are **three types of questions** like starred question, un-starred question and short- notice question.

> **Motions of the Parliament**
>
> - The term motion means a formal proposal made for the purpose of eliciting a debate and decision of the house.
> - There are some motions in the Parliament which are as follows
>   - **Adjournment Motion** It is introduced in the Parliament to draw attention of the house to a definite matter of urgent public importance.
>   - **No-Confidence Motion** The Lok Sabha can remove the Government from office by passing the No-Confidence Motion which needs a support of atleast 50 members.

Speaker of Lok Sabha

Speaker is the presiding officer of the Lok Sabha.

Election

- The Speaker of Lok Sabha is elected from its members by a simple majority of its members present and voting in the house.
- Usually, a member belonging to ruling party becomes the Speaker.
- The Speaker is elected for a term of five years.

Functions

- The Speaker presides over the meetings of the house, except when a resolution for his/her removal is being considered.
- The Speaker has the final power to maintain order in the house and to interpret its rules of procedure.
- He/she can ask a member to withdraw from the house for disordely behaviour.
- He/she decides whether a Bill is a Money Bill or not.
- The Speaker presides over a joint sitting of the two houses of Parliament.
- The Speaker appoints the Chairman of all parliamentary committees.

Rajya Sabha

The Rajya Sabha is also called the Council of States. It is the upper house of the Indian Parliament.

Term

- The Rajya Sabha never dissolves because it is a permanent body. But one-third (1/3rd) of its members are retired on the expiration of every second year.
- The members of Rajya Sabha are elected for a term of 6 years.

Composition

- The total strength of the Rajya Sabha is 250, out of which 12 members are nominated by the President of India and the remaining 238 are those who represents the States and the Union Territories.
- At present, there are 245 members in the Rajya Sabha.

Election of Members

The Parliament has prescribed that the members of Rajya Sabha are indirectly elected by members of an Electoral College for that territory, on the basis of proportional representation by means of the single transferable vote.

Qualifications for Membership

- The candidate should be a citizen of India.

- The candidate should not be less than 30 years of age.
- The candidate should have such other qualifications as may be prescribed by the Parliament from time-to-time.

Presiding Officers

- The Constitution stipulates (specify) that the Vice-President of India is the Ex-officio Chairman of the Rajya Sabha.
- A Deputy Chairman of the Rajya Sabha is to be chosen by the members from among themselves.

Power and Functions of Union Parliament

Legislative Powers

- The Parliament has exclusive power to make laws on all 100 subjects of Union List such as foreign affairs, atomic energy, defence, banking, etc.
- The Parliament can legislate the 61 subjects of State List only when
  - There is emergency in the country or President Rule or a State Emergency.
  - If two or more States ask for making a law. But this law will be applicable to States which have requested.
  - If laws in a State List become the national importance or it requires to fulfill international commitments.
- Parliament controls the Council of Minister in various ways. For example, Question Hour, Vote of No-confidence, Adjournment Motion, etc.
- The Parliament may alter the name or boundary of the state. It can also form a new state by merging or separating a part of territory of a state.

Financial Powers

The financial powers of the Parliament are as follows

- No money can be spent or no tax can be imposed without the approval of the Parliament.
- The Parliament passes the budget which contains the estimates of receipts and expenditure of the government for the financial year.
- The salaries and allowances of Ministers and members of Parliament are determined by the Parliament.

Amendment of the Constitution

- A bill for amendment can be initiated in either house of Parliament by a majority of total membership as well as by two-third majority of members present in voting.
- In some cases, amendments need ratification from half of the Legislative Assemblies of the states.

Control over the Executive

The Parliament controls the executive through the following powers

- **Interpellation or Inquiry** The Parliament can ask questions to the government about its policies and performance.
- **Adjournment Motion** To bring matters of urgent public importance, the Parliament can bring Adjournment motion.
- **Vote of No-Confidence** If a government does not follow the provisions of the Constitution, the Parliament can show No-Confidence to the government.
- **Monetary Control** The Parliament can bring cut motion during the budget session to disapprove any monetary policy of the government. It also examines the report of **Comptroller and Auditor-General** (CAG).
- **Censure Motion** It can bring Censure motion over the policies of the government.

Exclusive Powers of the Two Houses

Exclusive powers of the Lok Sabha and Rajya Sabha are

Exclusive Powers of the Lok Sabha

- A Money Bill can be introduced only in the Lok Sabha.
- Only the Lok Sabha can vote on the demands for grants in the budget.
- The Council of Ministers is collectively responsible only to the Lok Sabha. Thus, the Lok Sabha alone can vote a minister out of office.
- Only the Lok Sabha has the power to pass a resolution for the discontinuance of the national emergency.
- The Speaker of the Lok Sabha presides over the joint sitting of the houses.

- If a deadlock occurs between both the Houses over an Ordinary Bill, the Bill of the Lok Sabha normally prevails, as its strength is more than double to that of the Rajya Sabha.

Exclusive Powers of the Rajya Sabha

- Parliament can assume temporary power to legislate on State List subjects. It is done only if Rajya Sabha passes a resolution, which is supported by two-third (2/3rd) majority of its members present and voting.
- The establishment of All-India Services also depends on the Rajya Sabha. The House will pass a resolution which is supported by two-third (2/3rd) majority of its members, present and voting.
- During the Emergency, if the Lok Sabha is dissolved then Rajya Sabha becomes the sole de-facto (effective) and de-jure (legal because Rajya Sabha is a permanent body.
- The Constitution Amendment Bill has to be passed in each House by the specified special majority. Thus, the Rajya Sabha can prevent a Constitutional Amendment even if the Bill has been passed by the Lok Sabha.

Chapter 2 The Union Executive : The President and Vice-President

The President

- The President is the executive head of the Indian State and the Supreme Commander of the Defence Forces of India.
- He/She is the **first citizen of India** and acts as the symbol of unity, integrity and solidarity of the nation.

Qualifications for Election

- He/she should be a citizen of India.
- He/she should have completed 35 years of age.
- He/she should be qualified for election as a member of the Lok Sabha.
- He/she should not hold any office of profit under the Union Government or any State Government or any local authority or any other public authority.

Composition of the Electoral College

The President is elected by members of electoral college. It includes

- The elected members of both the Houses of the Parliament.
- The elected members of the Legislative Assemblies of the states.
- The elected members of the Legislative Assemblies of Union Territories of Delhi and Puducherry.

> **Reasons for Indirect Election of the President**
>
> - If elected directly, the President could become a rival Centre of power to the Council of Ministers.
> - An indirect election protects the President to become a nominee of the Ruling Party at the Centre.
> - The inclusion of members of State Legislative Assembly in the Electoral College makes the President the elected representative of the whole nation. A clear voice would be given to the states as well by this process.

Term of Office

- The President's term of office is 5 years.
- The President may resign before the completion of his/her term. In that case, he/she can submit his resignation to the Vice-President of India.
- The vacant seat of the President must be filled within 6 months.

Procedure for Impeachment

The President can be removed from office by a process of impeachment for violation of the Constitution of India.

Following is the impeachment procedure of the President

- To start the proceedings, a 14 days notice signed by not less than 1/4th of the total number of members of the house preferring charges should be given.

- Then a resolution containing the charges has to be passed by a majority of not less than 2/3rd of the total membership of the House.
- Either House of Parliament may prefer the charge of violation of the Constitution before the other House which shall then investigate the charges.
- During the investigation, the President shall have the right to defend himself/herself.
- After investigating the charges by other house, it has to pass a resolution by 2/3rd majority that the charges have been proved.

Powers and Functions of the President

The President of India has the following powers and functions

Executive Powers

- He is the head of the Union, who can take all the executive actions of the Government of India.
- He/she makes appointments to key post like Prime Minister of India and the Council of Ministers, the Attorney General of India, the Comptroller and Auditor General of India, the Chief Election Commissioners and so on.
- He/she is the administrator of the Union Territories and scheduled areas.

Legislative Powers

- The President of India summons or prorogue the Parliament.
- He/she addresses the Parliament.
- He/she sends message to the houses.
- He/she nominates members of both the houses. (e.g. 12 members of Rajya Sabha and 2 members of Lok Sabha).
- He/she has power related to bills.

Discretionary Powers

Though the President has no constitutional discretion, he/she has some situational discretion. These are as follows

- Appointing the Prime Minister when no party has a clear majority in the Lok Sabha or when the Prime Minister in the office dies suddenly and there is no obvious successor.
- Dismissal of the Council of Minister when it cannot prove the confidence in the Lok Sabha.
- Dissolution of the Lok Sabha when the Council of Ministers loses the majority in Lok Sabha.
- In case of sudden death, where the ruling party is unable to immediately elect a leader.

Emergency Powers

The President of India has the following Emergency Powers

- **National Emergency (Article 352)** The President has the power to make a **Proclamation of Emergency** on the ground of threat to the security of India weather by war or external aggression or armed rebellion.
- **President's Rule (Articles 356 and 365)** Article 356 of the Constitution authorise the President to make a proclamation of Emergency in the following situations
  - If he/she is satisfied that the government of a state cannot be carried on in accordance with the provisions of the Constitution.
  - If the State fails to comply with or give effect to any of the directions given by the centre in the exercise of its executive power. It is also called State Emergency or Constitutional Emergency.
- **Financial Emergency** Article 360 of the Constitution of India deals with Financial Emergency. The President can declare this Emergency if he/she is satisfied that a situation has arisen whereby the financial stability of the country or credit of India or of any part of its territory is threatened.

The Vice-President

According to the Article 63 of Indian Constitution, there should be a Vice-President for India, who occupies the second highest office in the country.

Qualifications

To be eligible for election as Vice-President, a person should fulfil the following qualifications

- He/she should be a citizen of India.
- He/she should have completed 35 years of age.
- He/she should be qualified for the election as a member of the Rajya Sabha.

- He/she should not hold any office of profit under the Union Government or any State Government or any local authority or any other public authority.

Term of the Office

The term of the office of the Vice-President can be understood through following points

- The term of the office of the Vice-President is 5 years. It may terminate earlier by resignation (addressed to the President) or removal.
- He/she may be removed by a resolution of Rajya Sabha passed by an absolute majority of its total members and agreed to by the Lok Sabha.
- The Vice-President can hold office beyond his/her term until his/her successor assumes the charge.
- He/she may be elected for any number of terms. Notably, no ground has been mentioned in the, Constitution for the removal of the Vice-President.

Powers and Functions

The powers and functions of the Vice-President are of two types

- **As an Ex-officio Chairman of the Rajya Sabha** The Vice-President acts as an ex-officio Chairman of the Rajya Sabha. In this capacity, his/her powers and functions are similar to those of the Speaker of the Lok Sabha.
- **Vice-President as President** The Vice-President acts as the President when vacancy occurs in the office of the President due to his/her removal or his/her death or otherwise. He/she can act as the President only for a maximum period of 6 months. When the sitting President is unable to discharge his/her functions, the Vice-President acts as the President until the President resumes his/her office. It only happens due to absence or illness or any other cause.

Chapter 3 The Prime Minister and Council of Ministers

- The Constitution of India provides for a Council of Ministers with the Prime Minister as its head.
- In the Parliamentary form of Government, the President is the head of the Union and the Prime Minister is the head of the Government.

Appointment of Prime Minister

- The Prime Minister (PM) is appointed by the President, who according to convention, invites the leader of the majority party or group in the Lok Sabha to form the government.
- The members of the majority group/party elect their leader in the Lok Sabha to be appointed as the Prime Minister.

Formation of the Council of Ministers

- The Constitution originally does not specify the number of the Council of Ministers.
- However, the Constitution (91st Amendment Act, 2003) put a ceiling on the size of the Council of Ministers to 15% of the strength of the Lok Sabha or the State Legislatures.
- The Council of Ministers is also called as the Cabinet.

Tenure

- The ministry shall hold the office so long as they continue to enjoy the confidence of the majority in the Lok Sabha, or so long the Prime Minister does not resign.
- The Council of Ministers is collectively responsible to the Lok Sabha.
- The Prime Minister can, at any time, demand a resignation from any minister and recommend the President to do so.
- Thus, the tenure of the ministry or a minister is not fixed. Generally, the maximum term for which a ministry can remain in office is 5 years i.e. one full term of the Lok Sabha.

Powers/Functions of the Council of Ministers

The Council of Ministers have the following powers and functions

Formulation of Policy

- The Council of Ministers is mainly a policy formulating body.

- It formulates both external and domestic policies of the government on important matters such as defence, economic policy, security needs and important reforms, etc.

Implementation of Policies

- When the policy decision on any subject is taken by the Cabinet, then, the Minister of State and the Deputy Minister of the concerned ministry scrutinise the policies properly and forward it to the civil servants to implement the decision.
- The Cabinet has the power to co-ordinate the activities of various departments and make important appointments by the President like Judges of Supreme Court and High Courts, Governor of States, Chief Election Commissioner and so on.

Legislative Powers

The Cabinet exercises the following powers

- Power of Initiating Bills (almost 95%)
- Amendment to the Constitution
- Issuing of Ordinance
- Summoning the Parliament
- Source of Information

Position and Powers of the Prime Minister

Position and powers of the Prime Minister can be seen through the following points

Prime Minister as the Leader of the Nation

- The Prime Minister represents the nation.
- He decides the kind of relation India would have with other countries.
- He tries to protect the interest of the country in international forums.
- He is the ex-officio Chairman of the **NITI Aayog** or National Institution for Transforming India Aayog that replaced Planning Commission of India.
- He is also the Chairman of Atomic Energy Commission.

Power in Relation to the Council of Ministers

- The President appoints only those persons as ministers who are recommended by the Prime Minister.
- The Prime Minister allocates and reshuffles various portfolios among the ministers.
- The Prime Minister can advise the President to dismiss a minister in case of difference of opinion.
- The Prime Minister presides over the meeting of Council of Ministers and influences its decisions.

Powers in Relation to the President

- The Prime Minister is the principal advisor to the President. The Prime minister chooses the ministers and on his advice the President appoints them. He acts as a link between the President and the Council of Ministers.
- The Prime Minister furnishes all the administrative affairs of the union, when the President may call for.
- The Prime Minister advises the President with regard to the appointment of important officials, such as CAG, members of UPSC, ECs, etc.

Powers in Relation to the Parliament

- The Prime Minister advises the President with regard to summoning and proroguing (discontinuing) the sessions of the Parliament.
- The Prime Minister can recommend dissolution of the Lok Sabha to the President at any time. Prime Minister announces government policies on the floor of the House.
- The Prime Minister is the leader of the Lower House in the Parliament and the Chief Spokesperson of the government in the Parliament.
- Whenever an unwanted situation arises in the Parliament, the matter generally ends with the intervention of the Prime Minister.

Collective and Individual Responsibility of the Members of the Cabinet

Collective Responsibility

- Article 75 of the Constitution clearly state that the Council of Ministers is collectively responsible to the Lok Sabha.
- This means that all the minister are jointly responsible to the Lok Sabha for all their acts of omission and commission.
- They work as a team and swim and sink together.

Individual Responsibility

- Article 75 of the Constitution also contains the principle of individual responsibility.

- It states that the ministers holds the office during the pleasure of the President, which means that the President can remove a minister even at a time when the Council of Minister enjoys the confidence of the Lok Sabha.
- However, the President removes a minister only on the advice of the Prime Minister.

Distinction Between the Council of Ministers and the Cabinet

Some distinguished features of the Council of Ministers and the Cabinet are as follows

Basis	Council of Ministers	Cabinet
Members	It includes all three categories of ministers i.e, Cabinet Ministers, Ministers of State and Deputy Ministers.	It includes only Cabinet Ministers.
Collective Function	It has no collective function, so that it does not meet as a body to transact government business.	It has collective function so that it meets as a body to transact government business.
Supremacy of the Cabinet	Its functions are determined by the Cabinet.	It directs the Council of Ministers by taking policy decisions which are binding on all ministers.
Implementation	It implements the decisions taken by the Cabinet.	It supervises the implementation of its decisions by the Council of Ministers.
Responsibility	It is collectively responsible to the Lower House (Lok Sabha) of the Parliament.	It enforces the collective responsibility of the Council of Ministers to the Lok Sabha.

Chapter 4 The Supreme Court

- Judiciary is the system of courts that interprets and applies the law in the name of the state.
- The Indian Constitution provides a single integrated Judicial system of courts for the Union and for the States.
- The Supreme Court is placed at the apex of the entire judicial system in India.

The Supreme Court

- The Supreme Court is the **highest court** in India. This single system of court was adopted in 1935, for enforcement of both central laws as well as state laws.
- It was inaugurated on 28th January, 1950 and succeeded the Federal Court of India which was established under the Government of India Act, 1935.

Composition

- At present, the Supreme Court consists of 31 Judges in which there is one Chief Justice and 30 other judges.
- Originally the strength was fixed to 8 (One Chief Justice and 7 other judges).

Qualifications of Judges

A person to be appointed as a judge of the Supreme Court should have the following qualifications

- He/she should be a citizen of India.
- He/she should have been the judge of a High Court or of two or more such courts in succession for at least 5 years.
- He/she should have been an advocate of a High Court or of two or more such courts in succession for at least 10 years.
- He/she should be a distinguished jurist in the opinion of the President.

Appointment of Judges

The President of India appoints the Judges of the Supreme Court through the following procedure

- When the President appoints the Chief Justice, he/she may consult with judges of the Supreme Court and the High Court.
- When the President appoints other judges of the Supreme Court, he/she consults with the Chief Justice of India.
- Usually, the seniormost judge of the Supreme Court is appointed as the Chief Justice of India.

Independence of Judiciary from the Control of Executive and Legislature

The Constitution of India has made some provisions to safeguard and ensure the independent and impartial functioning of the Supreme Court which are as follows

- **Appointment of Judges** The judges of the Supreme Court are appointed by the President after consulting the other judges of the Supreme Court and the High Court. Thus, it curtails the interference of executive and political considerations.
- **Security of Tenure** The judges of the Supreme Court are removed by the President only in the manner and on the grounds mentioned in the Constitution.
- **Removal of Judges** A judge can be removed by the President only for proved misbehaviour and incapacity.
- **Fixed Service Conditions** The salaries and other emoluments of the judges cannot be changed to their disadvantage during their term of office, except in case of financial emergency.
- **Ban on Practice after Retirement** After retirement, a judge of the Supreme Court shall not plead or act in any court or before any authority within territory of India.
- **Power to Punish for its Contempt** The Supreme Court can punish for the contempt of court if a person/authority makes an attempt to lower its authority and dignity. The Supreme Court has freedom to recruit its staff. It has freedom to announce decisions and decrees.

Jurisdiction and Functions/Powers of the Supreme Court

Jurisdiction is the power that a court of law exercises to carry out judgements and enforce laws. The jurisdiction and functions/powers of the Supreme Court are as follows

Original Jurisdiction

It means the power to hear and determine a dispute in the first instance. It happens in those cases, which cannot be moved in any court other than the Supreme Court.

These include

- Dispute between the Union Government and one or more states.
- The Centre and any state or states on one side and one or more states on the other side.

Writ Jurisdiction/Enforcement of Fundamental Rights

- The Constitution has constituted the Supreme Court as the guarantor and defender of the Fundamental Rights of the citizens.
- The Supreme Court is empowered to issue writs for the enforcement of the Fundamental Rights of an aggrieved citizen.
- These writs fall in the following categories such as-Habeas Corpus, Mandamus, Prohibition, Certiorari and Quo-Warranto.

Appellate Jurisdiction

The appellate jurisdiction of the Supreme Court extends to constitutional, civil and criminal cases such as

- **Constitutional Matter** In the constitutional case, as appeal can be made to the Supreme Court against the judgement of the High Court, if the High Court certifies that the case involves a substantial questions of law that requires the interpretation of the Constitution. Based on the certificate, the party in the case can appeal to the Supreme Court on the ground that the question has been wrongly decided.
- **Civil Matter** In this case, an appeal lies to the Supreme Court if the High Court certifies
  - that the case involves a substantial question of law of general importance.

- that the question needs to be decided by the Supreme Court.

- **Criminal Matter** The Supreme Court hear appeals against the judgement in a criminal proceedings of a High Court, if the High Court
  - has an appeal reversed an order of acquittal of an accused person and sentenced him/her to death.
  - has taken before itself any case from any subordinate court and convicted the accused person and sentenced him/her to death.
  - satisfies that the case is a fit one for appeal to the Supreme Court.

Advisory Jurisdiction

Under Article 143, the Constitution of India authorises the President to seek the opinion of the Supreme Court on two categories of matters. These are

- On any question of law or fact of public importance which has arisen or which is likely to arise. The advice is not binding on the President who may or may not accept it.
- On any dispute arising out of any pre-constitution treaty, agreement (contract), engagement, (warrant) or other similar instruments.

Revisory Jurisdiction

The Supreme Court has power to review its own judgement or order with a view to remove any mistake or error that might have crept (occur) in the judgement or orders. But it is not bound by its previous decisions.

Judicial Review

- The Supreme Court is the sole interpreter of the Constitution.
- It has the power to review any laws passed by the Union or State Legislature.
- If any law passed by the legislature is against spirit of the Constitution or contravenes any provision of the Constitution, the Supreme Court can declare such law as null and void.

Need for Judicial Review

Judicial review is necessary for the following reasons

- The Constitution is in written form thus, whenever the question of interpretation arises, the Supreme Court helps to sort it out.
- To uphold the principle of supremacy of the Constitution.
- To maintain federal equilibrium between the centre and the state.
- To protect the Fundamental Rights of citizens.
- The legislature may not possess the wisdom experience and impartiality, which are needed to explain meaning of the law. This function can be best performed by the Supreme Court.

A Court of Record

As a court of record, the Supreme Court has two important powers. These are as follows

- The judgements, proceedings and acts of the Supreme Court are recorded for perpetual memory and testimony.
- These records cannot be questioned when produced before any court. The judgements are in nature of precedents i.e., the High Courts and other courts are bound to give a similar decision in a similar case.
- It has power to punish for the contempt of court (which are of two types i.e, civil contempt and criminal contempt) either with simple imprisonment for a term of 6 months or fine upto ₹ 2000 or with both.

Chapter 5 The High Courts and Subordinate Courts

The High Courts

- The Constitution of India states that there should be High Court for each state, but the 7th Constitutional Amendment Act, 1956 authorised the Parliament to establish a common High Court for two or more States and Union Territory.
- At present, there are 25 High Courts in India, including those having jurisdiction of more than one state.
- Delhi is the only Union Territory that has High Court of its own. The other Union Territories fall under the jurisdiction of different state High Courts.

Composition

- Every High Court consists of a **Chief Justice** and such **other judges** who are appointed by the President of India time-to-time.
- The Constitution does not specify the strength of a High Court so that, the President of India determines the strength of High Courts which is depended upon the workload of these courts.

Qualifications of Judges

According to the Constitution, a person shall be qualified for appointment as a judge of a High Court under the following conditions

- He/she should be a citizen of India.
- He/she should have held a judicial office in the territory of India for 10 years.
- He/she should have been an advocate of a High Court for 10 years.
- He/she should not be over 62 years.
- It is noted here that, the Constitution does not describe the minimum age for appointment as a judge of a High Court.

Appointment of Judges

- The judges of the High Court are appointed by the President.
- The Chief Justice of a High Court is appointed by the President after consultation with Chief Justice of India and the Governor of that state.
- While appointing other judges, the President consults the Chief Justice of India, Governor of the concerned state and Chief Justice of that High Court.

Functions/Powers and Jurisdiction of High Courts

- High Court has extensive and effective powers like Supreme Court.
- It is the highest court of appeal in the state.
- It is the protector of the Fundamental Rights of the citizens as well as the interpreter of the Constitution.

Original Jurisdiction

High Court has original jurisdiction which means that it has power to hear disputes in the first instance, not by way of appeal.

Its power extends to the following

- Disputes relating to the election of members of the Parliament and State Legislatures.
- Regarding revenue matter or an act ordered or done regarding revenue collection.
- Enforcement of Fundamental Rights of citizens.
- Matter of admiralty, will, marriage, divorce, company laws and contempt of court.

Appellate Jurisdiction

- The appellate jurisdiction of a High Court is wider than its original jurisdiction.
- It means that a High Court has power to hear appeals against the judgements of Subordinate Courts functioning in its territorial jurisdiction.
- It has appellate jurisdiction in both civil and criminal matters.

Subordinate Courts

- In every state, besides the High Court there are number of Judicial Courts to administer justice.
- These courts function under the complete control and supervision of the High Court.

Types of Courts

Every district has Civil Courts, Criminal Courts and Courts of Revenue

- **Civil Courts** The cases related to land, property and money transactions, arbitration, guardianship, marriage, divorce and case involving a will, etc are exercised under jurisdiction of Civil Courts.
- **Criminal Courts** It exercises jurisdiction in case related to murder, robbery, theft, assault, etc.
- **Courts of Revenue** These courts deal with case relating to the maintenance of land records and assessment and collection of land.

Difference between Courts of the District Judge and Session Judge

Court of the District Judge	Courts of the Session Judge
It is the highest Civil Court of the district.	It is the highest Criminal Court of the district.
It is presided by a District Judge.	It is presided by a Session Judge.

Court of the District Judge	Courts of the Session Judge
The District judge and the additional District judges are appointed by the Governor in consultation with the Chief Justice of the High Court of the concerned state.	The Session judge and the Additional Session judges are appointed by the Governor in consultation with Chief Justice of concerned High Court.
Civil Cases related to land, property, money, transactions, arbitration, guardianship, marriage, divorce and will are decided by the District judge.	The cases such as murders, theft, dacoity, pick-pocketing, etc are decided by the Session Judges.

Lok Adalats

- It is a system of a alternative dispute resolution developed in India. It roughly means **People's Court.**
- The idea of Lok Adalat was mainly advocated by **Justice PN Bhagwati** (Former CJI).
- The **first Lok Adalat** was held at Junagarh, in Gujarat, on 14th March, 1982.
- The Lok Adalat accept the case pending in the regular courts within their jurisdiction which could be settled by conciliation and compromise.
- The Lok Adalat is presided over by a sitting or retired judicial officer as the Chairman, with two other members, usually a lawyer and a social worker.

The Lok Adalats have following advantages

- It delivers fast and inexpensive justice.
- It reduces the workload of other courts enabling them to deal with more serious matters. It promotes social justice by providing legal aid to weaker sections of the society.
- It works in the spirit of compromise and understanding where both the parties feel satisfied.

HISTORY

Chapter I The First War of Independence-1857

India's independence from British rule on 15th August, 1947 was the result of a long drawn out struggle for freedom. The years from 1757 to 1857 were marked by rapid expansion of English East India Company. But the year 1857, started a new chapter in Indian history when millions of soldiers, peasants, artisans participated in the uprising of British rule which is also called **First War of Independence**.

Causes of the Revolt

The Revolt of 1857 occurred during the Governor Generalship of Lord Canning. The revolt was a combination of political, economic, socio-religious and military causes.

Political Causes

- According to **Lord Dalhousie's Policy of Doctrine of Lapse**, the adopted heirs of kings could neither inherit king's title nor his property. This created dissatisfaction among native rulers. Kingdoms of Satara, Jhansi, Nagpur and Sambalpur were annexed in this way.
- Under the **Policy of Annexation**, Lord Dalhousie annexed Awadh in 1856 on the pretext of mis-governance.
- British refused to grant pension to Nana Saheb as he was adopted son. They also showed disrespect to Bahadur Shah Zafar. This infuriated the rulers of these states.

Economic Causes

- The East India Company purchased indigo, spices, cotton at very cheap rates from peasants and sold them at high prices abroad. Only indigo, tea, jute, cotton and opium were allowed to be grown by the Indians. People suffered due to shortage of food grains.
- The British officials were paid high salaries which were sent back to England.
- The British Government put restrictions on the import of Indian textiles in England besides imposing heavy import duties on such goods.
- In India, handmade textiles could not compete with machine made products from Britain. This ruined the Indian industries.

- Peasants had to bear the heavy burden of taxes which increased indebtedness and stagnated agricultural growth.
- Poverty and famines ravaged the country and British did nothing to reduce people's misery.

Socio-religious Causes

- British social reforms like Abolition of Sati (1829), Legalisation of Widow Remarriage (1856) etc, hurt the sentiments of the orthodox and conservative people.
- The orthodox Indians felt humiliated when they saw the conditions in the railway compartments, brahmins and people from the backward classes were made to sit side by side.
- British support to Christian missionaries who converted Hindus to Christians created dissatisfaction among the people.
- The Law of Property which enabled inheritance even to Hindus who converted to other religions was not received well by the people.
- Other socio-religious causes were taxing of religious places, government supports to Christian missionaries, fears regarding Western education and apprehensions about modern technology.

Military Causes

- The Indian and British soldiers were not treated equally. The salary of the Indian soldiers was too meagre to support their families, while the duties of both the British and the Indian soldiers were more or less similar.
- As per the General Service Enlistment Act, 1856 passed in British Parliament, Indian soldiers could be deported anywhere including overseas. Brahmin soldiers saw this as a danger to their caste as overseas voyages were restricted in their caste.
- The large proportion of Indian soldiers in British army and poor performance of British troops in other wars convinced the Indian soldiers to take up arms against British.
- The Bengal army consisted mainly of soldiers from Oudh, thus the annexation of Oudh hurt the feelings of the soldiers from that province.
- Indian and British soldiers were not treated equally, as British soldiers received salaries eight times higher than inteir Indian counter parts..
- Loss of British army in Afghan War convinced the Indian soldiers that the British could also be defeated.

Immediate Causes

- In 1856, the British authorities decided to replace the old fashioned musket (called the **Brown Bess**) by the new **Enfield rifle**. The cartridges to be used in the rifle were greased with fat. The loading process of the Enfield rifle involved bringing the cartridge to the mouth and biting off the top greased paper with the mouth.
- A rumour spread that the cartridges were greased with the fat of pigs and cows. Soldiers believed that these cartridges were intentionally greased with the animal fat to hurt their religious sentiments.

Main Events of the Uprising

- First instance that sparked the revolt started at Barrackpore, when most of the Indian soldiers refused to use the greased cartridges. As a result, a Brahmin soldier of the 34th Native Infantry at Barrackpore named **Mangal Pandey** led an attack on the adjutant of 34th Native Infantry on 29th March, 1857. After this incident, Mangal Pandey was arrested and hanged on **8th April, 1857**.
- This incident started uprising in various parts of North and Central India. The mutiny started at **Meerut on 10th May, 1857**. The occasion was the punishment of some sepoy for their refusal to use the greased cartridges. They broke open jails, murdered Europeans, burnt their houses and marched to Delhi.
- In **Delhi**, the sepoy seized the city and proclaimed Mughal Emperor Bahadur Shah II as the Emperor of India. However, the British surmounted Delhi and the old emperor Bahadur Shah was taken prisoner. As a punishment, he was ordered life imprisonment and deported to Rangoon, where he died in 1862.
- In **Lucknow** Begum Hazrat Mahal, the wife of the Nawab of Awadh led the uprising on 30th May, 1857. The city was recaptured by the British in March, 1858. Begum Hazrat Mahal fled towards the Nepal Frontier.

- At **Kanpur**, the revolt was led by Nana Saheb but he was defeated by the British in December 1857, after which he fled to Nepal.
- Kunwar Singh (Bihar), Rani Lakshmibai (Jhansi), Tantia Tope (Nana Saheb's General), Khan Bahadur Khan (Bareilly), Maulvi Ahmedullah (Faizabad), Azimullah Khan (Fatehpur), etc. were the other leaders who took command of the movement.

Consequences of the Revolt

The revolt was suppressed by the British and the leaders either died at battle or hanged. But the revolt shook the foundations of British empire in India. The consequences were

- **End of Rule** The revolt ended the rule of the East India Company by the Government of India Act of 1858.
- **Queen's Proclamation** The Queen's proclamation incorporating the transfer of governance from the East India Company to the British crown was made public at Allahabad, on 1st November, 1858, by **Lord Canning**, the first Viceroy of India.
- **Relations with Princely States** Doctrine of Lapse was abolished and the right to adopt sons and successors were given to the states.
- **End of Mughals and Peshwas** Mughal rule ended with the death of Bahadur Shah in 1862 and Peshwaship was abolished.
- **Changes in the Army** The strength of the European troops in India was increased from 45000 to 65000 and the number of Indian troops was reduced from 238000 to 140000. All big troops and artillery departments were reserved for the Europeans.
- Discrimination on the basis of caste, region and religion was practised in the recruitment to the army. Newspapers, journals and nationalist publications were prevented from reaching the Indian army to keep them separated from the rest of the population.
- **Policy of Divide and Rule** The British gave special protections and concessions to the Princely States, encouraging hatred and ill-feelings among the Hindus and the Muslims, so that the people of India could never challenge the British authority.
- **Economic Exploitation** The British aggressively initiated territorial expansion that gave place to the era of economic exploitation. India became a typical colony of the British, by exporting raw materials and importing British goods peasants, rural artisans, etc. were impoverished under the British rule.

Chapter 2 The Rise of Nationalism and the Indian National Congress

An important feature of the second half of the 19th century is the rise of nationalism as a result of economic exploitation and mal-administration by the British.

Nationalism

It is a feeling of togetherness and common consciousness based on political, historical, religious, cultural, psychological and other factors in a state.

Factors Leading to the Growth of Nationalism

There were several factors that led to the growth of Nationalism in India. Some of the factors are as follows

Repressive Colonial Policies

- **Vernacular Press Act** (1878) introduced by **Lord Lytton** forbade to publish any material that is against the British government.
- **Indian Arms Act** (1878) by Lord Lytton forbade the carrying of arms by Indians without license.
- In order to discourage Indians from competing for the Civil Service Examination, Lord Lytton lowered the maximum age of eligibility from 21 to 19 years.
- **Ilbert Bill** (1883) introduced by **Lord Rippon** sought to abolish judicial disqualification on the basis of racial discrimination. But it was with drawn as Britishers opposed it.

Socio-religious Reform Movements

- *Educated Indians realised the need for social reforms and to end superstitions attached with religion. Social movements emerged like abolition of caste system, sati, infanticide, child marriage, etc.*
- *Raja Rammohan Roy was the greatest social and religious reformer of the 19th century, who established the **Brahmo Sabha in 1828,** which was later renamed as Brahmo Samaj. Raja Rammohan Roy is also called as the 'Father of Modern India'. The Brahmo Samaj believed in 'Monotheism' or 'Worship of One God'.*
- *Jyotiba Phule was an urban-educated member of a so-called low caste. He promoted widow remarriage and worked for the education of women. In 1854, he established a school for untouchables and started a private orphanage for the widows. He founded the **Satya Shodhak Samaj** in 1873, with the aim of securing social justice for the weaker sections of society.*

Role of Press

A large number of newspapers were started in the latter half of the 19th century. Some of the prominent newspapers were The Amrit Bazar Patrika, The Bengali, The Tribune, The Pioneer, The Times of India, The Hindu and The Statesman in English. The press played an enormous role in fostering national unity and creating consciousness among the Indians.

Growth of Political Associations

Rise of nationalism led to the rise of many political associations as follows

- ***Landholder's Society** founded in 1838 by Dwarkanath Tagore was the first political organisation in India.*
- ***East India Association** and **Indian National Association** were the precursors and laid the foundation of Indian National Congress.*

Indian National Congress

*The Indian National Congress was formed by **Allan Octavian Hume** (AO Hume), an Englishman and a retired civil servant, in association with various national leaders, who called for a conference in Pune in December 1885.*

Immediate objectives of Indian National Congress

- *To consolidate a feeling of nationalism irrespective of caste, class or religious differences.*
- *To present popular demands before the government.*
- *To get public opinions through discussions and debates.*
- *To promote cordial relations between Congress workers.*

The First Congress Session

*It was held at Gokuldas Tejpal Sanskrit College, Mumbai from 28th December to 31st December, 1885 under the Presidentship of **Womesh Chunder Bonnerjee**. It was attended by 72 delegates.*

The Second Congress Session

- *It was held at Kolkata in 1886 under the Presidentship of **Dadabhai Naoroji**, some of the delegates were also received by Lord Dufferin as distinguished visitors to the capital.*
- *The Viceroy Lord Dufferin, favoured the formation of the Congress because he wanted it to act as a **safety-valve** for popular discontent, thereby, safeguarding the British interests in India.*

Chapter 3 First Phase of the Indian National Movement

The years after the formation of the Indian National Congress saw the rise of Nationalist movements. The people involved in the movements were called as early Nationalists.

The Early Nationalists (Moderates)

- *In the years from 1885 to 1905, the Congress was led by a group of leaders, who were called Early Nationalists or Moderates. The Moderates were drawn from the educated middle class consisting of professionals like lawyers, barristers, teachers and officials.*
- *The Moderates or the Early Nationalists were included from all parts of the country–WC Bannerjee, Rashbihari Ghosh, Surendranath Banerjee from Bengal, Pandit Madan Mohan*

Malviya from Uttar Pradesh and some other Moderates were from Maharashtra and Gujarat like–Dadabhai Naoroji, Gopal Krishna Gokhale, Justice Ranade, Pherozeshah Mehta, etc.

Demands of Moderates

- **Constitutional Demands**
  - A larger share in the government of the country.
  - Expansion of Legislative Council and Legislative Assembly.
  - Formation of Democratic self government.
- **Economic Demands**
  - Reduction in land revenue extracted by zamindars from peasants.
  - Development of banking, industrial growth and trade.
  - Abolition of salt tax and duty on sugar.
- **Administrative Demands**
  - More Indians should be appointed in higher posts.
  - Repeal of Arms Act and License Act.
  - Simultaneous examinations in England and India for the recruitment of Indian Civil Service.
  - Spread primary education among the maximum population in India.
  - Complete separation of executive and judiciary.

Methods of Struggle of Moderates

- Relying on constitutional and peaceful methods.
- Avoiding violence and confrontation.
- Making good use of 3 P's– Petitions, Prayers and Protest.

Beliefs of Moderates

- Belief in moderate politics.
- Loyalty to the British crown.
- Reforms within the framework of the British rule.
- Faith in British sense of justice and fairness.

Achievements of Moderates

Following reforms were led by the efforts of moderates

- In 1886, the Public Service Commission was appointed by the British.
- A Resolution was passed by the House of Commons in 1893 for simultaneous examination of the ICS in London and India.
- In 1895, the British government appointed the **Welby Commission** on Indian expenditure, under Sir Reginald Earle Welby.
- In 1892, the Indian Council Act was passed by the British.

Attitude of British towards Congress

- In the initial stage of the Congress, the British Government favoured the Congress. In fact, a few government officials like **Sir William Wedderbwin, Sir Henry Cotton** also attended the First Session of the Congress.
- In 1887, **Lord Dufferin** attacked the National Congress in his speech and ridiculed it as representing only a microscopic minority of the people. British officials criticised the National Congress and branded its leaders as **disloyal babus** and **violent villains**.

Prominent Early Nationalists

Among the prominent early nationalists, Dadabhai Naoroji, Gopal Krishna Gokhale and Surendranath Banerjee are especially notable.

Dadabhai Naoroji (1825-1917)

- He is known as **Grand Old Man of India**.
- He was founder of Bombay Association.
- He exposed India's economic exploitation in his book 'Poverty and Un-British Rule in India'.
- He exposed the economic implications of the British rule in India through Drain Theory also known as Drain of Wealth.
- He was elected as the President of Indian National Congress three times.

Gopal Krishna Gokhale (1866-1915)

- He was influenced by the ideals of Justice Ranade.
- He presided over the Varanasi session of Indian National Congress in 1905.
- He founded **Servants of India Society** in 1905.

Surendranath Banerjee (1848-1925)

- Advocated the use of constitutional methods for attainment of goals.
- He was the first Indian to qualify the Indian Civil Services Examination.
- He opposed the Arms Act, Vernacular Press Act and lowering of the age for ICS examinations.
- He also opposed the Partition of Bengal and Morley-Minto Reforms.

The Extremists or the Radicals

- They were new and younger group of leaders in the Congress.
- They did not agree with ideals of moderates.
- They wanted to extend Swadeshi and Boycott Movements.
- They were also called assertive nationalists.
- The famous trio were **Lal-Bal-Pal**.

Objectives of Radicals

- To make Indians aware about their self-respect and rights to freedom of speech, and right of property, etc.
- Fight against unfavourable policies of the British Government.
- To make a nationwide presence of the movements.

Methods of Struggle of Radicals

- Passive resistance and involvement with the masses.
- Non-cooperation with British government.
- Boycotting government services, courts, schools, colleges.
- Boycott of foreign goods.
- Promotion of Swadeshi goods.

Beliefs of Radicals

- Opposed to British rule and capitalism.
- Wanted self rule by the Indians.
- Total socio-economic transformation.

Achievements of Radicals

- Establishment of educational institutions headed by Indians.
- Brought the middle classes into the National Movement.
- Exposed the true character of the British rule.

Prominent Radical Leaders

The prominent extremists from 1905 to 1918 were Bipin Chandra Pal, Bal Gangadhar Tilak and Lala Lajpat Rai.

- **Bal Gangadhar Tilak** He started prominent newspapers–The Kesari (in Marathi) and The Maratha (in English). He organised the Ganapati festival and Shivaji festival to encourage nationalist ideas. He started the Home Rule League in 1916. He said 'Swaraj is my birth right and I shall have it.'
- **Bipin Chandra Pal** He started newspaper English weekly, New India and the journal Vande Mataram. He spreaded the message of Boycott, Swadeshi, National Education and Swaraj. He advocated widow remarriage and education of women. He was known as **Father of Revolutionary Thought in India.**
- **Lala Lajpat Rai** He started newspapers like Young India, Vande Mataram (in Urdu), Punjabi and People (English Weekly). He founded the National School of Lahore and presided over All India Trade Union Congress in 1920. He boycotted the Simon Commission and demonstrated against it in Lahore. He was known as **Punjab Kesari, Sher-e-Punjab.**

Chapter 4 Second Phase of the Indian National Movement

The second phase of the national movement began in 1905. The famous incident was Partition of Bengal.

Province of Bengal

Largest and most populous state of British India. It included Bihar, Orissa (Odisha), Chotanagpur, Assam.

Curzon's Scheme of Partition of Bengal

- Partition announced on 19th July, 1905 and implemented on 16th October, 1905.
- Bengal included the Western districts of Bengal proper, Bihar and Orissa. Calcutta was made its capital.
- Eastern Bengal and Assam consisted of the Eastern districts of Bengal proper and Assam. Dhaka was the capital of the new province of Eastern Bengal and Assam.

  Causes for the Partition were

  - To bring administrative efficiency as Bengal province was very large.

- To regulate the rising tide of nationalism in Bengal.
- To create a gap between Hindus and Muslims.
- To create a Muslim majority state.
- To destroy the political influence of educated middle class.

Anti-Partition Movement

- Partition opposed by Indian National Congress.
- Many protest meetings were organised by the prominent leaders like Surendranath Banerjee, Krishna Kumar Mitra, PC Ray, BC Pal and Ananda Mohan Bose.
- Anti-Partition Movement initiated on 7th August, 1905 in Calcutta.
- 16th October, when the Partition came into effect was declared as a **National Mourning Day**.

Repressions by the British

- Thousands of people arrested and put behind bars.
- Lala Lajpat Rai, Sardar Ajit Singh, Surendranath Banerjee and many other leaders were arrested.
- Government made use of other repressive measures such as the Prevention of Seditious Meeting Act, the Explosive Substances Act, the Criminal Law Amendment Act and the Newspaper Act.

Impact of Anti-Partition Movement

- People lost faith in the justice of British.
- People moved towards the idea of Swadeshi and Boycott.
- The Swadeshi Movement was an economic measure for the development of Indian industries.
- Tilak launched the boycott of British goods campaign.
- The Swadeshi and Boycott Movements brought into politics new classes of people. They encouraged the indigenous industries. This movement provided employment to many craftsmen in indigenous industries.
- The assertive nationalists or the extremists played a major role in this movement.

Chapter 5 The Muslim League and Lucknow Pact

- A Pact between the Indian National Congress and Muslim League in the Congress session held in Lucknow in 1916.
- A Pact between the two sections of the Congress to fight collectively i.e. Moderates and Extremists united.

Clauses of the Lucknow Pact

- There shall be self-government in India. Muslims should be given 1/3rd representation in the Central Government.
- The number of the members of Imperial Legislative Council was to be 150, of which 4/5th were to be elected and 1/5 nominated. 1/3rd of the elected members were to be Muslims.
- At the Provincial level, 4/5th of the members of the Legislative Council should be elected and 1/5th should be nominated. All members except those nominated, should be elected directly on the basis of Adult Franchise.
- In the Viceroy's Executive Council, half the members were to be Indian, elected by the elected members of the Imperial Legislative Council.
- Minorities should be given adequate separate representation in the elected bodies.

Circumstances Leading to the Lucknow Pact

- Muslims were unhappy with the unsympathetic treatment of Caliph or the ruler of Turkey by British in the First World War.
- All India Muslim League formed in December 1906 at Dhaka by **Nawab Salimullah**.
- The objectives of the Muslim League were
  - To promote a feeling of loyalty among the Indian Muslims towards the British Government.
  - To protect the political and other rights of the Muslims and present them before the Government in a mild language.

- To keep the Muslim intelligentsia away from the mainstream of the National Movement.

- Prominent Muslim leaders like Abul Kalam Azad and Ali brothers spread nationalist ideas among Muslims.
- Annie Besant and Tilak played significant roles in bringing the two organisations closer.

Significance of the Lucknow Pact

- It signified Hindu-Muslim unity.
- It gave strength to National Movement.
- Moderates and radicals were unified.
- Fear of Hindu-Muslim unity made British rethink their policies.
- British declared a policy of gradual development of self-government institutions in India on 20th August, 1917.

Drawbacks of the Lucknow Pact

- It emphasised separate political existence for the Hindus and the Muslims.
- 'Communal Veto' in legislation was provided by this pact because no legislature could proceed with any bill if 3/4th of the members of a particular community opposed it.
- The Congress lost its secular character by accepting separate electorates for Muslims and hence paved the way for communal tension in the future.

Chapter 6 National Movement and Mahatma Gandhi

The emergence of Mahatma Gandhi in India from 1915 onwards, gave a new direction to Indian National Movement.

Early Life of Mahatma Gandhi

- Mohandas Karamchand Gandhi was born in Porbandar, in the Kathiawad district of Gujarat on **2nd October, 1869**. His father Karam Chand Gandhi was the Diwan of the Rajkot State. His mother's name was Putli Bai.
- Gandhi in initial years after coming to India was guided by Gopal Krishna Gokhale and the latter was known as **Political Guru of Gandhi.**
- From 1893 to 1914, Mahatma Gandhi spent his time in South Africa and during this period, he was engaged in a heroic struggle against the racist authorities in South-Africa. He formed the Natal Indian Congress and suffered imprisonment.
- Later, Gandhi's novel methods of Satyagraha and Non-violence was adopted by the masses in India's freedom movement.

Significant Movements led by Gandhi

Many significant movements were led by Gandhi. Among them prominent is the Non-Cooperation Movement.

Non-Cooperation Movement

- Congress passed this resolution to start Non-cooperation Movement in its Calcutta session in September 1920.
- The programme of non-cooperation consisted of boycott of legislative councils, government schools and colleges, law courts, foreign goods, government functions and surrendering of titles.
- It was launched with the belief that if Indians refuse to cooperate than British rule would collapse.

Objectives of the Movement

The Non-Cooperation Movement was launched to press the following demands

- The Khilafat issue.
- The redressal of the Punjab wrongs.
- The attainment of Swaraj.
- Measures to promote Hindu-Muslim unity, removal of untouchability and Harijan welfare.

Suspension of Movement

- The movement suspended when 22 policemen were burnt alive in a police station at Chauri-Chaura village of Gorakhpur district in Uttar Pradesh. Gandhiji withdrew the movement on 12th February, 1922.

Impact of the Movement

- The Indian National Movement, for the first time in history, acquired a real mass base with the participation of different sections of the Indian society.
- It instilled a new confidence among the people and transformed the Congress from a deliberative assembly into a moral fighting force.

- *It fostered Hindu-Muslim unity by merging the Khilafat Movement with this movement.*

Causes of the Movement

- ***Khilafat Movement*** *(1919) Indian Muslims adopted an aggressive anti-British attitude against the unjust behaviour of the British towards Sultan of Turkey.*
- *Britain and its allies abolished the office of the Khalifa who was regarded as a spiritual head of the Muslims all over the world.*
- ***The Ali Brothers*** *The anti-British movement launched by Ali brothers in 1920 was supported by Gandhiji by starting the Non-Cooperation Movement.*
- ***Rowlatt Act*** *(1919) This act empowers the British government to detain any nationalist movement, activity or activist. It was opposed by the Indians.*
- ***Jallianwala Bagh Tragedy*** *(13 April, 1919) General Dyer's open fire to a peaceful meeting in Amritsar killed hundreds of people. This injustice inspired the Indians to fight more intensely against the British.*

Simon Commission

- *This commission was constituted under* ***Sir John Simon*** *in November 1927 to review the functioning of the constitutional system in India. It was constituted to suggest any changes and the need for any further constitutional reforms.*

Causes for Opposing the Commission

- *Indian leaders opposed the commission as there were no Indians in it.*
- *Congress felt that it was violation of the principle of self-determination and a deliberate insult to the self-respect of Indians.*

Events Related to the Commission

- *When the commission arrived in India in 1928, it was greeted with the slogan* ***Simon Go Back.***
- *The Muslim League and the Hindu Maha Sabha decided to support the Congress.*
- *The British used brutal suppression and police attacks to break the popular opposition.*
- *To dispense crowd gatherings, Police Lathin chergerd on the people. As a result, Lala Lajpat died due to police lathi charge.*

> **Declaration of Poorna Swaraj**
>
> - *All parties including the Congress and the Muslim League participated in the demonstrations. In an effort to win over them, the Viceroy Lord Irwin announced in October 1929, a vague offer of* ***Dominion Status for India.***
> - *In December 1929, under the Presidency of Jawaharlal Nehru, in the Lahore session of Congress the demand of Poorna Swaraj or full independence for India was formalised. It was also declared that 26th January, 1930 would be celebrated as the* ***Independence Day.***

Civil Disobedience Movement

- *It was started by Gandhiji in March 1930 in accordance with the decision taken at the Lahore Session of the Congress for 'Poorna Swaraj'.*
- *The movement started with the* ***Dandi March*** *on 12th March, 1930 because Gandhiji believed that the salt tax and the monopoly of the government on production of salt should be abolished.*
- *On 31st January, 1930, Gandhiji sent a letter to Viceroy Irwin stating eleven demands.*
- *Irwin was unwilling to negotiate, then Gandhiji took the decision and started a March from the Sabarmati Ashram on 12th March, 1930 for Dandi, the coastal town of Gujarat.*
- *He made salt from sea water and violated the salt law that had granted the government, the sole right to make salt.*

Impact of the Civil Disobedience Movement

- *It shattered people's faith in the British Government.*
- *It laid the social roots for the freedom struggle and popularised the new methods of propaganda.*
- *The Dandi March was significant indeed. Violation of the salt laws was soon followed by the defiance of forest laws in Maharashtra, Karnataka Central Provinces.*
- *The refusal to pay the rural 'chaukidari tax' in Eastern India.*
- *It ended the monopoly of the British over salt manufacturing.*
- *The movement discontinued with* ***Gandhi-Irwin Pact.***

Gandhi Irwin Pact

- *This Pact was an agreement between Gandhi and Lord Irwin on 5th March, 1931.*

- As per the pact, the British government withdrew all ordinances, prosecutions and released all political prisoners.
- Gandhi agreed to attend the Second Round Table Conference.

Second Round Table Conference

- It was held in London during the Viceroyalty of Lord Willingdon during September to December, 1931 and Gandhiji attended it on behalf of the Indian National Congress.
- The Conference, however, failed as Gandhiji could not agree with British Prime Minister Ramsay MacDonald on his policy of Communal representation and the refusal of the British Government for the basic Indian demand for freedom. The Conference closed on 1st December, 1931 without any concrete results.

Quit India Movement (1942)

- The movement was passed by All-India Congress Committee on 8th August, 1942 from Bombay.
- Gandhi gave a call for 'Do or Die' to his countrymen.

Causes of the Quit India Movement

- After the failure of the **Cripps Mission**, the Congress felt that the Communal problem in India would be solved only if the British were forced to quit India.
- The Congress believed that the Britishers were supporting the league and if they leave India, the people could sort out their differences.
- The Congress wanted the immediate withdrawal of the Britishers to save India from the Japanese invasion as Japan was an axis power and Britain was on the opposite fighting as an allied power.

Reactions of the Government to the Quit India Movement

Reactions of the Government to the Quit India Movement were as follows

- The Press was completely muzzled.
- Prisoners were tortured, 10000 people were killed and 60000 of them were arrested.
- Rebellious villages had to pay huge sums as fines.
- Gandhiji was detained at the Agha Khan Palace in Pune and other prominent leaders were sent to jail in Ahmednagar Fort.

Significance of the Quit India Movement

- The movement displayed national unity, nationalist feelings, people's spirit for sacrifice and determination.
- The movement attracted world attention and support in favour of India.
- It developed the feelings of political awakening and consciousness among the masses.
- It shook the foundations of the British rule in India.

Chapter 7 Forward Bloc and Indian National Army

Formation of Forward Bloc

- The party was formed on 3rd May, 1939 by **Netaji Subhash Chandra Bose.**
- Bose was President, S S Cavesheer as its Vice-President, Lal Shankarlal as General Secretary.
- A newspaper with same name was also published.
- Forward Bloc was declared as a socialist party.

Objectives of the Forward Bloc

- To unite all left-wing sections within the Congress.
- Liberation of India with support of the workers, youths and radical organisations.
- Support military action for struggle.
- To establish a socialist society by state planning.
- Abolition of landlordism.
- To provide benefits to working class.

Subhash Chandra Bose

- Subhash Chandra Bose was one of the greatest freedom fighters of India. He was born on 23rd January, 1897 at Cuttack in Orissa.

  After completing his studies in India, he went to England and passed the Indian Civil Services Examination.
- The Non-Cooperation Movement of Mahatma Gandhi attracted Subhash Chandra Bose and he became an active worker of the Freedom Movement. He criticised Gandhiji when he withdrew the Non-cooperation Movement in 1922.

- He was unanimously selected as the President of the Congress at the Haripura (Gujarat) Session in 1938. Subhash Chandra Bose inaugurated the Indian National Planning Committee in December 1938.

Rift with Gandhi

- Bose favoured large scale industrialisation while Gandhi favoured small scale industries to make villages sufficient.
- In the Tripuri (Madhya Pradesh) session of the Indian National Congress in 1939, Bose won the Presidential elections.
- However, Gandhiji supported Pattabhi Sitaramayya.
- Bose resigned from Congress Presidentship on 29th April, 1939 and formed the Forward Bloc.

Formation of Indian National Army (INA)

- The outbreak of the war in South-East Asia in 1941 caused a lot of concern and excitement great stir among the Indians in those regions.
- Indians, living in the territories captured by Japan, organised themselves into association, to contribute to the Liberation of India.
- The Japanese, after defeating the British in South-East Asia, took a number of Indian soldiers as Prisoners of War. In March 1942, a Conference of Indians was held in Tokyo and they formed the Indian Independence League.
- At the Bangkok Conference (June 1942), Rashbihari Bose was elected the President of the League. INA was formed by **Mohan Singh**.
- In July 1943, the leadership of INA was handed over to him.
- Provisional Government of Free India was formed on 21st October, 1943. It got its first independent territory in the form of Andaman and Nicobar Islands.
- Bose gave the call to his soldiers 'Give me blood and I shall get you freedom.' He gave the slogans 'Delhi Chalo' and 'Jai Hind'.
- The INA gave a tough fight to the British forces in the Assam hills and succeeded in capturing Ukhral and Kohima.

Surrender of INA

- The Surrender of Japan in the World War II sealed the fate of the INA.
- Early arrival of monsoon hampered the supply of ration and ammunitions for the army.
- It was supposed that Bose died in an air crash on 18th August, 1945.

Achievements of INA

- It inspired uprisings against the British in the armed forces of the country.
- As Hindus, Muslims and Sikhs in the INA fought as Indians, it indicated that Indians who waged an armed battle against the British were not at all affected by communal division.

Chapter 8 Independence and Partition of India

Demand for a separate state came up from Muslim League at the Lahore session in 1940. This was followed by the Wavell Plan.

Wavell Plan

- Lord Wavell invited Indian leaders for discussions in a Conference at Shimla in June 1945.
- The clauses were
  - Viceroy's Executive Council would consist of an equal number of Hindus and Muslims.
  - The Commander in Chief and the Viceroy would be British.
  - New Constitution would be framed by the Indians themselves.
  - India like other dominions would have a British High Commissioner.
  - The plan was not accepted by Muslims as no separate electorate for Muslims was mentioned.

Mountbatten Plan (3rd June, 1947)

- Mountbatten was the **last Viceroy of India** after Lord Wavell.
- The plan offered to form a Constituent Assembly to frame the Constitution of India.

Causes of the Plan

- Partition of India into two different and sovereign states—India and Pakistan.
- The plan provided Partition of Punjab and Bengal.
- Princely states were given the choice of joining either of the two countries or to remain independent.
- Existing Constitution would continue to work and draft the Constitution for free India.
- Creation of a Boundary Commission to decide the boundary of two dominions.
- India's independence to be preponed to 15th August, 1947.

Acceptance of Mountbatten Plan by the Congress

The Mountbatten Plan was accepted by the Congress because

- The large-scale of communal riots 'that engulfed the whole country convinced all that the only solution to communal problem lay in the Partition of India.
- Experience of working with the League had convinced the Congress that it could not have a joint administration with the League.
- The leaders felt that after Partition, India could evolve a truly secular and democratic polity.

Indian Independence Act (1947)

- The Bill containing the provisions of the Mountbatten Plan of 3rd June, 1947 was introduced in the British Parliament and was passed as the Indian Independence Act, 1947.
- The Act laid down detailed measures for the Partition of India and the speedy transfer of political powers to the new government of India and Pakistan.
- This act marked the end of the British rule in India and the Dominions of India and Pakistan came into existence on 15th August, 1947.

Clauses of the Act

- India would be partitioned and two Independent Dominions, India and Pakistan would be created from 15th August, 1947. The act provided legislative supremacy of both the dominions.
- The territories of the two dominions were divided in such terms that Pakistan would comprise Sindh, British Baluchistan, North-West Frontier Province, the West Punjab and East Bengal.
- India was to comprise all the remaining territories included in the British India.
- The exact boundaries of the dominions would be determined by a Boundary Commission.
- Both Bengal and Punjab would be divided.
- The Provincial Assemblies of the two parts would meet separately decide through a majority vote whether they wanted the division of province or not.
- A plebiscite would be held in **North-West Frontier Province** (NWFP) as well as in Sylet district (Muslim majority area) in East Bengal to determine whether they would like to join Pakistan or India.
- There would be a Governor-General, who would be appointed by the British king on the advice of the Cabinet of the concerned dominion.
- The Constituent Assemblies of both the dominions were to act as the Central Legislatures and would have full power to make laws for their respective dominion. They would act as sovereign bodies for legislative purposes.

Chapter 9 The First World War

The First World War began in 28th July, 1914 and lasted until 11th November, 1918.

Causes of the First World War

- Militant Nationalism refers to a strong love for one's own country country coupled with hostility towards others. This sentiment contributed to the outbreak of the First World War. It arose from increasing unrest among European countries as they sought to protect their national interests.
- **Division of Europe** Rising imperialism led to the capture of more colonies. Colonial rivalry led to division of Europe into two power blocs. These were
  - **Triple Alliance** Britain, France, Russia
  - **Triple Entente** Germany, Austria-Hungary, Italy

- ***Sarajevo Crisis*** It was the assassination of Archduke Francis Ferdinand, the heir to the throne of Austria-Hungary, at Sarajevo, capital of Bosnia, on 28th June, 1914. The assassination was planned and carried out by a secret society of the extremist Serbian nationalists called the **Black Hand** or **the Union of Death**. German Government pressurised Austria for an immediate declaration of war.

Events of the First World War

- War on the Western front between Germany and France.
- War on the Eastern front between Germany-Austria and Russia.
- Turkey joined Germany but was defeated by British army.
- US declared war on Germany.
- War ended by surrender of Austria-Hungary and Germany.

Results of the First World War

- Ruling dynasties of Romanov, Hohenzollern, Hapsburg ended.
- Ottoman empire came to an end.
- Signing of Treaty of Versailles.
- Great damage was done to the economies of industrialised nations of Europe.
- World War I was won by the Allied powers with the timely help of the United States. President of US, Woodrow Wilson issued his **Fourteen-Point Programme** to end the war.
- US emerged as a world power, militarily and economically. This position so long occupied by Great Britain.

Treaty of Versailles

- It was signed between Allies and Germany on 28th June, 1919, at the Paris Conference.
- The terms of the Treaty were
  - German power severely restricted and monarchy ended.
  - It was required to pay for the loss and damages incurred by the Allies, which came to be around 33 billion dollars.
  - The German Army was restricted to a force of 1,00,000 soldiers in a maximum seven infantry and three cavalry divisions.
  - The manpower of German Navy was not to exceed 15,000, including men for the fleet, coastal defences, signal stations, administration, other land services etc.
  - Rhine Valley was to be demilitarised.
  - Germany lost Alsace and Lorraine to France, Eupen-et-Malmedy to Belgium, and Schleswig to Denmark. Danzing became a free port.
  - The coal mines in the German area called Saar were ceded to France for 15 years.

Formation of the League of Nations

- Fear of another war convinced all leaders to promote international cooperation.
- League of Nations was created as a world organisation of all independent states in 1920.

Objectives of the League of Nations

- States were prohibited from entering into secret treaties and alliances.
- Member states were restricted in maintaining armies, warships and destructive armaments.
- The major aim of the League of Nations was to settle disputes among the member states and to maintain peace and order.
- The League of Nations was supposed to promote political, social, cultural and economic cooperation among the member states.
- All the states were to respect each other's independence.
- The member states had to heed the directions of the League against any state trying to disturb world peace and order.
- The league came to an end on 20th April, 1946.

Chapter 10 Rise of Dictatorship : Fascism and Nazism

After the war, European countries suffered from unemployment, social unrest, different and extreme ideologies. Ultimately dictatorship took prevalence. against ideologies of socialism and communism. In Italy - Fascism and in Germany - Nazism became prevalent.

Fascism

- The word Fascism has been derived from the Italian word fascio which is described as 'power in one hand'.
- It is a form of dictatorship in which all the power is in one hand and it is compulsory for all the others to respect its orders.
- Italy was ruled on the basis of Fascism, which was regarded as a nationalistic, anti-communistic and an anti-democratic movement.

Causes for the Rise of Fascism in Italy

- Italy suffered from economic crises, unemployment, shortage of foodgrains, shortfall of trade and commerce.
- Italy was not satisfied with the Treaty of Versailles because it could not get any part of the German or the Turkish empire.
- Italy was going through political crises as there was no stable government.
- Conflicts between the industrialists, capitalists, workers, labourers and peasants.
- Threat of socialist and communist ideas made the atmosphere explosive, lawlessness and uncertainty prevailed everywhere.
- League of Nations was a weak organisation.
- Mussolini with his charismatic personality won the confidence of his countrymen. He was regarded as the **Duce** which means the leader and provided a strong leadership.

Rise of Mussolini

- Benito Mussolini started as a socialist but later converted to an anti-socialist and formed Fascist party in 1922.
- King Emmanuel III offered him the post of Prime Minister in 1922.
- He ended democracy and started Fascism in Italy.

Objectives of Fascism

- It was an anti thesis of democracy.
- It supported the notion of **one party** and **one leader**.
- It favoured equal control in all the sections of the society.
- Fascists focused on nationalism and on individual institutions.
- Fascists believed that the interests of the state must get precedence over individual interests as the individual gets all the rights from the state.

Impact of Fascism

- It improved the economy, reduced unemployment and illiteracy.
- It curbed political freedom, censored press, prohibited freedom of speech.
- Catholic religion was made the state religion.
- Italy followed an Aggressive Foreign Policy.
- Mussolini became the dictator with military and civil powers. All political parties lost their existence except Mussolini's party.

End of Fascism

After defeat of Italy in Second World War, Mussolini was executed in 1945 which ended Fascism.

Nazism

- The word Nazi is derived from National Socialist Party, that was formed by Hitler.
- It is a form of dictatorship that is tightly controlled by the military.
- Germany was ruled on the basis of Nazism.

Causes for the Rise of Nazism

- The Versailles Treaty forced Germany to cede their territories to France, Belgium, Poland and Denmark and also pay heavy reparation, all of which humiliated the Germans.
- The Versailles Treaty created an economic crisis because of the raised tariffs against German goods, which created an economic crisis. It was felt that only a strong leadership could restore the past prestige of Germany.

- The Nazi party rose to power due to the absence of a strong opposition party. The agenda and the principles of Nazi party were propagated by its members.
- Hitler was known for moulding public opinion. He was a gifted orator who captivated the Germans by his emotional speeches.

Rise of Hitler

- Adolf Hitler, who had been a Corporal in World War I, joined the German Workers Party and soon became its leader. He changed its name to National Socialist Party or the Nazi Party.
- He was offered chancellorship by President Hindenburg. He formed the Nazi Government on 30th January, 1933.
- As the Nazi party was not able to win majority, he assumed dictatorial powers. Hitler abolished the Constitution and became the dictator of Germany.

Objectives of Nazism

- To use force and brutality.
- To praise war, extreme nationalism and dictatorship.
- To despise internationalism, peace and democracy.
- To uphold racial supremacy of the German race.
- To advocate rule by a great leader from a single party.

Impact of Nazism

- It improved trade, agricultural and industrial production.
- A Food Corporation was created to maintain buffer stock.
- It abolished all opposition parties, imposed a ban on the press, public speeches and formed secret police to check the activities of the citizens.
- Hitler through Nazism increased military by making it compulsory.
- Hitler openly condemned the peace treaty of Versailles and refused to pay war indemnity.
- Hitler acquired more and more territories for the Germans. He tried to expand in the South and East of Europe, as that region was economically useful for Germany. He also reclaimed the territory of Saar and Rhineland from France and annexed Austria by force in 1938.
- Nazism believed in superior German race and condemned Jews.

End of Nazism

After defeat of Germany in Second World War, Hitler committed suicide on 30th April, 1945, which ended Nazism.

> **Similarities between Fascism and Nazism**
>
> Fascism and Nazism as ideologies are similar in nature in the following ways
>
> - Both of these ideologies were against the democratic political system.
> - Both favored totalitarian rule.
> - Both of these ideologies believed in aggressive nationalism and imperialism.
> - Both wanted to uphold one party and one leader.
> - Both believed in state supremacy, which could suppress Fundamental Rights and individual freedom.

Chapter 11 The Second World War

The Second World War took place in 1939 and lasted upto 1945. It started in Europe, but soon America, Asia and Africa also got involved in the war.

Causes of the Second World War

- Dissatisfaction from the Treaty of Versailles gave rise to a spirit of revenge and Germany started looking for an opportunity to do away with the harsh treaty. Hence, the war became inevitable.
- The rise of extreme nationalism in Italy and Germany in the form of Fascism and Nazism, respectively contributed to the causes that led to the Second World War.
- Britain and France decided to accept the hostile demands of the aggressive nations to gain peace as they knew that for both Germany and Italy, the Treaty of Versailles was too harsh and humiliating.

- To check the rising tide of Communism and Russian Bolshevism, Britain and France, allowed Germany to re-arm and to re-militarise the Rhineland and capture Austria and Czechoslovakia.
- Japan to dominate East Asia, invaded Manchuria and Northern China. It joined the Berlin-Rome axis to further its policy of expansion.
- Countries of Europe lost faith in League's of Nation's usefulness as it failed to maintain International peace. The League was ignored and defied. Therefore, they themselves entered into mutual political and military alliances.
- Hitler with his army marched into Poland. France and Britain gave an ultimatum to Germany. In reply, Germany attacked France. On 3rd September, Britain and France declared war against Germany. Thus, the invasion of Poland marked the beginning of the Second World War.

Formation of Alliances

- Allied powers consisted of Britain, France and USA which entered later.
- Axis powers consisted of Germany, Italy and Japan.

Events of the War

- German forces completed its conquest of Norway, Denmark, Belgium, Holland and Southern France.
- Soon, the war engulfed entire Europe. Only Sweden, Switzerland, Spain, Portugal and Turkey remained neutral until the end.

Consequences of the War

- The Axis powers, i.e. Germany, Italy and Japan were defeated. Japan signed the Potsdam Declaration.
- Germany was divided into two zones under the army of each of the Allied Powers. The Federal Republic of Germany (West Germany) was administered by UK, France and the USA. **German Democratic Republic** (East Germany) was administered by the Soviet Union.
- Japan and Italy also became very weak. The American army was to occupy Japan until 1952. All lands acquired by Japan since 1895 were taken away.
- The meeting of Roosevelt, Churchill and Stalin led to the formation of United Nations Organisation on 24th October, 1945.

Cold War

- The harmony between USA and USSR declined and ideological difference emerged.
- Both the countries did not engage in actual fights, but there was a state of extreme political tension between the two. This state of tension is known as the Cold War, an atmosphere with no armed struggle, but the prevalence of a cold hostility. All these results divided the world into two blocs.
- One bloc was led by USA that believed in democracy and capitalism.
- The other bloc was led by USSR that believed in Communism based on Marxist theory.

Chapter 12 The United Nations and its Major Agencies

- The United Nations (UN) was formed on 24th October, 1945, at a conference in San Francisco.
- At present 193 countries are members of UN.
- All the organs of the United Nations are based in New York, USA, except the International Court of Justice, which is located at the Hague in Netherlands.
- The **UN flag** is light blue in colour and is portrayed in white. At its centre is the UN Emblem, a polar map of the world, embraced by twin olive branches. The flag was adopted on 20th October, 1947.
- UN consist of 6 organs—General Assembly, Security Council, International Court of Justice, Economic and Social Council, the Trusteeship Council and the UN Secretariat.

Purpose/Objective of UN

- To maintain international peace and security.
- To develop friendly relations among nations, based on the respect for the principle of equal rights and self-determination of people.
- To achieve international co-operation in solving various international, economic, social, cultural or humanitarian problems.

- *To be a centre for harmonising the actions of nations in the attainment of goals.*
- *To respect the sovereign equality of all its members.*

Organs of the UN

United Nations General Assembly, Security Council and International Court of Justice are the main organs of the United Nations.

General Assembly

- *It is the most important organ of the UN.*
- *All the member of UN are also members of General Assembly.*
- *It has 15 members (5 permanent and 10 Non-permanent)*
- *Each member has one vote*
- *The regular session of the General Assembly begins each year on the 3rd Tuesday of September and continues usually until the 3rd week of December.*
- *At the beginning of each regular session, the Assembly elects a new President, Vice-Presidents and the Chairman of the Assembly's six main committees.*
- *The Presidency of the Assembly rotates each year among the five groups of states: Africa, Asia, Eastern Europe, Latin America and the Caribbean, and Western Europe and other states.*
- *Functions of General Assembly are*
  - *To consider and make recommendations on the principles of co-operation as well as in the maintenance of international peace and security.*
  - *To consider and approve the budget of the UN and to apportion the contributions among members.*
  - *To elect the non-permanent members of the Security Council, the Economic and Social Council and the Trusteeship Council and to elect the judges of the International Court of Justice.*
  - *To appoint the Secretary-General on the recommendation of the Security Council.*
  - *To discuss and make recommendations on any issue affecting the powers and functions of any organ of the UN.*
  - *To make recommendations to promote international, political, social and economic co-operation.*

Security Council

- *The Council consists of 15 members out of which 5 members, viz., China, France, Russia, Britain and the USA are permanent.*
- *The non-permanent members are elected from Afro-Asian countries (5 Members), Latin America (2 Members), West European and other countries (2 Members) and East European countries (1 Member).*
- *Each member has one vote.*
- *Permanent members have Veto power i.e. a negative vote.*
- *Non-permanent members are elected for a term of 2 years by the General Assembly following a two/third (2/3) majority.*
- *Functions of Security Council are*
  - *To maintain international peace and security in accordance with the principles and purposes of the UN.*
  - *To investigate any dispute or situation, to take military action against an aggressor, and to recommend terms of settling disputes and any methods of adjusting them.*
  - *To call on members to apply economic sanctions and measures other than force, to prevent or stop aggression.*
  - *To recommend to the General Assembly for the appointment of the Secretary-General and to elect the Judges of the International Court of Justice together with the General Assembly.*
  - *To determine existence of any threats and to recommend actions for the same.*
  - *To exercise the trusteeship functions of the United Nations in strategic areas. One of the peace keeping forces of the UN is working in Afghanistan as* ***UN Assistance Mission in Afghanistan*** *(UN AMA), which is deeply concerned about the rising number of civilian deaths and injuries.*

International Court of Justice

- *Its headquarters are in* ***Hague*** *(Netherlands).*
- *The Court comprises of 15 judges elected for a term of 9 years by the UN General Assembly and Security Council sitting independently. Elections are held every 3 years for 1/3rd of the seats.*
- *A retiring judge may be re-elected.*
- *Functions of International Courts of Justice are*

- To settle in accordance with international law, legal disputes submitted by states.
- Only the Member States may apply to and appear before the Court. The Court decides cases in accordance with International treaties and conventions in force, and is competent to entertain a dispute if the parties so involved agree for it.
- The advisory procedure of the Court is open only to its 5 organs and 16 other authorised agencies of the UN family. The Court plays a significant role in the codification of International laws. The Court may recommend appropriate procedures/methods of settlement during or at the end of the case.

Major Agencies of the UN

- There are 18 specialised agencies to achieve economic and social progress.
- Important agencies are UNICEF, WHO and UNESCO.

UNICEF

- UNICEF stands for United Nations International Children's Emergency Fund. Later on, its name was changed to **United Nations Children's Fund**.
- It was created by the General Assembly, to provide long term benefits to the children of all developing countries. Its headquarters are in New York.
- The agency depends on voluntary contributions made by different governments, private agencies, through sale of greeting cards and via other fund raising campaigns, to finance its projects.
- UNICEF was also awarded the **Noble Prize for Peace** (1965) and the **Indira Gandhi Prize for Peace** (1989).
- The functions of UNICEF are as follows
  - It works for the protection of children in respect of their survival, health and well-being. It also supports child immunisation programmes.
  - It provides funds for training the personnel, including health and sanitation workers, teachers, nutritionists, etc.
  - It provides technical supplies, equipment and other aids to villages.
  - It assists governments to plan, develop and extend community services.
  - It provides help to children and mothers in case of emergencies.
  - It makes efforts to prevent diseases like TB, Malaria, eye diseases, skin diseases, etc.

World Health Organisation (WHO)

- It is the specialised agency for health, established on 7th April, 1948 with the objective of achieving the highest possible level of health for all.
- Its headquarters are at **Geneva** in Switzerland.
- Its aim is to help the governments raise the standards of public health and medical research.
- Functions of WHO are
  - It helps countries to improve their health system by building up infrastructure.
  - It gives important drugs needed for medical care. It launches programmes to immunise children against 6 major diseases-Measles, Diphtheria, Tetanus, Tuberculosis, Polio and Whooping cough.
  - It promotes research to cure and prevent diseases.
  - It works towards providing safe drinking water and adequate waste disposal.
  - It organises conferences, seminars and training activities for healthcare personnel.
  - It aims at fighting diseases and preventing them from spreading.
  - It publishes health journals to create health consciousness among people.

UNESCO

- It was established on 4th November, 1945 at **Paris**.
- The full form is **United Nations Educational Scientific and Cultural Organisation**.
- The main functions of UNESCO are as follows
  - Removal of illiteracy by encouraging adult education; distance education and open school education.
  - Financial assistance for the education of disabled children. It also lays special emphasis on the education of women and girls.
  - Encouragement of scientific education by providing regional training centres.
  - Advice about the production of textbooks, syllabus and teacher-training.
  - Help to establish library systems and also give fellowships.
- Scientific activities undertaken by UNESCO are as follows
  - It promotes research in fields like Geology, Mathematics, Physics and Oceanography.

- It helps in correcting the existing imbalances in scientific and technological manpower.
- It encourages the study of Social Sciences in orde to focus attention on combating all forms of discrimination, improving the status of women and helping the youth in solving their problems.
- It also organises conferences to bring scientists together.
- It circulates information through journals. **Courier** is the official monthly magazine of UNESCO.

- For the preservation of cultural heritage, UNESCO
  - provides technical assistance, equipments, fundsb for the preservation of monuments and works of art.
  - encourages artistic creations in literature and fine arts.
  - protects world inheritance of books, art work and manuscripts.

Chapter 13 The Non-Aligned Movement

Non-Alignment refers to the international policy of a sovereign state according to which it does not align itself with any of the power blocs.

Features of Non-Aligned Movement

- It is not aligned to any power blocs and it is against military alliances like NATO, SEATO, Warsaw Pact, etc.
- The belief that each country has the complete freedom to take independent foreign policy decisions.
- Non-alignment stands for action rather than passivism. It judges and issue on its merit. It is for the freedom and justice of the people.
- It actively participates in politics among nations.

Objective of Non-Aligned Movement

The main objectives of NAM are as follows:

- To eliminate causes that could lead to war.
- To protect the newly independent countries of Asia and Africa from colonial domination.
- To oppose colonialism, imperialism and racial discrimination.
- To support sovereign equality of all states.
- To advocate peaceful settlement of international disputes and protect human rights and the environment.
- To strengthen the United Nations as a organ of world peace.

Factors Responsible for Non-Aligned Movement

- Global tension caused by Cold War.
- Struggle against Imperialism and Neo-Colonisation.
- Right of independent judgement.
- Use of moderation in relations with all big powers.
- Restructuring of the international economic order.
- Formation of the Panchsheel.

Architects of NAM

- The founding fathers of NAM were inspired by the five principles of Panchsheel.
- The main architects of NAM were **Josip Broz Tito** of Yugoslavia, **Gamal** Kwome Naruna of Ghana and Sukarno of Indonesia **Abdel Nasser** of Egypt and **Jawaharlal Nehru** of India.
- The term NAM was coined by Nehru in 1954 in Colombo, Sri Lanka.

Achievements of NAM

- NAM helped in resolving tensions between the two power blocs and brought an end to the Cold War.
- NAM acted against the arms race of the superpowers during the Cold War years.
- NAM supported the cause of international peace, justice and freedom on all forums.
- NAM advocated the **New International Economic Order** (NIEO).